A COMPANION TO
HENSLOWE'S DIARY

Henslowe's 'diary' is a unique source of information about the day-to-day running of the Elizabethan repertory theatre. Philip Henslowe, a theatrical entrepreneur, kept records of his financial dealings with London companies and actors from 1592–1604.

The diary itself is difficult to decipher. Neil Carson's analysis is based on a much more thorough correlation of Henslowe's entries than has been attempted before, breaking down into clear tabular form the main items of income and expenditure and drawing conclusions about the management procedures of the companies, the professional relationships of actors and playwrights and the ways in which plays were written, rehearsed and programmed.

Previous speculation has dismissed Henslowe himself as ignorant, disorderly and grasping. Carson shows him to have been a benign and efficient businessman whose control over the actors' professional activities was much less extensive than has often been supposed.

A COMPANION TO
HENSLOWE'S DIARY

NEIL CARSON

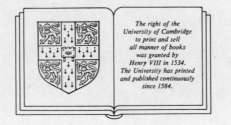

The right of the
University of Cambridge
to print and sell
all manner of books
was granted by
Henry VIII in 1534.
The University has printed
and published continuously
since 1584.

CAMBRIDGE UNIVERSITY PRESS

CAMBRIDGE

NEW YORK   NEW ROCHELLE   MELBOURNE   SYDNEY

Published by the Press Syndicate of the University of Cambridge
The Pitt Building, Trumpington Street, Cambridge CB2 1RP
32 East 57th Street, New York, NY 10022, USA
10 Stamford Road, Oakleigh, Melbourne 3166, Australia

First published 1988

Printed in Great Britain at the University Press, Cambridge

British Library cataloguing in publication data
Carson, Neil
A companion to Henslowe's 'Diary'.
1. Theater – England – History – 16th
century 2. Theater – England – History
– 17th century
I. Title II. Henslowe, Philip. Diary
792'0942   PN2587

Library of Congress cataloguing in publication data
Carson, Neil.
A companion to Henslowe's 'Diary'.
Bibliography
Includes index.
1. Henslowe, Philip, d. 1616. Diary. 2. Theater –
England – History – 16th century. 3. Theatrical managers –
England – Diaries. I. Henslowe, Philip, d. 1616.
Diary. II. Title.
PN2589.H43C37   1987   792'.0942   87–11650

ISBN 0 521 23545 6

TO MY MOTHER AND THE
MEMORY OF MY FATHER

CONTENTS

PREFACE

NOT SURPRISINGLY the editing of Henslowe's diary has always taken precedence over its explication. Commentaries have been rudimentary or have lagged well behind the publication of the original material. Edmond Malone, the first to make scholarly use of the manuscript, apologized that it was not in his power 'to arrange those very curious materials in their proper places', but did not wish that 'the publicke should be deprived of the information and entertainment' they would afford (1790: I, Part 2, 289). Malone's extracts printed in his edition of *The Plays and Poems of William Shakespeare* (1790) were the only selections from the diary and papers available to most scholars until J. Payne Collier's edition of the diary, published in 1845. Collier's commentary was devoted almost entirely to an explanation of the document's relevance to the study of Shakespeare. Furthermore, it was coloured by his attitude to its author whom he described as 'an ignorant man, even for the time in which he lived, and for the station he occupied'. Collier's assessment seems to have been based entirely on the fact that Henslowe 'wrote a bad hand, adopted any orthography that suited his notion of the sound of the words . . . and kept his book, as respects dates in particular, in the most disorderly, negligent, and confused manner' (1845: xv). Collier himself made no attempt to improve the order of the work, however, and added materially to its confusion by introducing a number of forged entries.

The first serious effort to see some kind of pattern in the document was made by F. G. Fleay in his *Chronicle History of the London Stage 1559–1642* (1890). Fleay drew up an abstract of the performance records and loan accounts, but ignored most of the non-theatrical material which he described as being 'of no conceivable interest to anyone'. His analysis of the Henslowe records had an important influence on later work, as did his call for a new edition of the diary. 'Collier's edition', he wrote, 'is a disgrace to English literature, and the Dulwich authorities would do well to have it re-edited by a competent hand, with careful elision of his numerous forgeries, and with the matter arranged in serviceable consecution . . . without infringing on the accuracy of the text' (1890: 95).

Greg's editions of the diary (1904), and papers (1907), and his volume of commentary (1908) more than met the need Fleay identified. They have now served nearly three generations of scholars and in some respects will not likely be superseded. The Foakes–Rickert edition of the diary (1961) introduced many new readings, and the Scolar facsimiles of the diary and papers (1977) enable students to puzzle out their own interpretations of the text. But Greg's discussions of the many individuals mentioned in the diary will probably stand for many years, as will his account of the lost plays.

Nevertheless, a reassessment of Greg's assumptions and some of his interpretations is overdue. As Foakes and Rickert observed, scholarship in the last eighty or more years has suggested new possibilities of interpreting difficult entries. Furthermore, there is a compelling need for a functional abstract of the diary's contents to which scholars can refer. The absence of an agreed-upon basis for analysis and comparison means that each scholar must do this preliminary recasting of the accounts himself, and can only with great difficulty check the conclusions of others. The purpose of this volume, then, is to present the matter of the diary in that 'serviceable consecution' advocated by Fleay without, it is to be hoped, the infringement of accuracy he warned against.

ACKNOWLEDGEMENTS

Specialists and non-specialists alike will recognize how much this work owes to previous scholars. I would like to acknowledge particularly the advice and assistance of Carol Chillington Rutter whose challenging questions and criticism were invaluable, and the support and encouragement of William Ingram and R. A. Foakes.

I am also grateful to the Social Sciences and Humanities Research Council of Canada for financial support, and to the University of Guelph for a period of leave during which I was able to complete a first draft of the manuscript.

ABBREVIATIONS

ES   *The Elizabethan Stage* by E. K. Chambers. 2 vols. London: Oxford University Press, 1923.

HD   *Henslowe's Diary* edited by R. A. Foakes and R. T. Rickert. Cambridge: Cambridge University Press, 1961.

HP   *Henslowe's Papers* edited by W. W. Greg. London: A. H. Bullen, 1907.

Mun. Muniments in the Henslowe papers.

Ms   Manuscript(s) in the Henslowe papers.

PRO   Public Record Office

SR   *A Transcript of the Registers of the Company of Stationers of London: 1554–1640* edited by Edward Arber. London, 1875–94.

A NOTE ON STYLISTIC CONVENTIONS

Pagination. To avoid confusion between modern editions, references to Henslowe's diary are to the original manuscript in the form f. 1 (folio 1 recto) or f. 1v (folio 1 verso).

Currency. English currency dates from Saxon times when the basic unit was a silver penny known as a sterling. Large amounts were estimated in pounds of sterlings each one containing two hundred and forty pennies. In Norman times the 'pound' was divided further into twenty shillings and the three basic units were referred to in Latin manuscripts as *libra*, *solidus* and *denarius*, terms which were shortened to '£', 's' and 'd'. By Elizabethan times a bewildering number of coins had been introduced, but all of them could be related to the basic units. Henslowe occasionally refers to unfamiliar coins such as marks, but his accounts are kept in the traditional form, and his calculations in pounds, shillings and pence. Frequently he substitutes hyphens for the more usual symbols and it is this system (1-10-6) that has been adopted in this commentary.

1 · PHILIP HENSLOWE AND HIS 'DIARY'

PHILIP HENSLOWE was the fourth of seven children of Edmond and Margaret Henslowe (or Hensley) of Lindfield, Sussex. We do not know when he was born, but it is likely to have been between 1550–60, which would have made him about sixty when he died. He appears to have acquired little of either education or patrimony, and to have begun his career as an apprentice or servant to a London dyer by the name of Henry Woodward. Philip's diligence in the execution of his duties must have recommended him (at least to his mistress), for on 14 February 1579 (a mere two months after her husband's death), Agnes Woodward and Philip Henslowe were married. At a stroke, the former servant acquired not only a readymade family (6-year-old Joan and 4-year-old Elizabeth), but also a substantial estate.

Henslowe was probably in his mid- or late twenties at the time of his marriage; his new wife was considerably older. No record of Agnes' birth date survives and the only clue we have to her age is a deposition made after Henslowe's death in 1616 alleging that she was then a hundred years old. This testimony by Philip's nephew is almost totally untrustworthy, however, since it would make Agnes fifty-nine years old at the time her second daughter was born (and sixty-three when she married Philip). It is more likely that she was in her early fifties in 1579.

Whatever their relative ages, the Henslowes appear to have suited one another, and with his newly acquired resources Philip began to prosper. In June 1584, he negotiated for the purchase of 60 dozen goat skins (Mun. 86, 87). The following year he secured what was probably his first piece of real estate, a property in Southwark known as the Little Rose (Mun. 15). It was described as tenements with two gardens, and according to Greg may have been a brothel (1904: II, 3). As early as 1593 he may have owned an inn called 'the ffolles head' (f. 1v); two years later he acquired the adjoining 'Jemes is head' (f. 3v), and sometime subsequently a property known as The Barge, the Bell, and the Cock, and also possibly one called The Unicorn (Greg 1904: II, 25, 26). He also invested in numerous rental properties, and his income from this source rose steadily in the seventeenth century.

Henslowe's elevation from 'servant' to prosperous burgher is pleasantly edifying, but it is not entirely the story of a self-made man. Quite apart from his good sense in marrying money, Henslowe was fortunate enough to become allied to another shrewd and ambitious entrepreneur in the person of Edward Alleyn. This came about in October 1592, when the actor married Henslowe's step-daughter, Joan Woodward. Alleyn and Henslowe obviously had much in common, for they became partners in a variety of highly successful business enterprises. Of the two men, it was probably Henslowe who gained most by the alliance. According to testimony given in 1616, the

1

'Industrie and care' of Alleyn contributed greatly to the 'Bettering of the Estate of the said Philip Henslowe' (PRO STAC8/168/18).

It would be unfair, however, to attribute all of Henslowe's success to his relatives by marriage. In the course of his life he won a series of honours which were no doubt in good measure a result of his own efforts and ability. In 1592 he was appointed Groom of the Chamber to Queen Elizabeth, a post that required him to spend considerable time at court (Ms I, 11). Following James's accession, he became Gentleman Sewer of the Chamber, and in 1607 he was elected vestryman (along with Edward Alleyn) of the parish of St Saviour. A year later he became a churchwarden, and in 1612 he was appointed one of six governors of the Free Grammar School of the parish. By the second decade of the seventeenth century, therefore, the poorly educated apprentice had attained what Greg describes as 'an assured and honoured social position among his fellow citizens' (1904: II, 15).

What can we deduce from all this? Such a position is not, of course, incompatible with the ignorance and greed sometimes attributed to Henslowe. To determine whether or not these worldly honours were hollow we need to know more about Henslowe's personal life. Here the documents illustrating Henslowe's relations with his extended family are valuable. The complicated and sometimes acrimonious dealings reflected in letters and legal documents provide some clues to the motives and feelings of the man. While the evidence is not always as unambiguous as we might hope, it does provide a useful background against which to judge his activities in the theatre.

Philip was the second youngest of five sons, and in worldly terms quite likely the most successful. He had no children of his own, but, owing to rather tragic circumstances, he became involved in the raising of several nieces and nephews. The first of these was Francis, son of his eldest brother, Richard, who died in 1574. Sometime about 1590, when Francis would have been about twenty-four, Henslowe received an appeal for assistance to obtain his release from prison. He obliged at a cost of 16s. 4d. (Ms III, 5). Between January 1593, and May 1594, Henslowe employed Francis in his pawnbroking business, at the end of which period he advanced him £15 to pay for a share in the Queen's Men (f. 2v). The following June, Francis borrowed another £9 for half a share in an unnamed acting troupe (f. 3v). In December 1597, Philip lent him £7 to help him buy a house on the Bankside (f. 62). By 1604 he was performing with the Duke of Lennox's Men (f. 100), but sometime after that he was again in prison (this time for stealing a horse), and had to borrow £5 from his uncle to obtain his freedom. There is no record that Francis repaid any of these debts. Then in 1606 Francis and his wife died, probably of the plague, and an undated note among Henslowe's papers records charges 'laid owte' for their funeral (Mss IV, 57, 58).

The relationship between Henslowe and his second nephew, John, is, if anything, even more poignant. Philip had been of assistance to his second brother, Edmond, and on a number of occasions had loaned him money to buy real estate and to pay off his creditors (f. 122v). But he became more deeply involved in the family affairs when Edmond fell sick sometime in 1591. Henslowe rode down to the family place in Sussex, paid for Edmond's care and for the threshing of his crops, and finally underwrote the costs of his funeral and the legal expenses connected with his will (f. 122v–123).

Edmond's estate was substantial. He owned a 'mansion house' and shop at Buxtead, and from the sale of this and his household goods he hoped to endow his family. He bequeathed £20 to his wife, and to his daughter, Anne, he promised a dowry of £100 to be paid one month after her marriage. Apart from several small legacies, the remainder of the estate was to be divided equally between his wife and his two other children, John and Mary, the former to receive his portion on reaching maturity and the second a month after her wedding. Perhaps the most curious provision of Edmond's will, however, was his wish that Philip in his capacity as executor should assume responsibility for the care of his children during their minority. The terms of the will are very specific:

I make my brother Philip Hensley sole exequutor and doe desire him to deale for my childrenns behalfe the beste he can Prouided allwaies that he sustaine no lesse theareby But that out of the said goodes, he shoulde be paide all suche iuste costes and charges as he shalbe at in compassinge anie of thease bequestes, ffor I would have him and his wiefe, take my childrenn as theire owne and with them theire seuerall porc[i]ion, and to see them broughte vp in the feare of god till suche time as they shall come to age themselves.

(PRO, P.C.C., PROB 11/79, 212–212v probated 15 Dec. 1591, cited by Cerasano (1985) in an unpublished appendix.)

Not surprisingly, perhaps, Edmond's widow Margery had other ideas about the raising of her children. As Henslowe reports it, she 'ded desyer to haue the bordinge & bringyn vp of her owne iij chelldren after al the good weare [ap]praysed wch the one halfe was to her sealfe & the other halfe vnto John & mary wch was valewed to 30 li, & for that halfe she was contented to bord them & scolle them' (f. 124). The wording is ambiguous, but the phrase 'that halfe' presumably refers to John and Mary's portion which Margery kept in addition to her own.

The arrangement seems to have worked well until Margery's death three years later. At that time the children 'cameal vp to . . . London'. Henslowe claimed sometime after 1595 that they had 'bene euer since at [his] carges & as [he had] payd for ther borde to ther mother [he looked] a cordynge to the will to be a lowed yt agayne' (f. 124). The phrase 'to ther mother' is puzzling, but Henslowe seems to be claiming only those expenses incurred after the children arrived in London on 27 February 1595. According to the detailed calculation drawn up, probably in the summer of 1595 and set out on folios 122v to 123v, Henslowe spent some £85 on his brother's family, but appears to have benefited little from the will. The portions of John and Mary seem to have been consumed paying for their upkeep; of Anne's legacy of £100 there is no further mention; and Philip reports that he 'never had any thinge of [Edmond's] but the howse' (f. 41v) which contrary to the provisions of the will was not sold until after Margery's death when it brought £80, less than Henslowe's expenses until that time.

It is not known how old the children were when they came to London, but the two eldest were quickly apprenticed (John to a dyer and Mary to a seamstress) which suggests they were in their mid-teens (f. 124v). Of his two nieces, Ann was eventually married, but Mary fell ill of a 'dead pallsey' in 1605 and was rendered 'lame' and unable to work. Henslowe lent John money to take his sister home to his house. Thereafter he paid two shillings a week for her keep until she died in 1607.

Up until this point Henslowe's dealings with his poor relatives seem to be marked by a sense of responsibility and possibly even generosity. His subsequent relations with his nephew John, however, are more complex. After Francis's death in 1606, John was the sole surviving male in the Henslowe line and the most obvious heir to Philip's fortune. Not improbably there were considerable hopes and pressures centred on the young man. Unfortunately he seems not to have been able to live up to them. At some time after his arrival in London he left his master, and Philip apprenticed him again, this time to a waterman. About 1598 he 'layd owt' £5 to buy a boat, and several years later in 1605 he paid £14. 16s. to buy John a place as one of the King's watermen (f. 124). The year before that, Edmond's will had again been challenged in the courts and Philip had financed John's legal defence (f. 123v).

Any of these transactions might have caused friction between the two men. But it was apparently John's taking his uncle to court that produced an irreparable rupture. The details of the case are unknown, but, according to witnesses in 1616, it was the source of a bitter breach between uncle and nephew. Jacob Meade asserted that Henslowe 'heild a very hard conceipt of [John because] . . . in former tymes [John] had sued & troubled [his uncle] for goods wch were some tyme the plaintiffs fathers . . . as the comp[lainant] pretended' (PRO C.24/431/23 and ST.CH. 168/18 cited Chillington 1979). Not improbably the litigation grew out of John's suspicion that he had been cheated of his inheritance in some way by his uncle. Whatever the cause, it seems to have permanently poisoned relations between the two, for when they met 'by chance or otherwise in any place . . . [Philip] would scarcely vouchsafe to speake vnto [John] or so much as to take notice of [him] otherwise then by some slight careless salutation or a nod of his head or such like'. As a consequence of this hostility, Henslowe by the time of his death had vowed that John 'should not have a foote of the land or one peny worth of the goods wch were [Henslowe's]'. Accordingly he effectively disinherited his nephew by passing part of his estate (which was officially valued at £1700. 12s. 8d. but may have been worth as much as eight times that amount) to John's son and the remainder to his wife, Agnes, who in her turn willed it to Joan and Edward Alleyn.

The picture which emerges from these documents is not simple. Clearly Henslowe was capable of what looks like vindictiveness, but we know little of the circumstances that aroused it. His treatment of his relatives apart from John seems to have been fair and the tone of his letters to Alleyn is simple and warm (Mss I, 10, 12, 13, 14). Whereas the provisions of Edmond's will would seem to have opened the way for Henslowe to appropriate the inheritance to his own use until the children were old enough to claim it, he does not appear to have done so. On the contrary, he seems to have treated his sister-in-law, Margery, with consideration and tact. While there is no reason to suppose that he treated his business associates with the same tolerance he showed to members of his family, neither is there any irrefutable evidence that he did not. The complaints of actors about his hard dealings in 1615 constitute a special case which will be dealt with later. During the period the diary covers, however, Henslowe's relations with players and playwrights seem to be marked by the same patience and fairness he showed towards his own relatives.

THE 'DIARY'

If for the sake of convenience we continue to use the word 'diary' to refer to Henslowe's theatrical account book, we must do so with the understanding that it is a misnomer. The volume which Philip acquired from his elder brother John he used for various purposes after 1592. Indeed, one of the first things to strike a modern reader primarily interested in the theatre is just how much of the volume is given over to non-theatrical affairs. Memoranda, receipts, recipes, and notations on a multitude of subjects from real estate to family business abound. While at first these auxiliary interests seem to present a bewildering confusion, it is possible to group them under a few general headings.

To begin with, the volume frequently served Henslowe as a sort of 'commonplace book' in which he recorded interesting and miscellaneous bits of information. These range from aphorisms (f. 1), to card tricks (f. 18v), to medications (ff. 16v, 17v, 18, 136v), to memoranda of events such as the wedding of Edward Alleyn and his step-daughter Joan (f. 2). Closely related to these entries are various memoranda which Henslowe made to help him remember such things as the measurements of the wainscoting in Alleyn's house (f. 2), the fact that he had put his horse to grass (f. 24v), and the details of a farm he may have considered buying (f. 111v).

The incorporation of such apparently irrelevant material into an account book seems strange to a modern reader and is sometimes seen as evidence of Henslowe's dis-organized mind or sloppy methods. But account books of the sixteenth century were neither so neat nor so homogeneous as today's ledgers. Merchants frequently inter-mixed their financial statements with various personal matters, such as rules for conduct or treatments for coughs and other ailments (Yamey 1940: 5). The account book of the leading sixteenth-century merchant of Ipswich was little more than a rough book whose erasures and cancellations make it almost indecipherable. Even the most successful and eminent merchants of the period often show very elementary techniques and slovenly execution (Ramsay 1956: 186). Sir Thomas Gresham, for example, used a mixture of roman and arabic numerals (the latter gradually replacing the former in England in the sixteenth century), and mixed company and personal business in his books. In this respect, at least, Henslowe's practice in his diary is perfectly normal for his time.

Another use Henslowe soon found for his volume was as a depository of various legal and semi-legal records. These include several agreements and contracts which were signed and witnessed, and would therefore have had some weight in a court of law if the terms were ever challenged. Entries range from simple signed acknowledge-ments of indebtedness such as that of Arthur Langworth (f. 88), to more specialized memoranda. Henslowe recorded payments received as rent (f. 43), or on private debts (f. 103), and collected signed testimony relating to payments he made for 'the bargain for the tenements on the Bankside' (f. 98v). He also itemized various bonds committing one individual to underwrite the debt of another (f. 2), or agreeing to a forfeiture in the case of non-payment of debt (f. 259v), or the failure to fulfil a promise (f. 97v). Elsewhere in the diary he transcribed agreements which would not have had legal status in the form in which we find them. For example, a partnership between Alleyn and Henslowe on the one hand and John Ackley and Nicholas Dame on the other seems to be no more than a summary of the terms of the contract (f. 204). Entries relating to an agreement between Alleyn and Langworth (ff. 24, 25) would also appear to be merely descriptive, since neither of the parties has signed them. In these cases, Henslowe is probably simply reminding himself of the terms of official documents deposited elsewhere.

A better notion of Henslowe's use of the diary for business purposes can be derived from the accounts relating to his dealing with, and on behalf of, his son-in-law, Edward Alleyn. These accounts are recorded on folios 238–23 where Henslowe reversed the book and began working from the back towards the middle. The record has the appearance of a ledger. One page contains a series of expenses incurred by Edward Alleyn in connection with his house during an indeterminate period before and after 24 November 1592. On the facing page a column of figures adds up to £13-04-02 (exactly £5 less than the actual amount of Alleyn's expenses). An account of further expenses described as charges 'as hathe bene layd owt a bowt edward alenes howsse' begins on folio 237 and appears to list items paid for by Henslowe (possibly after Alleyn left to travel in the provinces after 31 January 1593). The accounts go back to 4 November, and extend to September 1594 (probably an error for 1593) (f. 235). Henslowe drew up an account of what he was owed on folio 234v, and repeated it on 234.

These pages are interesting because they are much more systematic than most of the accounts in the diary. Expenditures are carefully itemized, and it would appear that they have been transcribed from other sources. This is suggested by the fact that five items paid for by Alleyn appear in exactly the same phraseology in Henslowe's accounts, although the mistake was caught and the duplicate entries are crossed out. Henslowe made no effort to total the expenses until very near the end of the account when he entered a sub-total and then a final total in the left margin opposite the last entry. The sum (£154-12-00) seems to be 12s. 1d. too high, but it is possible that Henslowe was making some kind of correction which he has not shown in the book. The figure has been carried over to the top of folio 234v, but Henslowe reckoned Alleyn's debt using a very different set of figures from those on the previous pages. What is significant about these entries is that they show that as early as 1592 Henslowe was capable of neat and meticulous book-keeping, of bringing all expenditures relevant to a particular enterprise together, and of drawing up a balance of debits and credits. The *raison d'être* of the Alleyn accounts was clearly to provide a comprehensive record of expenditures so that Henslowe could reclaim his money.

A similar need explains the series of records relating to Henslowe's activities as executor of his brother's estate. As we have seen, Henslowe attended his brother in his last sickness, and after his death assumed increasing responsibility for the family. In 1595, after the death of his sister-in-law he arranged for the sale of the house, and about the same time drew up 'A Juste note of what [he had] Lent vnto edmond Henslowe . . . & Layd owt . . . [for his] children' (f. 122v). The account was compiled from different parts of the diary where he had recorded expenditures from 1592 to 1595, and was presumably prepared so that he could present a claim against the estate (f. 124).

In the two examples so far discussed Henslowe was acting as an agent, and in such circumstances he demonstrated that he was reasonably painstaking. In the second case, for example, he meticulously retranscribed the expenditures on folios 39, 40, 41, and 41v, although presumably he could have done his calculations without going to this extra trouble. Why he did so is not clear unless it was to present the account to other eyes which might have been confused by the original entries made over a number of years. The transcription is, perhaps, a tacit acknowledgement of the occasional or irregular nature of the original accounts.

Henslowe probably learned his book-keeping techniques as an apprentice. Since he is referred to on different occasions as a citizen and dyer, the business in which he developed his skills was what today we would describe as a service industry. Material brought to the shop was presumably processed and returned and the only book-keeping necessary would be to keep track of the changing inventory of material to be dyed, and to record payment for the process. The system Henslowe learned, therefore, was probably a fairly simple one, for English business practices were in considerable flux in the mid-sixteenth century. Early account books frequently record only credit dealings, the entries being crossed out when payment was received. Such entries often did not occur in chronological order, since the costliness of paper necessitated the use of every empty space available (Yamey 1940: 5). Nevertheless, these primitive methods of book-keeping were adequate for most business requirements and lasted in England well into the seventeenth century.

The need of merchants to take frequent inventories, and their desire to be able to reckon their current financial position more readily, led as early as 1211 in Florence to a system of double-entry book-keeping. This method called for the recording of every transaction both as a credit and a debit, and made possible a regular balancing of the accounts. For example, instead of a sale of cloth being entered only once as an increase in cash, it would be listed twice (as a cash increase and as a deduction from the stock). In this way the total of current assets (stock plus cash and accounts receivable) can be more easily compared with current liabilities. The more efficient double-entry system made its way slowly from the large Italian mercantile firms to the smaller businesses of Europe. It appears that it had become established in the more up-to-date counting houses of London by the middle of the sixteenth century (Ramsay 1956: ciii), but individual tradesmen clung to the older methods for another hundred years.

The most relevant feature of the double-entry system for our purposes is its use of a variety of different kinds of books. Originally, one volume would have been used to record transactions as they occurred. In such a book, sales and purchases, cash and credit entries might follow one another chronologically without distinction. From an early date, however, merchants tended to replace a single comprehensive book with a number of separate volumes each devoted to a particular type of transaction (Defoe 1738: 34). A complete system required three volumes: a journal or day book listing credit transactions; a cash book for cash transactions; and a ledger in which the entries from the journal and cash books would be summarized in separate accounts for each customer.

It is very probable that the book-keeping system that Henslowe learned as a young man was not adequate for the enterprises of his maturity. After his marriage to Agnes Woodward, Henslowe lived almost entirely on investment. His wealth consisted of his capital, held partly in real estate, partly in loans and partly in cash. His real annual income would be what he received in rent and interest less the amount he spent to earn that income. To determine his financial position at any time he would have had to be able to total his assets in property, credit and cash, and deduct from them his current liabilities in expenses or bad loans. It would have been extraordinarily difficult to do these things using the diary alone. For example, Henslowe made no distinction between cash and credit transactions. The sale of a jewel to William Sly (f. 15) was recorded in the same way as a loan to Richard Jones (f. 34v). And yet in the first case the item should be deducted from some inventory of jewels, while in the second the amount should be subtracted from the cash on hand. The existence of a rent book from the years 1504–1611 (Ms XVIII, 6) and a 'building book' referred to by Alleyn (Ms IX, 24 Dec. 1621) suggest that the diary contains only a partial record of Henslowe's financial dealings. There is no consolidation of entries to present a more or less comprehensive financial picture, and, indeed, it is difficult to deduce why some of the records were kept at all.

This is certainly the case with many of his real estate transactions. Documents relating to this aspect of Henslowe's business have survived among the muniments and manuscripts preserved at Dulwich College. Greg has collated all the evidence to put together as complete a picture of Henslowe's speculations in property as is possible. Here we will consider the diary entries only as evidence of Henslowe's book-keeping methods. The fullest accounts are those with Mrs Keyes in April and May of 1599. On folio 42v, Henslowe itemized what he had 'payd for mrs keayes' and on folio 43 what he had 'Receud of mrs Keayes Reant'. This is a conventional record of income on the right hand side and payments on the left. Thus receipts totalling £4-6-0 are offset by expenditures amounting to £4-7-8. These latter are made up of rent paid on Mrs Keyes' behalf, a loan of £1-00-0, and the transfer of certain rents received. The accounts are not totalled or balanced, but the debit side is crossed out. Once again, the more complete form of these accounts may be a result of the fact that they were prepared for someone other than Henslowe himself.

Such a conclusion might be supported by the lacunae in the remaining real estate records. Where Henslowe listed his own payments (to John Malthouse for example) he did so without explanation and without reference to any income. His 'Reconynge' drawn up on folio 19 shows various legal expenses incurred in connection with the purchase of tenements which may have been part of the messuage on the Bankside known as The Barge, the Bell and the Cock (Greg 1904; II, 297). There he itemized various charges amounting to £4-7-02 (which he incorrectly totalled as £4-11-11 at the bottom of the account). That these costs are only part of the expenses involved in the transaction is suggested by the 'ttottalis' £131-06-11 entered at the bottom left of the account, but there is no indication in the diary of what this total represents or how it was arrived at. It is clear, therefore, that the 'malthouse Recknyge' is only a partial record of Henslowe's transactions relating to The Barge, the Bell and the Cock, and that further accounts including the purchase price of the property, expenses for repairs and amounts received in rent must have been kept elsewhere. Like the other reckonings for Alleyn and Mrs Keyes, this was probably prepared as a kind of statement of account.

The majority of the real estate entries seem to be memoranda of some kind, but in most cases it is difficult to see why they were preserved and impossible to deduce their relationship to Henslowe's investments as a whole. They seem to fall into three categories: statements of expenses (including rent), reminders of agreements (ff. 24, 25, 98) and accounts of rental income. There are several brief summaries of expenses, such as the cost of repairs for The Fool's Head (f. 1v), the amount paid for painted cloth, wainscoting and turned pillars for The James' Head (f. 3v) and costs for repairs to Hugh Daves' house (ff. 6–6v), mending a wharf (f. 21) and building a house on the Bankside (f. 32). Few of these accounts are added up, and when they are, as in the case of the Bankside property, the addition is inaccurate. It is also interesting that sometimes entries are made before the cash is actually paid out and then subsequently cancelled by writing 'no' in the left-hand margin (f. 32). These cancellations have been taken into consideration when the account was totalled, but there is no indication of what income (if any) the sums were charged against.

Another expense incurred by Henslowe was his annual rents. The only record of these is a memo on folio 178v showing yearly charges of £52-14-8 beginning in 1602. There is no indication of when these rents were due, or how often they were paid, and no evidence of an attempt to balance these expenses against income received from the properties. That Henslowe was in receipt of rents is shown by accounts on the facing page. There he enters 'A note of alle my tenentes & what they paye yearley' (f. 178). This entry has the appearance of an *aide memoire* rather than an active account, although a series of dots and strokes following each name may indicate instalment payments. On the whole, therefore, the diary entries relating to Henslowe's investments in real estate appear to be little more than casual jottings for particular purposes rather than a systematic attempt to keep track of his changing financial position.

The same could be said of the extensive records of personal loans. From very early in his business career Henslowe found it necessary to extend credit to his associates and customers. Though not as widespread as today, the use of credit was an integral component of sixteenth-century business and trade. There were three main types of credit instruments: the bill of debt (a promissory note in English usually written by the debtor himself), the 'obligation' (a note drawn up in Latin by a scrivener and signed, sealed and witnessed), and the bill of exchange (usually reserved for transactions with the continent) (Ramsey 1962: xlix). Some of the diary entries would qualify as the first, but most are simply notes of what Henslowe was owed together with (occasionally) a record of repayments.

One of the simplest forms of credit is instalment buying whereby the purchaser in effect borrows money from the vendor. One such transaction is described on folio 16, where Henslowe records the sale of a doublet to Steven Magett. Between 23 January and 3 May 1596, Magett paid sums of from one to four shillings amounting in all to sixteen shillings. When the total price of the doublet was paid, Henslowe crossed out the account as an indication that it was closed. It is possible that an amount for interest was included in the sale price, but I think it unlikely. It is more probable that Henslowe was making allowances for the irregular income of those associated with the theatre, as he appears to have done when he sold Richard Bradshaw a quantity of copper lace in December 1600, and agreed to accept payment when Bradshaw returned to London after a provincial tour (f. 84v).

Henslowe recorded relatively few sales in his diary. He was constantly lending money in other ways, however, and there are a number of minor peculiarities about his accounts. To begin with, records of loans are not restricted to a particular part of the volume. Furthermore they are only rarely consolidated, and many of them seem to be incomplete. Several appear to have remained unpaid, while in other cases there are acknowledgements of payments for debts which have not been recorded. Finally, almost all of the loans are to individuals whom Henslowe would have known personally. These scattered records do not look like the accounts of a professional moneylender; they have more the appearance of the rather casual efforts of a man to keep track of his personal loans.

This is not to suggest that Henslowe was indifferent to the losses which might result from bad debts. He tried to minimize such losses in several ways. One of the most common entries was a simple notation of an unsecured loan such as 'lent vnto mr harey draper the 4 of aprell 1593 in Redey money the some of xvjli' (f. 3). Such a memorandum would have had little validity in law, since it is unsigned and unwitnessed. This particular entry has not been crossed out which may indicate that the loan was never repaid, or may simply be evidence of Henslowe's carelessness. Since Draper did not put his name to the memo, he might not have known of it, and would have had no reason to insist that it be cancelled when the debt was paid.

Somewhat more binding in effect would be the witnessed notes of indebtedness. These took various forms. There were the signed memoranda such as 'Lent mr Richard ffuller my attorney the 24 of aguste in Readey money . . . & witneses to the leandynge herof mr shealden player & mr fullers man' (f. 40v). In this case presumably the borrower could not sign for the debt himself since the money was being picked up by a servant, but the signatures would no doubt be legally binding. In many cases the indebted party would himself sign an acknowledgement. Such promissory notes were often entirely in the hand of the borrower and constituted a formal receipt such as

'Borrowed of phillip Henchlowe xxs the vijth of Aprill anno dom 1599 — Henry Porter' (f. 62). At other times the acknowledgement might be in the form of a bond, setting out the conditions of repayment as in the following: 'Be it knowne vnto all men by theise p[rese]ntes That I Henry Porter do owe and am indebted vnto Mr Phillip Henchlowe in the some of Twenty shillynges of good and lawfull money of England, ffor the wch true and good payment I bynd me my heiers and executore, where vnto I have set my hand this present seaventene of January, a. do. 1598 per me, Henry Porter' (HD: 265). Some of these bonds (but not Porter's) have been cancelled, which in most cases is the only evidence we have that the debt was retired. It seems clear that in these transactions Henslowe was attempting to ensure repayment, but it is questionable whether he was always successful. One debt, that of Gabriel Spencer acknowledged on 20 April 1598 (f. 42), remained uncancelled in the diary and was almost certainly unpaid at the time of Spencer's death on 22 September of that year. Other uncancelled accounts probably indicate similar outstanding debts.

Some insight into Henslowe's lending practices and his methods of recording his loans may be gained by examining his relations with the actor William Bird. Bird joined the Admiral's Men in the autumn of 1597 when the company incorporated several of the leading players from Lord Pembroke's Men. Between then and 1603, Bird was involved in several legal and domestic difficulties which necessitated frequent recourse to Henslowe for 'redey money'. Altogether he borrowed £30-00-0, repaying all but £4-00-0 by 12 March 1602 (f. 89v). A number of these transactions are itemized in the diary.

The earliest records of loans to Bird appear on folio 38 immediately below a list of expenditures related to 'the changinge of ower comysion' (possibly a reference to Henslowe's efforts to secure the Mastership of the Bears (Greg 1904: II, 37). At the bottom of the page are two memoranda of loans to Bird witnessed by third parties (including 'thomas dowten biger boye whome fecthed yt fore hime'. This latter loan was for a short period (19–24 December), and was apparently collected by one of the boy actors on Bird's behalf. The following February Henslowe advanced Bird a further £1-00-0 for a waistcoat, but this loan was not witnessed.

On 9 April 1598, Bird, along with Spencer and Downton, borrowed a total of £6-00-0 which they acknowledged in a bond drawn up partly by Henslowe and partly by Downton, and signed by the three debtors (f. 42). Possibly the money was needed to defray legal costs involved in a court case between the three of them and Martin Slater. At any rate, Henslowe appears to have advanced the trio another sum of £1-10-0 for this purpose on 8 March. In recording this second advance in Bird's account, Henslowe turned to a new page (f. 39) and retranscribed all of the actor's debts under the heading 'wm Bornes alles [alias] birde Recknynge . . . at severall times lent as folowethe 1597'. The original items were probably crossed out about this time, and Henslowe carefully carried forward the details of the loans, including the fact that they should have been repaid the previous Christmas Eve. Between 25 and 29 March Henslowe advanced Bird an additional 18s. 4d. which he added to the actor's growing debt.

Running out of space at this point, Henslowe continued Bird's account on the facing page under the heading 'wm borne alles birde 1598 Deatte as folowth'(f. 38v). Between 29 March and 27 November he added seven small loans totalling £3-14-8. Overlapping with these accounts are a series of secured loans on folio 41v. These advances differ from earlier loans in that Henslowe began to take articles of clothing and jewellery as security for his money. That this was more of a formality than a serious attempt to protect his investment, however, is suggested by the entry 'Dd vnto wm Birde ales borne ij gewells of gowld wch he layd to me to pane [pawn] for xs wch I dd to hime agayne wth owt money wch he owes me.' In succeeding years, Bird's needs appear to have been more sporadic. Henslowe made memoranda of loans on 22 April 1599 and 26 November 1600 (f. 42v). Then on 11 July 1601 he drew up a final statement which Bird signed acknowledging a total debt of £23-00-0.

It is difficult to see how Henslowe arrived at this figure. Between April and December 1598, Bird borrowed a total of £14-18-0. His recorded loans in 1599 and 1600 totalled another £5-00-0. In addition, the actor borrowed sums of £6-00-0 and £3-00-0 jointly with Spencer and Downton. The final acquittal given by Henslowe mentions 'another debte of vj li or thereaboutes. vppon a bond' (f. 89v) which probably refers to the first of these joint loans (f. 42), so it is possible that the second may have been incorporated (in whole or in part) in Henslowe's reckonings. This would give a total of £22-18-0 which Henslowe might well have rounded out to £23-00-0. But the diary also records several irregular repayments which should have been credited against this sum. Between 25 February and 4 March 1598, Bird managed to repay ten shillings on his debt of £1-00-0 for a waistcoat (f. 39v). Then on 17 June of the same year Henslowe collected five shillings which he obviously expected to be the first of many such payments, since he entered it under the heading 'Rd of wm Birde at severalle times' (f. 33). In June 1601, Bird again began to repay his debt and managed to turn over £1-11-8 before Henslowe recorded that he 'pd him backe a gayne this mony' (f. 102v). It would appear that either Henslowe did not credit these payments to Bird's account (deliberately or otherwise) or that the diary entries constitute only part of the record of the actor's transactions. That the latter is the case is suggested by the reference to 'ij gewells of gowld' which Henslowe noted he had returned (f. 41v), but nowhere recorded having received.

Sometime before 18 October 1601, Bird borrowed another £5-00-0, and instead of adding this amount to the £23-00-0 Henslowe entered it separately along with a column of several repayments (f. 103v). Once again the payments cease after about a month so it is something of a surprise to learn that by 12 March 1602, Bird had reduced his debt to £4-10-0 and stood 'cleere of all debtes & demaundes except theis debtes and suche stocke & covenentes as I maie clayme & challendge of him by reason of his coniunction wth the Companie' (f. 89v). This latter is obviously a reference to Bird's obligations as a sharer as distinct from his personal debts.

Generalizing from these records, I think we can draw several conclusions. First, Henslowe used a variety of strategies (witnessed notes, bonds, receipts and collateral) to secure his loans, but there is no evidence that he foreclosed on any of them, or even that he charged interest. Their personal nature is borne out by the casual record-keeping, and by the fact that the entries are intermixed with family matters, such as his activities on behalf of his brother's children (ff. 39v, 40). If Henslowe were the flint-hearted moneylender he is sometimes made out to be, it is unlikely that he would have been so apparently indifferent to repeated delays and defaults in repayments.

The non-theatrical accounts reveal much about Henslowe's book-keeping methods and his 'style' of doing business. It would appear that the diary is less a formal account book (such as a ledger or a journal, both of which would need to be kept more systematically) than a personal memorandum book. Occasionally it contains extensive records like a complete list of expenditures, or a series of loans, but even in these cases there is no effort to incorporate the information into a comprehensive financial statement. It is difficult to imagine how Henslowe could have supervised his various business enterprises without a fuller set of books including, at the very least, a ledger in which he would have recorded his transactions with individuals. If such books existed, possibly they became separated from the diary at the time of Henslowe's death. Whatever the truth, we must recognize, I think, that the diary contains only a partial record of Henslowe's activities, albeit a record maintained by a reasonably painstaking individual.

2 · THEATRICAL LANDLORD

WE DO NOT KNOW how Philip Henslowe, 'citizen and dyer', recent bridegroom and speculator in sheepskins, became attracted to the new business of the theatre. Nothing we have learned of his other interests would suggest a literary bent, nor does his enterprise or ambition in marrying his master's widow betoken a Bohemian personality. Whatever the cause, whether shrewd foresight, love of art, naked greed or a combination of all three, on 10 January 1587 Henslowe entered into partnership with one John Cholmley, grocer, to share expenses in the building of a playhouse. According to the terms of their agreement Cholmley was to have the use of a small tenement or dwelling-house on the property for storage, and the exclusive right to sell bread and drink to patrons. He was also to get one half of all the money collected from the audience attending the plays. In return he agreed to pay Henslowe an annuity of £816 in quarterly instalments of £27-10-0 over a period of eight years and three months. For his part, Henslowe promised to pay all rents and to repair the bridges and wharfs belonging to the property by the following Michaelmas (Mun. 16).

The purpose of the partnership from Henslowe's point of view was to insure himself against fluctuations in the rate of return by selling an uncertain gain for a smaller but guaranteed income. Cholmley, no doubt, would be attracted by the prospect of making a double profit, one on the food concession and a second on his share of the box-office revenue. As it stands, however, the agreement seems unworkable since the terms make no provision for a share of the receipts to go to the actors. Not unlikely this is a reflection of the relative ignorance of both partners of the nature of the business upon which they were embarking.

The agreement specified that the theatre should be erected by John Grigges, a carpenter, with 'as muche expedicon as may be' but did not name a precise completion date. At the same time, it bound Cholmley to quarterly payments beginning on the feast of St John the Baptist, and added that failure to meet these payments would constitute a breach of the agreement and the termination of the partnership. There is no record of when the Rose theatre was finished although it was certainly standing by 1588 (ES: II, 407). Henslowe seems, therefore, to have lived up to his side of the bargain, but no sign of Cholmley's participation in the enterprise can be found a few years later when we first get a glimpse of its operations.

What Henslowe did with his new playhouse during the first four years of its existence is not known. Between March and April 1592, however, he recorded expenditures in his newly acquired account book amounting to some £108. These related to charges for what by that time he was referring to as 'my playe howsse' (f. 4). It is difficult to see why major repairs should have been required a mere five years after the

14

construction of the building so it is more likely, perhaps, that these expenses point to some alterations of the basic structure, possibly the construction of a 'heavens' and lords' rooms over the stage. Charges for a 'maste' (likely a flagpole), for thatched roofing, for two dozen turned ballasters, and for 'sellynge' (ceilings) in the lords' room and the room over the tiring house (f. 5v) all support such an interpretation. When the work could have been done, however, is difficult to see since the theatre was in constant use by Strange's men between 19 February and 23 June (Table II.1). I am inclined to think that alterations were completed before the company moved in. The receipts are for large bills which were probably presented some months after the work was completed. The other expenses listed on folios 4–5 have the appearance of an account retranscribed from other sources like that prepared for Edward Alleyn.

Just as mysterious as the date of these entries is their purpose. They seem to represent Henslowe's attempt to determine his current financial position. But in order to ascertain whether or not he was earning an adequate return on his investment, Henslowe would have had to add to these figures his original capital outlay together with yearly fixed costs, and set the total off against income. Possibly he did draw up some kind of balance sheet like the one on folio 235v, but if so it has not survived. In order to understand Henslowe's activities in relationship to the theatre and the players, therefore, it is necessary to attempt to reconstruct his theatrical finances.

INCOME

As we have seen, Henslowe originally envisaged splitting all of the income from the theatre with his partner Cholmley. What he probably intended was that the owners of the theatre would divide the admission fees paid to enter the galleries, while the players would take the receipts collected at the outer door. This, at least, was the custom at the Theatre according to Cuthbert Burbage who went on to say that at some later point the owners' or 'housekeepers'' share was reduced to one half of the gallery income (PRO LC/5/133, pp. 50–1; cited Schoenbaum 1975: 104). Precisely when this change took place is not known. Depositions taken in a case involving James Burbage and the widow of his former partner, John Brayne, make ambiguous reference to the manner in which the owners shared the income from the theatre. Mrs Brayne was authorized by the court to appoint collectors to stand at the door 'that goeth vppe to the galleries' to take 'half the money that shuld be gyven to come vppe into the said galleries at that door' (ES: II, 392). Since we do not know if there was more than one door to the galleries, however, we cannot be sure what proportion of the takings Mrs Brayne was claiming. By 1597 the Swan owner, Francis Langley, received only one half of the gallery money as rent (Wallace 1910: 352). It seems likely, therefore, that Greg is right (1904: II, 134) when he estimates that the figures recorded in the diary after 19 February 1592 represent one half of the receipts collected in the galleries. Whether those receipts belonged to the actors or the owner is a more complex problem, to which we will return.

There are several puzzles related to these accounts. The first is why Henslowe kept them at all. Was he perhaps compiling a financial statement to show to a silent partner as Burbage apparently did at the Theatre (Wallace 1966: 85)? Another problem is the method used. Did Henslowe collect the money daily and record it immediately, or did he consolidate this list from other reckonings as we have seen him do with some of his non-theatrical activities? As Foakes and Rickert point out (HD: xxvii), Henslowe seems sometimes to have written his dates prior to entering titles and income (f. 9v). An error in the dating of entries from 8 May to 3 June 1592 (f. 7v) might suggest that he recorded these items in batches. On Monday 9 May, Henslowe wrongly transcribed the date as 7 May. During the next two weeks, each date is two days behind the calendar. Following the entry for 18 May, however, Henslowe again misread his figures and began the next series of receipts with the date 10 May. He carried on chronologically until he reached the bottom of the page where he recorded receipts for 22 May (twelve days behind the actual date). At the top of the next leaf he continued with 24 May, but at last realized his error. Discovering the mistake following 18 May, he went back and corrected the entries to 22 May. This left his new date still three days behind the calendar, a fact he must have known since he corrected 24 May to the actual date, 5 June (f. 8).

It is easy to see how this series of mistakes began, but difficult to understand how it could have continued so long undetected if Henslowe entered his receipts every day. He could hardly have gone for almost a month not knowing the date, especially since he was engaged in business transactions in the same period (ff. 6v, 123v). Altogether more probable is the hypothesis that Henslowe made his diary entries at irregular intervals. I suspect that he began a group of entries on 6 May, and got out of sequence when he confused the VI of 'harey the vj' for the date of the preceding day. He continued this batch of entries until the week following Whitsun, carefully skipping a day between the sixth performance of one week and the first of the following. He indicated this break by a line across the page between what he recorded as 11 and 13 May (Thursday and Friday), although, as Greg has shown, the interruption in playing almost certainly took place between 13 and 15 (Saturday and Monday). Sometime later he began again and made a second mistake when he misread 18 as 8 and commenced the following week's receipts with the date 10 May.

Support for the theory of periodical entry is provided by what looks like a sub-total located on folio 7v. This figure is one of several numbers jotted in the margins of folios 7v and 8. In certain cases, the figures are quite clearly references to sums of money, as 'Rd li 24' or 'Rd 32.14.' Other figures such as '9', '34' or '066.' are more ambiguous. The entry in question reads 51-10 (a correction of 49-10) and very probably means £51-10-0. How Henslowe arrived at this figure is not clear. It is very close to the total receipts collected between 17 April (the date following the first marginal entry) and what Henslowe records as 15 May. This sum amounts to £51-9-6, and it is easy to believe that the figure was rounded out. But it is difficult (perhaps impossible) to reconcile the other 'sub-totals' with the accounts. For example, 'Rd li 24' should probably read '23', while 'Rd 32.14' might be a miscalculation for £32-8-6. Possibly '34' is a rough estimate, but I can find no correlation between subsequent marginal figures and the actual sub-totals of the receipts recorded. Furthermore, all such jottings disappear after 22 June 1592, so if someone was attempting to keep track of receipts, the effort was abandoned.

A change in Henslowe's method of recording income took place in the early summer of 1594 when he entered into an association with the Admiral's and Chamberlain's Men. Beginning 3 June 1594, he started each entry with a symbol followed by the date and the name of the play. (The form of entry bears a strong resemblance to a series of pawn accounts (f. 73), to be discussed later, in which Henslowe began using the same symbol and date systems in December 1593.) Entries in this new form run without significant interruption until 22 January 1597. In the earliest of them there is evidence of an attempt to keep track of receipts by recording totals at the foot of the page (ff. 9v, 10, 10v). Interestingly, these are in a different ink from the surrounding entries, which may indicate that the calculations were carried out at a different time and even, perhaps, by a different hand. The totals recorded (111-6-0, 60-06-3, 58-08-0) correspond only approximately with the actual totals (104-15-6, 67-18-6, 58-04-10). We notice here, however, a feature that is characteristic of many of Henslowe's accounts – that the three incorrect totals add up to a figure very close to the real one (£230-00-3 for £230-17-6). Either Henslowe's totals do not sum up the pages as they now exist, or he discovered his mistake and silently corrected it.

After 14 December 1594, receipts were no longer totalled, but two interlined entries on folio 12v suggest some kind of a review of the figures. The first of these ('post 83 li') appears between the date (10 June 1595) and the sum recorded on that day. It corresponds fairly closely to the total collected from 10 March up to and including 'whittson daye' by which Henslowe probably meant Monday 9 June. The purpose of this sub-total (if it is one) is obscure, but the occurrence of the word 'post' is extremely interesting. In a commercial context the word later referred to the action of transcribing an entry from a journal or day book to a ledger, and it is entirely possible that Henslowe is using it in this sense. If he is, then this would be fairly convincing evidence that the diary is only a book of original entry, and that Henslowe (or an associate) maintained another set of books in which accounts might have been laid out in a more systematic manner. The flaw in this argument is that the word occurs only one other time in the diary (at the bottom of folio 12v), and there it is difficult to see how Henslowe arrived at his total of 173-00-0. A figure which looks like a sub-total appears on folio 14 without the preceding 'post', and once again it is not easy to see what the sum represents.

Another puzzling feature of these income accounts is the presence of several notations referring to payments to the Master of the Revels. These payments were of various kinds. Between 26 February and 10 May 1592 Henslowe paid Tilney five shillings a week, after which time the sum gradually increased until it reached six shillings and eightpence by the end of Strange's first season. Thereafter no further mention of payments to the Master is to be found until 10 March 1595, at which time there is an interlined notation '17p from hence lycensed' (f. 11v). This seems to refer to the seventeen 'ne' plays introduced into the Admiral's Men's repertoire since June

1594 and may be an indication that licence fees for all these works were paid in a lump sum. More likely, perhaps, it may simply indicate that the company was paid up until that time. On 31 May a curt note 'pd' may refer to some sort of payment to the Master of the Revels; that is certainly the meaning of entries on 7 November, 18 December, 30 January and at the end of February 1596, when Henslowe reported 'the master of the Revelles payd vntell this time al wch I owe hime' (f. 14v).

The relationship between these three styles of entry is obscure. Weekly remittances in 1592 were probably licence fees for operating the theatre paid by the owner. The play licences mentioned in the second entry are quite distinct, and the cost of such licences should normally be a charge on the actors rather than the landlord. Subsequent notations probably refer again to fees for operating the theatre, but there is no indication of what sum was being paid out. Between 26 April and 12 July 1596, Henslowe recorded several other payments in the income accounts and collected signed acquittances in other sections of the diary where the money paid to the Master is sometimes described as 'paye' (f. 20v), and sometimes as being for the Master's 'use' (f. 23v). From these receipts it would also appear that by 1596 the theatre licence fee had risen to 10 shillings a week.

The playhouse income accounts continue unchanged until 22 January 1597, when there is a sudden and dramatic alteration in their form. On that date Henslowe changed from roman numerals (Rd at Joronymo . . . xixs) to a system of five columns of arabic numbers (Janeway 1597 tt at Nabucadonizer 0 09 02 00 – 03). There is fairly general agreement that this change must reflect an alteration in Henslowe's relationship to the company, but no consensus as to what that change might be. Wallace (1910: 361) followed by Baldwin (1927b: 71) suggested that the first two figures represent pounds and shillings and record half the gallery income, while the last three columns (representing pounds, shillings and pence) record the outer door receipts. This theory was attacked by Chambers (ES: II, 143 n.) on the grounds that the players' income would not go through Henslowe's hands, and that there is not the kind of correlation between the two amounts which we would expect if they were both collected on the same day. In his turn, Chambers put forward the suggestion that the greatly fluctuating sums in the last three columns were loans to the players. As Foakes and Rickert point out, however, Henslowe already had a separate loan account with the players (ff. 22v–23), and would be unlikely to open a duplicate one. These writers seized on Chambers' observation that during the first seven weeks of playing (24 January–14 March) there is a rough correlation between the first two and last three columns on a weekly basis which disappears after the players cease borrowing from their landlord. They conclude that for the duration of these entries, Henslowe was responsible for collecting all the receipts, listing the half gallery income in the first two columns, and entering the door receipts due the players in the last three. The fact that the latter figures vary greatly (sometimes being reduced to zero) they explain by supposing that Henslowe was repaying himself out of these takings and turning over to the players what remained (HD: xxxiv).

It seems unlikely that Henslowe should change from the fairly detailed description of advances he used before and after this period to a system so open to error and abuse. Perhaps the conclusive argument against the theory that these figures conceal Henslowe's loans to the company, however, is the size of the amounts involved. Presumably the highest figures in the last three columns would be those from which small or no deductions had been made, and which would therefore be close to the total amount taken in at the outer door. These figures average about £20 per week so it should be possible to estimate the players' weekly borrowing by subtracting the actual weekly total from a hypothetical average. When this is done we see that the supposed loan repayments amount to about £14 a week, far above the sums borrowed from Henslowe at any other time.

Whatever the true nature of these entries, they cease as abruptly as they began when the amalgamated Admiral's–Pembroke's Company started performing at the Rose in October 1597. At that time, apparently, the landlord prepared to continue his five-column system by making a marginal note 'the xj of octobe be gane my lord admerals & my lord of penbrokes men to playe at my howsse 1597' (f. 27v). Beneath this entry he inscribed a column of 'tt at's in readiness for recording titles and income. Three plays (*Joroneymo*, *the comody of vmers* and *doctor fostes*) were entered, but then the entries cease until the end of the month when Henslowe listed six performances ending on 5 November together with the usual five columns of figures. A peculiarity of this last sequence of income accounts is that it overlaps with a very different system of recording receipts found elsewhere in the diary. This alternative set of figures is described as 'A Juste a cownte of all Suche monye as I haue Receued of my lord admeralles & my lord of penbrocke men as foloweth be gynynge the 21 of october 1597' (f. 36v). It differs from previous records in that it gives only a weekly total, but eventually it is this method which prevails, and the records of daily performance disappear. The accounts of the week ending 5 November, however, are in both systems and it is possible therefore to compare the figures. On folio 27v the first two columns yield a total of £5-12-0, whereas the amount recorded in the weekly accounts for the same period is £2-18-10 (f. 36v). This confirms the impression that the new totals average only about half what was collected between 1592–7 (Table IV).

These new weekly accounts run until 8 July 1598, by which time Henslowe had received exactly £125 (a total rounded off by the last payment of £2-11-07). Three weeks later he began yet another income account with the words 'Here I Begyne to Receue the wholle gallereys ffrome this daye' (f. 48). These latter receipts continued until 13 October when Henslowe acknowledged he had collected £358-03. A week later he continued the account (f. 62v), and by 13 July 1600, the players had paid an additional £207-02-0 which they acknowledged left them just £300 in Henslowe's debt (f. 69v). Here the income receipts cease altogether with the exception of two isolated entries on folio 83 under the heading 'My Lordes of penbrocke men begane to playe at the Rosse the 28 october 1600.' These report income of 'xjs 6d' and 'vs' taken at 'licke vnto licke' and 'RadeRicke'. What is puzzling is that they show a return to an earlier system of daily rather than weekly receipts, presumably reflecting an agreement between Lord Pembroke's Men and the owner of the Rose similar to that struck between the Admiral's Men and Henslowe in 1594–7.

What can we deduce about Henslowe's relations with the players from his chameleon-like records of income? The accounts themselves seem to progress through five stages, as follows:

> 1592–94 daily income: 'Rd at (title and date)   xxii'
> 1594–97 daily income: '(date) Rd at (title)   xvii'
> 1597–97 daily income: '(date) tt at (title) 03 04 01 03 00'
> 1597–98 weekly income: 'Rd the (date)   vli js xjd'
> 1598–1600 weekly income: 'wholle gallereys'   xli xiiij'

It has been assumed that these entries are Henslowe's receipts compiled for his own (or possibly a partner's) information. Such an interpretation is supported by outside evidence that Francis Langley was in receipt of one half of the gallery takings at the Swan (Wallace 1910: 352); that Henslowe took one half of the gallery income at the Hope as rent (Mun. 52); and that Burbage kept a 'Booke of Reconinges' between himself and his partner, Brayne (Wallace 1966: 85). But there are a number of difficulties with this theory. Cholmley is nowhere specifically referred to in the diary, and Beckerman's suggestion (1971: 42) that the accounts were needed to settle with Alleyn ignores the fact that the actor seems to have withdrawn from active management between 1597 and 1600. Foakes' theory that the information was compiled for the Master of the Revels (HD: xxix) may be true, but he bases his argument in part on his contention that the cessation of daily entries coincided with a change in the manner of paying the Master. In fact, as we have seen, Henslowe returned briefly to a system of daily entries in October 1600, when, according to Foakes, such records would no longer be required. Another problem is the relationship between this 'rental' income and the 'wholle gallereys', sums collected by Henslowe between 1598 and 1600 as repayment for loans to the players. Greg has demonstrated that these latter sums almost certainly represent only half of the income from the galleries. He suggests that Henslowe's rental income was a constant figure and that there would be no need in these years to record it in the diary (1904: II, 134). Apparently he did not see how seriously this fact undermines his basic assumptions. For as Foakes rightly points out, 'If there was no need for Henslowe to keep a record [of his rental income] at this time [1598], it may be wondered why he should have troubled to keep one earlier' (HD: xxviii).

It is time to ask whether the seemingly confusing features of the diary accounts cannot be explained by a simpler hypothesis than the ones so far proposed. Is it possible that this income was not Henslowe's after all, but that from first to last the landlord was recording money collected by him but due to the players? We recall that Cholmley and Henslowe originally intended to collect all the income to the theatre (by which they perhaps understood only the gallery income), and that Burbage and Brayne seemed to be doing the same at the Theatre. If we suppose that the gatherers at the

Rose were divided between those who collected in the galleries and returned their receipts to the owner, and those who collected at the outer doors and gave their revenue to the players, then some of the puzzling features of the entries disappear. The daily income records can be seen as a statement, not of what Henslowe earned, but of what he owed the actors out of the total gallery income. This is perhaps more consistent with the non-theatrical accounts which are mostly statements of expenditures rather than income. The enigmatic five-column entries may also be more easily understood as the players' income. If we assume that the first two columns represent the actors' half gallery income (which Henslowe continued to record, but in this novel form), then perhaps the second three columns represent the outer door takings (less whatever the players needed to pay current production expenses). I suspect that this system reveals an increasing reliance on the part of the Admiral's Men on the services of Henslowe as treasurer and banker. When Alleyn retired and the Pembroke's actors joined the Company (fresh from their painful experiences with Langley), there was perhaps less willingness on the part of the newly formed company to trust Henslowe with the handling of so much of their income and the five-column system was abandoned.

The reorganization of the Company also coincides with the sudeen change from a daily to a weekly method of entry. Starting in October 1597, Henslowe recorded money 'Receued of' the players. The sums collected between 21 October 1597 and 8 July 1598 differ from all other income accounts in the diary. Unlike the daily sums listed earlier, and the 'wholle gallereys' collected later, these entries are about half as large as the usual weekly totals and regularly include odd pence. Furthermore, the amounts seem to be discretionary, since the final payment appears to have been calculated to bring the total to exactly £125 (ff. 35, 36v). Finally, it is not at all clear whether the money belonged to Henslowe or the players. The amounts are not deducted from the actors' debt which might suggest (as it apparently did to Greg) that they represent payments for rent. But why are they so much smaller than earlier 'rental' figures? And why were they so carefully rounded off? One possibility is that the money was being held in trust by Henslowe and like Humphrey Jeffes' half-share (for which Henslowe also rendered a 'Juste acownte'), it was 'payd backe agayne vnto the companey' (f. 36). Perhaps the new Admiral's—Pembroke's Men insisted on a new method of gathering and dividing the receipts. But what that method was we cannot say. Not unlikely, the players began collecting the money from the outer doors themselves, and possibly turned over one-half of their gallery takings to Henslowe to be held in trust for some now indeterminable purpose.

The accounts with the Admiral's Men cease when the Company moved to the Fortune where Alleyn (as part owner) probably took over the responsibilities of dealing with the players. When Pembroke's Men began performing at the Rose in 1600, Henslowe assumed that he would once again collect the receipts in the galleries and turn over one-half of them to the players, but, for whatever reason, the system was not continued.

INVESTMENT

Throughout the period that Henslowe was receiving income from the theatre he must have been concerned with the double problem of safeguarding and investing his money. Regular deposit banking does not appear to have developed in England until the next century, so presumably currency was stored in strongboxes in individual homes and shops. Since Henslowe does not seem to have been engaged in manufacturing or commerce, he must have been continually on the lookout for suitable opportunities for profitable investment. In a period when interest charges were legal but frowned on, such investments may have been difficult to find.

There is some indication that Henslowe's financing of the actors may have grown out of, or dovetailed with, his pawnbroking business. The diary contains a number of accounts related to this curious side of Henslowe's affairs dating between January 1593 and April 1596. The earliest appears on folio 55, where Henslowe lists a loan to his nephew, Francis, 'vpon A peticote of Read wth iij belementes laces of A womon dwellinge in londitche'. The transaction is peculiar and requires some interpretation. It seems clear that the money is being secured by the woman's gown although the payment is actually made to Francis. Henslowe was apparently underwriting a pawnbroking business, but it is far from clear just what his relationship to that business was.

Little is known about pawnbroking in England in the sixteenth century, and it has even been suggested that it did not exist as a separate, self-sufficient trade until the reign of James II (Hudson 1982: 32). Elsewhere in Europe pawnbroking was widespread, even becoming a licensed monopoly in the Low Countries as early as the fourteenth century. Records from medieval Bruges and nineteenth-century London suggest that the methods and problems of the business did not vary much from age to age. The pawnbroker's clientele was drawn from all classes, but it was the poor who predominated. Records surviving from Pistoia in the fourteenth century show that in one five-day period, a pawnbroker made eighty loans of which nearly half were for less than £1-10. Pledges were mostly articles of clothing, followed by tools, jewellery, arms, bedding and household utensils. Regulations under which the pawnbrokers operated specified that pledges had to be kept for a year and a day after which they became forfeit and could be sold. The customary rate of interest allowed by law was 2d in the pound per week or 43 per cent (De Roover 1948: 121–5). Although the rate seems usurious (and was frequently attacked as such), it has been argued that it was not excessive in view of the expenses involved. These would include licence fees, rent, wages, interest on capital borrowed, storage charges and depreciation on pledges (De Roover 1948: 128).

To keep track of the large number of small articles, the pawnbrokers at Bruges issued a document for each loan on which they recorded the names of lender and borrower, a description of pawned articles, the amount due, the signature of the lender and the date (De Roover 1948: 132). This medieval equivalent of a pawn ticket would be retained by the borrower and presented along with a payment covering principal and interest to reclaim the article pawned. How these latter were stored is not known. One would assume that some numerical identification would be necessary to simplify the process of recovery from storage, but since no actual pawn ticket has survived it is impossible to know the truth. An extant fragment of an account book belonging to a Tuscan pawnbroker in 1417 indicates that the lender kept a folio record of loans and wrote the dates of repayment in the margin (De Roover 1948: 122).

Against this background it is possible to begin to reconstruct Philip Henslowe's activities in the pawning business between 1593 and 1596. Once again, one is struck by the partial nature of the surviving records. The first set containing his dealings with Francis suggests that he was underwriting his nephew by advancing money on unredeemed pledges. This would permit money which would otherwise be tied up to be put out at interest a second time. Henslowe would collect interest from the date he advanced money to Francis until the time the pledge was redeemed. Francis, in the meantime, would advance the borrowed money on a second loan. But what was Henslowe's role? It seems on the face of it that he would not have been involved in the day-to-day supervision of the business. On the other hand, he may have received and stored goods, for he recorded marginal notes in his diary such as 'DD [delivered] vnto frances mayde' (f. 74v). This particular action may have deserved some notice because it was unusual. There is no indication of whether pledges were redeemed by Francis or by the parties themselves. Whoever finally collected the pawned article paid an amount of interest which seems to have varied considerably. Charges were calculated by the month from the date received, and ranged from sixpence to fourteen pence, but seem normally to have been sixpence or eightpence in the pound. Henslowe kept no record of when a pledge was redeemed, simply crossing out an entry (or in many cases a whole page of entries) when he received his money. This last suggests to me that the articles were collected (possibly in large lots) by the agent. At various times there were more than one agent, and over the years Henslowe had dealings with four women in addition to his nephew Francis. The accounts were kept separate, but whether or not the individuals were partners or salaried employees, and whether they worked at one shop or several, is difficult to determine.

Henslowe's pawn entries, although less scattered than his other loan accounts, do not have the appearance of a complete set of pawnbroking records. Not only are the dates on which pledges were redeemed missing, but there is nowhere any calculation of profit or loss on the operation. In addition to the interest he collected, Henslowe also appears to have claimed unredeemed pledges. Sometime in March 1595, he returned to Goody Watson several garments described as 'my owne' which he asked her to sell at specified prices (f. 19v). These articles are almost certainly unredeemed pledges on which Henslowe had lent Watson money on 27 October, 5 and 29 November and 16 December 1595 (ff. 80–80v). The prices he asked were from two to four shillings more than the sum borrowed, amounts which probably represent interest for the three or four months he held the articles. The relatively brief period between the loan and the sale may indicate that the articles had already been in the pawnshop for many months before they were brought to Henslowe. Or it may simply mean that regulations concerning the sale of pledges were less stringent in London than they were on the continent. The full story of Henslowe's pawnbroking activities is unlikely to be recovered. In any case, it is probably not a coincidence that the last pawn transaction is dated 12 April 1597 (f. 133), and that the earliest recorded loan to the players is made the following month (f. 71v).

At first Henslowe's dealings with the Company took the form of personal loans. Between 2 May and 25 May 1596, he recorded six advances to Edward Alleyn 'for the company' which altogether added up to £21-13-04 (f. 71v). He entered this figure in arabic figures at the foot of the column and again to the right of the heading describing the loans. Part way down the page he began an income account with the heading 'Receaued agayne of my sonne EA of this deate abowe written as foloweth'. Between 10 May and 11 June, he recorded repayments amounting to £25-10-00, which he sub-totalled in the left margin. Sometime later Alleyn borrowed an additional £10-09-0, but by 8 July the Company had paid Henslowe a total of £39-09-00, which he entered incorrectly as £30-10-00 to the left of the heading. When he balanced the figures he discovered that the actors had repaid £7-06-08 more than they had borrowed and he returned that sum to Alleyn.

The account is interesting for what it reveals about Henslowe's book-keeping methods. First, he seems to have made a distinction between expense sums which he recorded on the right, and income sums which he entered on the left. Secondly, he carried his totals to the top of the account where he sometimes had to correct them by crossing out one set of numbers and entering another. A puzzling feature of this other-wise fairly accurate account is the figure 033-00-04 at the head of the page. In that position it would appear to be intended as the corrected total of loans made, but it is 17 shillings too large. Since Henslowe obviously used the correct total in estimating what to repay Alleyn, it is possible that he originally intended to charge the Company interest.

The next series of transactions between Henslowe and the players took place between 14 October 1596 and 25 March 1597 (ff. 22v–23). It marks an interesting development from the method of recording personal loans, and seems to reflect Henslowe's search for a more satisfactory way of keeping track of his advances and repayments. The account begins on folio 23 beneath the heading 'A note of Suche money as I haue lent vnto thes meane whose names folow at seaverall tymes edward alleyn martyne slather Jeames donstall & Jewbey'. There follow four items totalling £2-12-8 which appear to be separated off from a further five loans and three repay-ments which are grouped together by a large bracket in the left margin. Perhaps these first advances were repaid separately, since they do not figure in subsequent calcu-lations. Sometime after 1 November, Henslowe shifted his loan entries to the facing page (f. 22v) leaving space at the bottom of folio 23 for additional repayments. By early December he had advanced a further £15-15-0 which he correctly sub-totalled in the left margin and noted that the entire debt, including £7-00-0 still owing on 'the other side', came to £22-15-0. On 16 December he drew up another sub-total in the left margin, this time adding up all his advances (except the first four) which gave him a sum of £35-15-00. In January, the players were able to repay £18-00-0, but by

14 March they had had to borrow another £8-11-0, bringing their total debt to £44-06-0, which Henslowe noted in the margin. On Good Friday the landlord and his tenants drew up a reckoning for the season, at which time Henslowe advanced the players a further £5-14-0 which brought their loans to an even £50, just £30 more than they had managed to repay.

Here we see Henslowe modifying his method of recording personal loans to adapt it to changing circumstances. Individual items were listed at the top of a page and repayments below them. When he ran out of space (presumably because he did not expect to be called on so frequently), he transferred the account to a facing page so it was all visible. Periodic sub-totals were compiled, but only on the first occasion did Henslowe deduct what the players had repaid him to give a current balance. Subsequent estimates were of his advances only. The final reckoning was worked out without totalling the income account, and the balance entered at the head of the account on folio 22v, where it was witnessed by Edward Alleyn.

The next series of loan accounts show Henslowe working out a relationship to the new combined Admiral's–Pembroke's Company. About this time Edward Alleyn retired from active participation in the troupe, and Henslowe had to deal with the new leading players, Robert Shaa and Thomas Downton. Both Shaa and Downton had been part of the ill-fated Pembroke's Men at the Swan Theatre, and it is not improbable that they brought a different style of management to the Rose. This is suggested in part by the change we have noticed in the method of collecting the gallery income. It is borne out by the players' increased reliance on Henslowe as a banker. One important point of contention between the Pembroke's Men and the owner of the Swan was Langley's assertion that he was owed some £300 for costumes. In their deposition in the suit in the Court of Proceedings, Shaa and Downton asserted that Langley had no claim on them because he had already been repaid. What is particularly interesting about this case is that the method of repayment used was the allocation of a certain portion of the players' gallery takings for this purpose. The system is described as follows:

yf the said Def[endan]t were at charges for the provyding of apparell . . . the same was vppon his owne offer . . . And that the Deft should be allowed for the true value thereof out of the Compl[ainan]tes [i.e. the players'] moytie of the gains for the severall standinges in the galleries of the said howse [the Swan] . . . which [they] have faithfullye performed from tyme to tyme.

(Wallace 1910: 352)

The statement is interesting for several reasons. It is the earliest description we have of the method of financing production expenses out of the gallery receipts which became common in the seventeenth century. Furthermore, it is the first example of a company financing itself by borrowing from a theatre owner. Finally, the evidence suggests that such procedures were not continuous, but were resorted to only 'from tyme to tyme' presumably as normal methods of financing proved inadequate. We will discuss later what factors may have forced the players to turn to Henslowe for support. Here it is worth considering how the theatre owner responded to what were almost certainly new demands on his resources.

The accounts with the new Admiral's–Pembroke's Company begin as what appear to be personal loans to the two leading players. Between October and December Henslowe entered a number of advances to Shaa at the top of folio 37 and to Downton at the bottom of the same page. Since the former loans are all described as being 'for the company' (or for theatrical purposes) and the latter are vague or personal, it would seem that Henslowe was at first uncertain about the nature of the loans he was making. This uncertainty is also reflected, perhaps, by the fact that no less than three of the loans were witnessed by Edward Alleyn.

Anticipating that the Company would want to borrow more money, Henslowe left some space to record further loans, and on 1 December noted the players' first repayment of £1-00-0 (which was subsequently cancelled) (f. 37v). Shortly after the second loan to Shaa, Henslowe made an advance to Thomas Downton of £12-10-0 to get two cloaks out of pawn. Instead of recording this transaction with the advance to Shaa, however, he entered it at the bottom of the page, thereby implying some kind of distinction between the two loans. Thereafter, Henslowe continued to enter the advances to Shaa at the top of the page, and those to Downton at the bottom. By 8 December, he had run out of space on Shaa's half of the page, and continued the account overleaf about an inch beneath the first repayment entry. Twenty days later, this second page had also been filled, and Henslowe was forced to turn to a blank space in the diary. There, instead of simply continuing his records, he began all over again, transcribing the entries from folios 37–37v into a new account beginning on folio 43v.

This fresh start must have been made sometime between 28 December 1597 (the date of the last entry on folio 37v), and 5 January. Henslowe specified that the money was being advanced to the Company, consisting of the ten named players 'borne gabrell shaw Jonnes dowten Jube towne synger & the ij geffes' (f. 43v) which he thereafter referred to simply as the Admiral's Men.

From these entries it is possible to catch a glimpse of his day-to-day relations with the players. On 8 December he advanced money to 'the littell tayller' to enable him to buy 'tafetie and tynsell' to make a costume for the play *Alice Pierce*. Since the tailor could not authorize the advance on his own, the entry was witnessed by Edward Alleyn, who apparently still had some authority in the Company. At another time, Henslowe gave Ben Jonson £1 as an advance on a play he was writing for Christmas. Jonson had apparently shown a plot of the work to the Company and it had authorized payment by Henslowe. How this authority was communicated to the landlord is not explained. Henslowe's dealings continued to be with a wide variety of individuals, ranging from sharers such as Shaa, Borne, Juby, Spencer, and Downton to dramatists (Munday and Drayton), and 'ij yonge men'.

By the end of 1597 it had become apparent that the new company was going to rely more heavily than its predecessor on money borrowed from Henslowe. To accommodate his growing business with the players, Henslowe turned to an empty space in his volume (f. 43v) and began the account anew. The most striking difference between this and earlier accounts is that for the first time Henslowe made no provision for recording repayments. And indeed, he appears to have received none, for sometime after 8 March 1598 he totalled his advances accurately as £46-07-03 (f. 44v) and the principal sharers of the new Admiral's Men acknowledged their indebtedness for the entire amount.

Two questions suggest themselves. First, why would Henslowe continue to lend money to an organization which seemed unable or unwilling to repay him? Was he content to wait because he would collect interest on his money? On at least one occasion Henslowe included what he called 'forberance of my mony' in a loan to the Company. On 6 December 1602, he bought from Robert Shaa 'iiij clothe clockes layd with cope lace for iiij li a clocke' (f. 118). The cloaks were for the use of the Company, so Henslowe added the sum to the players' account. As he explained, however, he included a sum of five shillings 'vpon euery clocke' which meant that the amount entered in the diary was £17. It is not impossible that similar interest charges are hidden elsewhere in the diary. On the whole, however, this entry appears to be an exception, so it is unlikely that Henslowe was profiting from his moneylending. It would appear that the landlord was satisfied to lend money to the players in order to keep them at his theatre, where he earned a more than satisfactory income from rent. A second question is whether or not the newly constituted Admiral's Men inherited the debt of £30 incurred by the previous Company under Alleyn's leadership. Once again, there is no evidence in the present accounts, although Henslowe's later calculations suggest that the debt was assumed.

Beginning with the Spring–Summer season of 1598, Henslowe seems to have provided most of the money spent on playbooks, costumes, and properties by the Admiral's Men. The accounts run more or less continuously from 13 March 1598 (f. 45) to 13 October 1599 (f. 64v). In that time, the financier made periodic reckonings of both loans and repayments, but it is not until the latter date that he struck a balance in order to estimate the players' indebtedness. Because his calculations were partial and irregular it is difficult to follow Henslowe's footsteps. Nevertheless, where we can trace his figuring it is remarkably accurate. For the first few months, Henslowe contented himself with periodic sub-totals. His first (£104-12-8) appears on folio 47v, and is exactly ten shillings too high. By 28 July 1598 (f. 48) he had added a further five-shilling error, to give a total of £120-15-4 (Table IV.12). Significantly, this total does not include the already acknowledged debt of £46-07-3, so that the Company's total indebtedness exceeded £167. The following day Henslowe received the first weekly instalment of 'the wholle gallereys' which he recorded as repayment against this debt.

This latter income account appears on folio 48, and is set up like the Alleyn repayment account on folio 71v. At the top of the columns of dates and figures are two amounts, one on the left and one on the right. According to convention, these should be respectively repayments and loans. Since we do not know when the figures were entered, however, there is no way of confirming that Henslowe was following the convention. Nor is it obvious what the figures represent. The left-hand total of £160-15-4 is exactly £40 greater than Henslowe's estimate of the Company's debt on

28 July, but this may be nothing but coincidence. The corrected total on the right-hand side is the same as the sub-total of income drawn up on 16 December, but again there is no obvious reason why a sub-total should be entered here.

The first attempt to draw up a balance occurs on 24 February 1599. On that date Henslowe correctly totalled the sums he had received from the players' half galleries as £247-03-00 (f. 48v). He subtracted this from his estimate of what he had lent the Company and entered the result as 'dew £233-17-17'. His method of arriving at the total of his advances is rather cumbersome. His first sub-total made between 4 and 8 October (£152-14-00) appears to be just £10 too large. A second marginal sub-total of £80-12-00 (f. 52) is accurate, except that it includes two personal loans of £1 each which were subsequently cancelled (f. 51v). At the bottom of that page Henslowe recorded a further sub-total which he miscalculated as £88-10-0 (instead of £89-10-0). On 22 January 1599 he reverted to his former method and entered correct marginal sub-totals on 22 January (£42-12-00) and 16 February (£39-00-0). These give a sum of £314-18-0 which, together with the earlier debts of £46-07-3 and £120-15-4, comes to £482-00-7. Deducting £247-03-0 from this amount would give a balance of £234-17-7 rather than £233-17-7. These figures, which are within ten shillings of my calculations (£155-13-7 + £77-14-0, Tables IV.12 and IV.13) indicate that Henslowe could be extremely accurate when he made the effort.

The next balance was drawn up prior to the summer break between 8 and 21 June 1599 (f. 63). The £76-04 borrowed by the players between that date and 24 February should yield £558-04-7, but Henslowe entered a total of £586-12-7. This looks very much as though accounts containing loans of £28-8-0 may have been entered on leaves missing between folios 54v and 63. This is supported by the fact that the diary contains no loans between 16 April and 26 May 1599, although the income records indicate that playing was continuous through this period (f. 48v). Henslowe subtracted what he had received from the players and obtained a balance 'dewe' of £262-12-7 (f. 63). This figure is £27 higher than it should be, since Henslowe deducted the wrong sub-total from folio 48v (£324 instead of £357).

A more official balance was entered on 13 October 1599, when Henslowe reckoned that he had 'layd owte for [Lord Nottingham's Men] the some of vj hundred & thirtie two pownds' and that the players had paid 'of this deatte iij hundred & fiftie & eyghte powndes' (f. 64v; 48v) leaving a balance of £274-00-0. Once again Henslowe arrived at his total by calculating a sub-total (£41-12-04), then adding a subsequent loan of £3 to give a grand total of £631-04-11 which he rounded off.

The loan accounts continue without interruption after the October balancing. From this point, however, Henslowe began recording the total of his loans at the bottom of each page. This considerably simplified the procedure of balancing which he next did on 10 July 1600. At that time eleven sharers of the Company acknowledged a debt of £300 (f. 69v). It is difficult to see how Henslowe arrived at this figure. His own sub-totals added to his previous reckoning yield a grand total of £842-18-5 which, after repayments of £565-05 have been deducted, leaves a balance owing of £271-13-0. It is possible that there are some hidden expenses which do not show up in the diary, or possibly the players agreed to round off the figure, thereby including a sum for interest in the final payment. A third possibility is that Henslowe is including the 1595 debt of £30.

It would appear that this marks the end of the Admiral's Men's tenancy at the Rose. On 28 October 1600, Henslowe began an account with Pembroke's Men, who 'begane to playe at the Rosse' on that day (f. 83). But the daily receipt entries continue for only two days, which suggests to me, not that Pembroke's deserted the theatre, but that it did not require Henslowe's services as banker in the same way as its pre-decessors. Henslowe continued to lend the Admiral's Men money, but it becomes more difficult to envisage just how the business was carried on. I imagine that during most of this period Henslowe conducted his affairs in his own home, and that players or playwrights wishing to borrow money came to the landlord's counting-house. This would have been a relatively simple matter when the Company was located on the South Bank. When it moved to the Fortune, however, I think it is possible that Edward Alleyn took over some of the day-to-day administrative duties, such as supervising the owners' gatherers. The Company's expenditures on plays and costumes did not abate, but no repayments are recorded. By February 1602 the Company had borrowed an additional £304-10-4, all of which Henslowe added to their debt, bringing it to a daunting £604-10-4 (not including £50 paid to Jones and Shaa when they left the Company).

By 15 September Henslowe estimated that the players' debt had climbed to £718-12-10 (f. 107v) which, using the uncorrected total at the foot of folio 107, includes all the loans made since February. At Christmas 1602, however, Henslowe once again cast up his accounts and estimated that 'all Recknengs a bated' the players owed him £226-16-8 plus £50 lent to give Jones and Shaa (f. 108v). This statement can hardly mean what it says. Total loans to that date amounted to £774. That the Admiral's Men can have paid off more than £500 of its outstanding debt in such a short time seems most improbable. That it did not is indicated by Henslowe's last major balancing, which he carried out on 5 May 1603 (f. 109v). On that day he totalled all advances made to the Company since 23 February 1602 as £188-11-6. Then he added that figure to £211-09-0, which he called a 'Some vpon band' to get £400-00-6. The second amount is the same as a mysterious figure at the top of the column of sharers' names on folio 104, and it may be that the Company signed a formal bond to repay this amount which Henslowe then treated separately, as he did the £50 advance to Jones and Shaa. The numbers seem impossible to reconcile with the final statement of debt which Henslowe reckons at £197-13-4. Finally, almost a year later, in March 1604, Henslowe acknowledged that with the exception of £24 he was 'descarged to them of al deates' (f. 110). How the players can have reduced their financial obligations to Henslowe so rapidly, and in a period when playing was severely curtailed because of the plague, is a mystery which we cannot solve with infor-mation from the diary. Unfortunately Henslowe's records are sketchy at the very point when we would expect them to be most detailed. Whether the players had money in reserve, or sold their costumes to raise cash, or gave Henslowe a share of the theatrical stock as payment of their debt we will never know. That Henslowe may indeed have taken some payment in kind is suggested by his phrase 'all Reconynges consernynge the company in stocke generall descarged' (f. 110). But what exactly this rather ambiguous phrase means we can hardly say.

An examination of Henslowe's activities as theatrical landlord and banker shows that the popular conception of the man as a crass and illiterate promoter hardly fits the facts. While it is dangerous to generalize from Henslowe's book-keeping to his personality it is, perhaps, fair to say that the diary is a much more systematic and accurate document than is sometimes implied. It seems clear that it formed only part of Henslowe's accounting records, which included also formal bonds and very likely one or more ledgers. The diary and papers reveal glimpses of a man conscientious in his family responsibilities, and undemanding in his business dealings. While he undoubtedly earned interest on the money he invested in a pawnbroking business, that interest (although higher than the legally allowable 10 per cent) was not more than was customarily charged abroad. There is no evidence that Henslowe's pawnbroking activities continued once he began lending money to the players. Partial as it is, the evidence which survives gives no indication that Henslowe charged interest on these loans except in exceptional circumstances. Certainly there is no suggestion that he was guilty of usury, and there is no contemporary allusion to such a charge ever being brought against him.

3 · THE PLAYERS

A s WE HAVE SEEN, Henslowe's diary entries were made for very limited purposes, and attempts to arrive at deductions of a sweeping kind necessitate a certain amount of correlation and inference. Nowhere is the process of analysis more delicate than when applied to questions of theatrical management. For on many important matters, such as the division of administrative authority, the methods of making and enforcing decisions, or the procedures by which a script was transferred to the stage, the diary is ambiguous or silent. The most crucial question to be considered in this context is the nature of the relationship between Henslowe and the various companies performing in his theatres. Was the landlord, as some commentators assume, involved in the day-to-day business of the theatre, hiring actors, buying plays, choosing costumes and properties? Or was he simply a property-owner, whose major interest was in collecting rent? Many of the prevailing negative assumptions about Henslowe's tyranny over the players have been derived from documents linked to the Lady Elizabeth's Men, c. 1613–15. The first of these, entitled 'Articles of agreement', sets out the responsibilities of Henslowe and Jacob Meade who had 'raised' the Company, on the one hand, and Nathan Field and his fellow players on the other (Mun. 52). According to its terms, Henslowe and Meade were to provide playing premises, and to supply the actors with costumes and properties (both in London and on tour) from Henslowe's private stock. In addition, Henslowe and Meade were to choose 'ffower or ffive Shareres', who would act as a kind of management committee, and to pay out money approved by this body to purchase 'apparrell' or plays. They also undertook to arbitrate in matters of dispute between members of the Company, expelling disobedient or recalcitrant actors at the request of the majority, and turning over to the players any fines collected for infractions of Company rules or discipline. The theatre owners must also have supervised the collection of some or all admission charges, since they agreed to render up an account of such takings 'every night'. The Company, for its part, promised to repay Henslowe for expenditures made on any play 'vppon the second or third daie whereon the same play shalbe plaide'. They agreed to turn over one-half of the gallery receipts to Henslowe in repayment for a debt of £124, and also probably covenanted to pay the other half for rent (although this latter provision is not incorporated in the surviving document).

The way in which this agreement actually worked out in practice may be surmised from two further documents entitled 'Articles of Grievance and Oppression against Philip Henslowe' (Ms I, 106). These articles were drawn up by Lady Elizabeth's Men, probably in 1615, and likely refer to a later company than the one represented by Nathan Field. The actors' complaints focus on Henslowe's autocratic and high-handed methods. The basic financial arrangement is familiar: the actors agreed to pay Henslowe one-half of the gallery income as rent, and the other half as payment for a debt of £126 and towards ongoing expenditures on properties and costumes. While the players remained in Henslowe's debt, he would retain their costumes and playbooks as security for his money. Once the debt was retired, which the players estimated would be in three years, the stock was to be turned over to the Company. The players charged that Henslowe deliberately broke the Company in order to avoid surrendering the stock.

This last point is of particular interest for the light it throws on the way in which Henslowe was able to interfere in the autonomy of the acting troupes. Ostensibly Henslowe was only an agent of 'fower of the sharers'. In fact, however, the landlord was in the habit of securing bonds from individual players to protect his investment. Since these bonds were drawn up in Henslowe's name rather than in the name of the Lady Elizabeth's Men, Henslowe was apparently able to 'withdraw' the hired men and to 'turn them over to others'. Just what these terms mean is not entirely clear, but the implication that Henslowe was able to make and break companies in this way is evident enough. Also it appears that Henslowe occasionally threatened to prosecute players for bonds in his possession and used this power to influence the decisions of the sharers.

These articles were drawn up shortly before Henslowe's death, and no answer to the charges has survived. It would be naive, therefore, to take them at face value or to ignore the possibility that the players overstated their case. When settlement was finally reached after Henslowe died, the actors agreed to pay Alleyn £200 of the £400 Henslowe had said they owed him, which suggests that there was some right on the landlord's side. When due allowance is made for hyperbole, however, it would appear that there must have been a kernel of truth in their accusations. It seems fairly safe to conclude that by 1615 Henslowe had a considerable stock of playing apparel (and possibly playbooks) which he had no doubt accepted as settlement for various playhouse debts. He had also learned how to protect his capital by sequestering or impounding costumes and playbooks as security for outstanding loans, and by taking bonds to guarantee the performance of various obligations. The question at issue is whether Henslowe employed these practices from the beginning, or whether they were the result of long and bitter experience dealing with irresponsible (or indigent) players.

The view that Henslowe always exercised considerable control over the activities of the players occupying his theatres is not without foundation. To begin with, the terminology of many entries in the diary implies that Henslowe had some kind of managerial role in the companies he dealt with. As early as 1597 we find a note of an advance to Ben Jonson 'vpon a Bocke wch he was to writte for vs' (f. 37v). In November 1599 Robert Wilson gave a receipt to Henslowe for £8 for 2 *Henry Richmond* which was 'sold to him & his Company' (f. 65), although the pronoun might equally well apply to Robert Shaa, who authorized the payment. William Birde sold a play called *Jugurth* with the proviso that 'if you dislike Ile repaye it back' (f. 67v). Here the allusion must be to Henslowe, and the implication is that he had some say in the choice of scripts. A similar implication underlies the entry of 28 February 1599, in which Henslowe recorded that Henry Porter gave 'his faythfulle promysse that I shold haue alle the boockes wch he writte' (f. 54).

Outside the diary, several other surviving documents suggest that Henslowe played a managerial role. After the death of Gabriel Spencer in September 1598, he wrote to Alleyn that he had 'loste one of my company' and requested his son-in-law's 'cownsell', presumably concerning a replacement (Ms I, 24). In the autumn of 1597 Henslowe recorded agreements with several of the individual members of the Pembroke's–Admiral's Company which look suspiciously like those described in the Articles of Grievance of 1615.

The bonds in question are not in existence, but a series of memoranda in Henslowe's hand reproduces their terms, and the signatures of various witnesses to them (ff. 230v–233). The entries are curious, since in the form in which they exist (neither signed nor sealed) they would not have any legal force. Nevertheless, they no doubt reproduce the agreements between Henslowe and several players as Henslowe understood them, and frequently the wording implies that the landlord exerted some sort of authority over his tenants.

The earliest of the memoranda is dated 27 July 1597, and is the most extreme in its terms. Henslowe recorded that 'I heayred [hired] Thomas hearne . . . to searve me ij yeares in the qualetie of playenge . . . & not to departe frome my companey tyll this ij yeares be eanded' (f. 233). It may be that the wording reflects the uncertainty of the time (following the Privy Council's proclamation to close the theatres in the summer of 1597), but there is little doubt about how Henslowe viewed his relationship to Hearne. By 6 August the political situation may have been clearer, for on that date Henslowe recorded that 'I bownd Richard Jones . . . to contenew & playe with the company of my lord admeralles players . . . & to playe in my howsse only' (f. 232v). The phrase 'to contenew & playe' is puzzling, since Jones is one of the players who deserted the Admiral's Men to join Pembroke's at the Swan. Otherwise this bond distinguishes more sharply between Henslowe as theatre owner and the Company as the producing organization. Henslowe's role in 'binding' Jones in this case seems more that of an agent of the players. Shaa and William Birde were similarly bound to act with the Lord Admiral's Men about this time, but on 6 October Henslowe reported that 'Thomas dowten came & bownd hime seallfe vnto me . . . to playe ‹wth me› in my howsse & in no other . . . wth owt my consent' (f. 232). Here the correction of 'wth me' to 'in my howsse' is surely significant. Henslowe obviously knew, but tended to forget, that while the theatre belonged to him, the Company did not. Consequently phrases such as 'my consent' probably mean 'the consent of four or five of the sharers. Support for this interpretation comes from the fact that the signatures Henslowe reproduced were those of the witnesses rather than the individual bound by the agreement. It seems unlikely that Henslowe would have sought out as many as six and seven members of the Company if he had had the necessary authority himself to hire these actors as his 'covenante searvantes'.

The widely held impression that Henslowe ran the companies in his theatre is clearly wrong. In fact, the theatre owner's knowledge of the inner workings of the acting companies was fairly shaky. The most convincing proof of the landlord's distance from the day-to-day management decisions is his apparent ignorance of specific details. Frequently he does not know the name of a play, and the title is inserted later (f. 118), sometimes in a different hand (f. 69v), sometimes interlined. He is often unfamiliar with the playwrights working for the theatre, referring at one point simply to 'the other poet' (f. 118v). And on at least two occasions he even mixes up the companies, entering Worcester's transactions in the Lord Admiral's accounts (ff. 108, 109). But the final proof that Henslowe was acting on the players' orders rather than the other way around is the form of the accounts themselves. The money paid out is 'for the vse of the compayny' (f. 65), and expenditures are approved by individual sharers. The cumulative debt is acknowledged by the sharers and ultimately repaid by them.

COMPANY ORGANIZATION

If the business decisions reflected in the diary are those of the players, what do the entries tell us about the way those decisions were reached? An Elizabethan acting company was a two-tiered organization consisting of eight to twelve 'sharers' and a variable number of apprentices and hired men. As the term suggests, the sharers had invested in the company and collectively were responsible for its debts. The hired personnel, on the other hand, had no such legal or financial obligations, and simply worked for their weekly wages. This structure was a consequence of the evolution of the professional acting companies during the preceding century. Originally retainers in the noble households of medieval and Tudor England, the players became more and more independent as acting moved out of private halls and into inn yards and public theatres. By the 1590s the 'domestic' status of the players had become something of a legal fiction, as the 'servants' of the Lord Admiral or the Lord Chamberlain devoted almost all of their time and energy to mounting plays in London.

These plays were produced in a highly complex repertory system requiring meticulous planning. Plays had to be purchased, rehearsals organized, actors and craftsmen hired and supervised, performances planned, production schedules overseen, box-office revenue collected, salaries paid and profits estimated. In addition it was necessary to arrange for the transcription and licensing of playbooks, to keep track of the costumes and properties needed for each performance and to organize provincial tours. Management practices that might have served a small group of players in the first half of the century would have been hopelessly inadequate to meet the demands of a large professional organization in the last decade. It is likely, therefore, that in addition to any articles of agreement entered into with a theatre owner, the players would have worked out some kind of 'composition' among themselves, outlining the rights and obligations of various parties to the contract. Although no example of such a contract from the period survives, the loan accounts in Henslowe's diary provide us with considerable information about the ways in which Elizabethan players governed themselves and their hired men.

The clearest reflection of the actors' management procedures is to be found in the patterns of authorization. Generally speaking, responsibility for approving payments was shouldered by two leading sharers (Shaa and Downton, then Shaa and Rowley, and finally Alleyn and Downton). One member of the pair was usually more active than the other in approving expenditures on scripts, but the evidence does not indicate that there was a clear distinction between what we might call a 'literary manager' and a 'production manager'. Probably the leading player assumed a directorial role analogous to that of the later actor-managers, and was assisted by several subordinate 'officers'. The way in which the four or five executive sharers may have divided their responsibilities is suggested in the deposition of Ellis Worth, Richard Perkins, and John Cumber in the case of Smith vs Beeston (1619). These actors describe how the Queen's Men managed their affairs at the Red Bull in the years around 1612. The ordering and setting forth of plays, they explained, 'required Divers officers and that every one of the said Actors should take vpon them some place & charge' (Wallace 1909: 35). What this probably means is not that every other actor assumed a managerial post, but only that every one of the four or five principal sharers did so. In fact, only one of these management positions (the one responsible for 'the prouision of the furniture & apparrell') is described in the deposition. The duties of this office included deducting from 'the colleccions and gatheringes wch were made continaully whensoeuer any playe was acted a certen some of money as a comon stock towardes the buyeing & Defraying of the charges of the furniture & apparrell'; purchasing 'the furniture, apparrell & other necessaries' needed for the production; rendering an account of his activities to the company, and returning any surplus to the sharers 'according to there place & qualitie' (Wallace 1909: 36). Christopher Beeston, the holder of the office in the Queen's Men for a period of some seven or eight years (from 1611/12 to 1619) was apparently empowered to act 'wthoutt the privitie Direccion or knowledge' of any of his fellows. Not surprisingly, perhaps, this independence led to corruption (or at least the suspicion of corruption) so that by the time the Company dispersed at the death of Queen Anne, some of the sharers were convinced that Beeston had considerably 'enritched' himself at their expense.

Several other details of this case throw light on the administrative practices of the Queen's Men in the years 1612–19. It appears that offices in the Company were not permanent, but that the 'vsuall manner was, that sometymes one, and sometymes another . . . Did provide Clothes and other necessaries for the setteing forth of the actors' (Wallace 1909: 40). Since the case concerns an alleged debt to a mercer, the emphasis is on the business transactions most directly related to that suit. The fact that no mention is made of the purchase of plays or the paying of hired men does not necessarily mean that Beeston did not also have responsibility for such activities. But the reference to 'every one of the said Actors' strongly suggests a group of officers of which Beeston was only one.

An interesting feature of the management of the Queen's Men is that it was completely internal (Beeston was himself a sharer) and that it was conducted without the help of an outside financier. A production fund was created by setting aside a portion of the box-office revenue, and the depositions make it clear that the Company did not go into debt since 'Beeston would nott haue engaged himself for any stuff vnlesse the said Beeston had formerlie receaued outt of the colleccions aforesaid as much money as would haue answered for the same' (Wallace 1909: 38).

This raises questions about the Company's financial management. How was the 'certen some' deducted from the daily takings? Was this money kept separate from the rest of the cash? Who supervised the operations? Nowhere in the documents surviving from the sixteenth century is there unequivocal reference to a company treasurer. And yet logic dictates that there must have been one. James Burbage maintained a 'Booke of Reconinges', but the volume seems to have dealt only with his activities as partner (Wallace 1966: 129). Henslowe's diary makes very infrequent reference to the payment of salaries or shares. That a record of such things was kept in some of the theatres is established by the testimony of Roger Clarke, who said that at the Red Bull the hired men's rate of salary was 'sett downe in their booke' (Sisson 1954: 63). What this suggests is that there may have been several sets of records, and that the accounts of production expenses may have been separate from those setting out the salaries and share dividends. Evidence from a much later period shows how Thomas Cross, a treasurer in the Duke's Theatre, was responsible for 'paying the whole charge of the House weekly, that is to say, the Salaries of all hireling Players both men and Women, Music Masters, Dancing Masters, Scene-men, Barbers, Wardrobekeepers, Doorkeepers and Soldiers, besides Bills of all kinds as for Scenes, Habits, Properties, Candles, Oil, and other things, and in making and paying (if called for) all the Dividends of the Sharers' (Milhous 1979: 13–14).

While it would be rash to cite Restoration evidence as proof of Elizabethan practice, it would be foolish to ignore it altogether. Theatrical practices evolve slowly, and there is reason to suppose that some kind of continuity existed between the Elizabethan and the Restoration theatres. At the very least, it seems safe to assume that while theoretically each sharer was entitled to a say in management decisions proportionate to his investment, in practice there must have been considerable delegation of responsibility. Company affairs were probably run by a small 'executive committee' of senior sharers which in turn probably designated several 'officers' to supervise particular areas such as finance, production, and possibly 'script development'.

Since the sharers could not themselves produce a theatrical season, it was necessary for them to recruit a number of hired men and apprentices to swell their ranks. The number of such non-sharing members in an acting troupe is difficult to determine and probably varied from season to season and from company to company. By 1624, for example, the 'musitions and other necessarie attendantes' required by the King's Men was twenty-one (Adams 1917: 75). Since every such 'attendante' represented an additional expense, however, there was considerable incentive to keep the companies small. The author of the anonymous *Fair Maid of the Exchange* shows how the twenty-two roles in that comedy could be played by eleven (in fact twelve) actors, and it has been convincingly argued that, with two exceptions, all of Shakespeare's pre-Globe plays could be produced with a standard cast of twelve men and four boys (Ringler 1968: 126). This rather low estimate of company size is based on a theory of minimal staging which assumes that 'crowds' on the Elizabethan stage rarely numbered more than two. Shakespeare's own reference in *Henry V* to 'four or five ragged foils' might lend some support to such a theory, but at least one plot of the period seems to contradict it. Part Two of *The Seven Deadly Sins* (probably performed at the Curtain or the Rose as early as 1592) required between twenty-two and twenty-nine actors (McMillin 1973: 236). If we add a backstage staff of eight or so (some of whom might have appeared on stage as supers) then it is unlikely that the company that performed *2 Seven Deadly Sins* can have been much smaller than thirty. This agrees with David Bevington's estimate (1962: 30) and is probably a suitable number to take as a basis for discussion.

There have been attempts to distinguish between the 'hired men' who were actors and other backstage personnel, but such distinctions are misleading. Everyone in a company who was not a sharer or an apprentice was 'hired' whether he earned his salary by acting, opening trap-doors, making costumes, playing a musical instrument, or collecting money for admission. As employees, the hired men played no official role in the management of a company. Their duties were likely prescribed, but were rarely set out in formal contracts before the eighteenth century (Milhous 1980: 29). Among the most important (and certainly the most public) of the hired men were the salaried actors. The detailed casting information provided by the plots of *2 Seven Deadly Sins* (c. 1592), *Frederick and Basilea* (1597), and *The Battle of Alcazar* (1602?), shows that some actors doubled as many as seven roles in a single production. Since an average season might include ten new plays and perhaps some twenty old works, a secondary player might need to have as many as a hundred parts committed to memory. Likely some form of unofficial precedence existed in a company so that the experienced members played the more important roles and were frequently excused from doubling. It has been argued that these distinctions were rigid, and that the leading sharers invariably played the leading roles (Baldwin 1927b: 177), but the evidence hardly supports such a theory. In the case of the Admiral's Men, at any rate, Richard Alleyn was almost certainly not a sharer in 1597 when he played one of the title roles in *Frederick and Basilea*.

Some clues to the actors' methods of work can be gleaned from the terms of an agreement between Philip Henslowe and Robert Dawes. Although Dawes was a sharer in Lady Elizabeth's Men at the time of the agreement in 1614, he had only recently been elevated to that position and seems to have had no administrative duties. His responsibilities as an actor, therefore, would not likely have differed much from those of the hired men. He agreed to 'attend all such rehearsall which shall the night before the rehearsall be given publickly out', and to pay specified fines for arriving late, for absenteeism, for missing a performance, for drunkenness, or for taking any of the costumes out of the theatre. It is no doubt a reflection of the interests of the parties drawing up the contract that the penalty for missing a performance was one-fortieth of the fine for removing costumes from the premises (HP: 123–5).

Salaries paid to hired personnel varied little during the period. On 2 July 1597 Thomas Hearne covenanted to 'searve . . . ij yeares in the qualetie of playenge' for five shillings a week in the first year and six shillings and eightpence a week in the second (f. 233). This salary seems to have been fairly standard, and to have remained the same for almost forty years. Stephen Gossen complained in 1579 that 'hirelings' stood in 'reversion of 6s by the week' (1579: 15), while Roger Clarke testified in the next century that he had been promised the same weekly salary by the Queen's Men in the years 1621–3 (Sisson 1954: 63). More experienced actors were undoubtedly able to earn a bit more. William Kendall contracted for ten shillings a week in 1597 (BL Ms Egerton 2623: 19) as did Richard Baxter in 1623 (Sisson 1954: 63). Thomas Downton's servant was able to demand eight shillings a week in 1599 (f. 20v), but all of these figures appear to have been flexible. When playing ceased, for example, or a company went on the road, salaries were sometimes halved (f. 20v). Even during the regular seasons the hired players might be called on to share in hard times. Roger Clarke, a 'hyred servant' in the Queen's Men in 1623, testified that 'When they hyred me they agreed to give vnto me six shillings a weeke so long as I should continue their hired servant and they did so sett downe in their booke and when good store of Company came to the playes that the gettings would beare it, I was truly payed my vjs a week but when company fayled I was payed after the rate of their gettings which sometymes fell out for my part iis vjd a week.' He further maintained that such 'prorating' of the hired men's salaries was the common practice with 'all other companyes of players in and about London' who, notwithstanding their agreements, regularly paid out 'no more then it will fall out to their Shares as Company doe come in to playes' (Sisson 1954: 63).

John King in the same case claimed that during his thirty years as a hired man with the Red Bull Company he had lost more than one hundred pounds, because it was understood that in poor times he was expected to 'beare [his] part of the losse . . . aswell as the company and to have a part proportionablie only to those gettings' (Sisson 1954: 64). This testimony suggests a rather inequitable distribution of financial risks between investors and employees, but the picture may not be as one-sided as it appears. King also referred to continuous employment for a period of thirty years (c. 1593–1623), which may mean that he was kept on some kind of retainer through periods of idleness.

Fully as indispensable as the hired actors were the various stagehands and craftsmen who laboured behind the scenes. The so-called 'tiremen' probably looked after costumes (Ms I, 104), purchased material (f. 92v), possibly made costumes (ff. 115v, 117v), and sometimes borrowed money on the company's behalf (f. 22v). The players also had dealings with a number of craftsmen. Whether these workmen were on the company payroll or functioned as independent businessmen is difficult to say. The tailors Radford and Dover, and the property-maker William White, collected money directly from Henslowe on many occasions (ff. 86v, 92, 92v, 93) which might suggest a residential status of some kind. On the other hand, Henslowe made similar direct payments to other craftsmen not likely attached to the company, such as Mr Heath and Mr Stone, mercers (ff. 87, 92v, 108v), Mrs Gosson, a milliner (f. 95v), and to unnamed lacemakers (f. 49v), a carman (f. 22v), and a 'sylke man' (f. 68).

An interesting example of how the players may have dealt with theatrical craftsmen and tradesmen is provided by the case of William Freshwater, a tailor who supplied Worcester's Men in 1602–3 (ff. 115, 119). Some twenty years later, he testified about procedures followed in Queen Anne's Men in the years 1612–16. Described in the deposition as a tailor and workman for the Company. Freshwater explained that he himself had often gone to a mercer's house 'some tymes by direccon from the sayd Beeston & some tymes as sent by others of the sayd Company, for diuerse stuffes, wch they had occasion to vse. And when he [had] asked the pl.[ain]t[ive] for the stuffes . . . [the mercer] often tymes refused to delyuer the same . . . without some token from . . . Beeston' (Wallace 1909: 46). Witnesses in the case testified that they had seen Beeston examine the mercer's 'shopp book or Bookes of accompt' at which time Beeston had acknowledged receipt of the material and promised to pay for it. Such acknowledgement must have been merely verbal, however, for although the relevant account book was introduced into the court as evidence, Beeston was able to deny that he had seen it. Smith seems to have been less successful in his proceedings against the players than his fellow mercer, John Willett, who in 1603 finally collected a bill of eight pounds ten shillings from Worcester's Men by having John Duke arrested and thrown into the Clink (f. 120v).

Further light is shed on the lower ranks by a letter from William Birde to Edward Alleyn complaining about one John Russell, whom Alleyn had appointed as a gatherer. When Russell proved untrustworthy in this capacity, the actors 'resolued he shall neuer more come to the doore yet [for Alleyn's sake], he shall haue his wages, to be a necessary atendaunt on the stage, and if he will pleasure himself and vs, to mend our garmentes, when he has leysure, weele pay him for that to' (Ms I, 104). From this letter it would appear that while Alleyn as theatre owner selected the gatherer, it was the players who paid his salary. Whether that salary was the same as a 'necessary attendaunt' would receive, or the actors had decided to transfer Russell to an entirely different job with a different salary, is not clear. What is interesting is that Russell's new responsibilities did not take all of his time, so he was free to earn extra income during his 'leysure'.

INCOME

A major problem attending any attempt to reconstruct the financial management of a troupe such as the Lord Admiral's Men is the difficulty of estimating their income. The actors generally received the revenue from the outer door (the house money) plus half of the receipts from the galleries. Admission to the theatre appears to have been paid in instalments, everyone paying a penny at an outside door for admission to the yard, after which those who wished could pay an additional penny for access to the galleries, and a third 'for a quiet standing' – presumably in one of the so-called 'lords' rooms' – (Lambarde 15: 359). Money paid at these various entries was collected by gatherers who then participated in a division of the income between company and landlord. The way the system operated in the Restoration is described in the Agreement drawn up between Sir William Davenant and several actors in 1672. According to that agreement, 'Sir William Davenant, his Executors, administrators, or assignes, shall at the generall Chardge of the whole Receiptes prouide three persons to receive money for the said Tickettes, in a roome adioyning to the said Theatre; And that the Actors . . . shall Dayly or Weekely appoint two or three of themselues, or the men hirelinges deputed by them, to sitt with the aforesaid three persons . . . that they may suruey or giue an accompt of the money receiued' (Adams 1917: 98–9). The most thorough attempt to work out the theatre door receipts from evidence in Henslowe's diary and papers is that of T. W. Baldwin (1927c: 42–90) who concludes that the outer door returns amounted to one and two-fifths of the gallery receipts, or about £1-17-9 a day. Since this figure seems surprisingly low, and the average attendance it implies (453) smaller than we would expect at the public theatres, it is worth reviewing the evidence.

The major part of Baldwin's rather complicated argument is based on the interpretation of the five-column figures on folios 26–27v of Henslowe's diary. As we have seen, Baldwin believed these figures represent one-half of the gallery income (in the first two columns) and the outer door money (in the last three). A study of the entries reveals that there is a change in the figures, beginning about 12 March. The daily takings for the first five weeks are as shown below:

Date		Title	Gall.	Outer
Jan.	24	that wilbe	0-17-0	0-19-7
	25	blind beager	0-19-0	3-08-0
	26	Nabucadonizer	0-09-0	2-00-3
	27	woman hard (ne)	2-11-0	6-07-8
	28	long mege	0-07-0	1-30-11
	29	woman hard	2-03-0	4-14-0
	30	[Sunday] Totals	[7-06-0]	[20-00-5]
	31	Joronymo	1-04-0	1-15-6
Feb.	1	woman hard	1-05-0	2-11-2
	2	what wilbe	1-18-0	1-03-0
	3	oseryke	1-09-0	3-02-1
	4	woman hard	1-08-0	4-03-0
	5	valteger	1-09-0	5-13-9
	6	[Sunday] Totals	[8-13-0]	[18-08-6]
	7	oserycke	0-14-0	7-16-0
	8	woman hard	1-09-0	1-02-1
	9	Joronymo	0-17-0	4-15-2
	10	stewtley	0-18-0	1-01-0
	11	elexsander (ne)	3-05-0	0-17-0
	12	elexsander	1-14-0	9-13-0
	13	[Sunday] Totals	[8-17-0]	[25-04-3]

LENT

Mar.	3	what wilbe	0-09-0	0-16-0
	4			
	5	elexsander	<u>1-15-0</u>	<u>0-13-0</u>
	6	[Sunday] Totals	[2-04-0]	[1-09-0]
	7	woman hard	1-05-0	6-02-1
	8	Joronymo	1-01-0	0-03-4
	9	lodwicke	1-16-0	7-04-0
	10			
	11			
	12	valteger	<u>0-18-0</u>	<u>9-01-4</u>
	13	[Sunday] Totals	[5-00-0]	[22-10-9]

Here we see a rough (though not complete) correlation between the first and second set of figures, and average daily revenues of about £1-00-0 and £3-00-0 respectively. Contemporary estimates of theatre attendance and the players' income are not entirely reliable. Samuel Kiechel, a traveller whose knowledge of the subject cannot have been extensive, estimated the daily takings at the public theatres to have been between £10-00-0 and £12-00-0 (ES: II, 358). A more informed estimate is provided by Thomas Heywood, actor, playwright, and sharer with almost thirty years' experience, who declared in 1623 that the income at the Red Bull in 1612–13 had been about 'eight or nyne pownds in a day received at the dores and Galeries' (Sisson 1954: 64). Whether or not we believe that the diary entries from 24 January to 12 March give us the exact admission figures at the Rose, I think we must conclude that the receipts from the outer door were very probably higher than Baldwin estimated, and that they amounted to between £3-00-0 and £4-00-0 daily from some eight hundred to a thousand spectators.

The problem facing the sharers who collected this income was how to allocate their resources between fixed and variable costs. In addition to theatre rental, the players had to pay the salaries of their hired men and secure a continual supply of new scripts. They also had to license their plays and secure the properties and costumes needed for their productions. Only when all these running expenses had been met would the principal players know whether or not there was a profit for them to share. In order to live themselves, they had to draw a salary, but how could they estimate what that salary should be when neither future income nor future expenses could be accurately predicted? If they drew too much from current receipts, they might not be able to pay their bills at the end of the season. If they drew too little, they might earn less than their hired employees. The solution they appear to have found was to divide among themselves a certain portion of the total receipts, thereby varying their own income as the total revenue varied.

The way this system worked is suggested by a series of entries on folio 36 headed 'A Juste acownte of the moncy wch I haue Receued of humfreye Jeaffes hallffe sheare beginynge the 14 of Jenewary 1597' (actually 1598). Jeffes seems to have been a new member of the combined Pembroke's–Admiral's Men formed in the Fall of 1597, and his name first appears in the diary in the list of players drawn up between 28 December 1597 and 5 January 1598 (f. 43v). For some indeterminable reason, Henslowe collected small sums (presumably Jeffes' share of the income from the gallery) at weekly intervals between 14 January and 4 March 1598, at the end of which period he returned to the Lord Admiral's players all but 6d. of the total to be shared 'a monste them'.

It is impossible now to ascertain why Henslowe should have been collecting the receipts from Jeffes' share, and why the money should have been returned to the company as a whole rather than to Jeffes himself. In spite of this, the figures are invaluable for what they suggest about the players' income and the size of the troupe at this time. Some light is thrown on these subjects by a comparison of the income from Jeffes' share with what Henslowe described as 'A Juste a cownte of all Suche monye as I haue Receued of my lord admeralles & my lord of penbrocke.men' (f. 36v).

We can assume that these weekly sums recorded by Henslowe (about half of what he was collecting from 1592 to 1597) represent one-quarter of the total gallery income. If we also assume that the sharers normally divided part of the gallery income among themselves, then there should be a constant ratio between the 'Juste a cownte' and Jeffes' half share. A glance at the list below shows that this is in fact the case and that Jeffes' half share is consistently about one-seventeenth of the half-gallery income.

Date		1/4 Gall.	1/2 Gall.	Share	Fraction
Jan.	21	3-09-0	6-18-0	0-08-0	1/17
	28	1-08-9	2-17-6	0-03-4	1/17
Feb.	4	5-00-0	10-00-0	0-11-7	1/17
	11	2-16-4	5-12-8	0-06-7	1/17
	18	3-09-0	6-18-0	0-08-0	1/17
	25	4-15-0	9-10-0	0-10-0	1/17
Mar.	4	5-11-3	11-02-6	0-13-0	1/17

If the ten players mentioned in the loan accounts (f. 43v) have all invested in the Company, then the distribution would be seven full and three half shares for a total of seventeen half shares.

Confirmation that the sharers were deriving their personal income from the gallery receipts is provided by a brief account on folio 33v of 'gabrell spencer . . . his share in the gallereyes' between 14 April and 24 June 1598. Once again, three of these weekly payments amount to a constant fraction of the gallery receipts for the same period.

Date		1/4 Gall.	Share	Fraction
Apr.	14	5-02-0	0-07-0	1/14.5
	27	3-04-0	0-04-0	1/16
June	17	3-36-0	0-05-0	1/15

In this case, the fraction is roughly 1/15 rather than 1/17, which suggests a change in the composition of the troupe. (Possibly a sharer has left.) The sums are probably one-half of Spencer's share of the half galleries assigned to Henslowe as repayment of a private debt. All these figures show that a full share in the Lord Admiral's Men during the Spring and Summer of 1598 returned between seven and twenty-six shillings a week.

The value of an individual's share in the common stock of playbooks, properties, and costumes varied with the success of the Company, but there is evidence that it rose steadily in the sixteenth century. Six sharers in a company that may have been Pembroke's Men owned joint stock worth £80-00-0 (£13-06-0 per share) in the 1580s (Edmond 1974: 129–36; McMillin 1976: 174–7). Francis Henslowe borrowed money from his uncle for theatrical shares in 1593 and again in 1595. On the first occasion he paid £15-00-0 for a full share in the Queen's Men (f. 2v). Two years later, when joining an unnamed company, he had to pay £9-00-0 for half a share (f. 3v). Richard Jones and Robert Shaa had £50-00-0 'at their goinge' which suggests that the value of a share in the Admiral's Men in 1602 was £25-00-0 (ff. 108v, 109v). Departing sharers were paid £80-00-0 by Queen Anne's Men in 1612, and £70-00-0 by the Prince's Men in 1613 (ES: I, 352).

There is also some indication that company income at the Fortune was somewhat higher than it had been at the Rose and that the principal players benefited from this increase. Sometime in November 1600 Edward Alleyn rejoined the Admiral's Men, and Henslowe noted a payment to him of £1-12-0 'for the firste weckes playe the xj parte of xvij li ix s' (f. 70v). About a year later, in February 1602, Henslowe recorded another payment to Alleyn 'owt of the gallery mony' of £1-07-6 which may also have been a weekly share (f. 105). In the summer of 1601, several sharers paid off their 'privat deates' by giving Henslowe weekly sums which probably amounted to one-half of their shares (ff. 102v–103v). These repayments ranged between £0-10-7 and £1-00-0 which suggests that the players may have been collecting weekly shares of between £1-00-0 and £2-00-0.

BORROWING

In normal times the professional acting companies appear to have lived within their means. This was clearly the practice of the Queen's Men in 1612 when Christopher Beeston 'would nott haue engaged himself for any stuff vnless [he] had formerlie receaued out of the colleccions [from the gallery] as much money as would haue answered for the same' (Wallace 1909: 38). All the evidence seems to indicate that the Admiral's Men followed a similar practice at the Rose from 1594 to 1596. Beginning in the latter year, however, Henslowe's diary reflects a change in the players' methods of purchasing playbooks, costumes, and properties which constitutes a radically different approach to company finance. The earliest evidence of this change is found on folio 71v, where Henslowe recorded a series of loans 'vnto my sonne edwarde allen', already discussed. Just why the players should suddenly have found it necessary to borrow money from their landlord cannot be known. Some light may be thrown on the question, however, by examining the Company's revenue during this period. Income from performances had been slowly declining (from an average of £1-14-0 in 1592 to £1-07-0 in the summer of 1596) (Table V.1). Furthermore, the first few weeks of the 1596 Spring–Summer season seem to have been particularly poor. Easter week netted Henslowe only £8-08-0 (compared to £15-06-0 the previous year), and the next two weeks brought in only £13-07-0 (compared to £20-10-0 in 1595). This slide in revenue may have been sufficient to leave the players unable to meet their current expenses and in need of outside capital.

When we bring together information from Henslowe's daily performance records (f. 15v) and the schedule of loans (f. 71v), we can see that the first advances to the players were probably made to enable them to pay production expenses for 1 *Tamar Cham* and *Phocas* (Table IV.8). A comparison of income and repayments, however, demonstrates that the company tried to pay off its debt to Henslowe as rapidly as possible. From 10 to 27 May the players made almost daily repayments as follows:

Date	Title	1/2 Gall.	Repay
May 10	Julian Apostata	1-06-0	1-10-0
11	fortunatus	0-18-0	1-00-0
12	tambercame	2-05-0	2-06-0
13	blind beger	2-00-0	2-06-0
14	Jew of Malta	1-04-0	1-06-0
15			1-04-0
16	chynone	1-13-0	1-16-0
17	tambercame	2-06-0	2-10-0
18	beger	2-09-0	2-13-0
19	ffocasse (ne)	2-05-0	
20	Julyan	0-14-0	
22	pethagoros	1-07-0	1-08-0
23	ffocasse	1-19-0	2-00-0
24	ffortunatus	0-14-0	1-02-0
25	tambercame	1-00-0	1-05-0
26	hary the v	1-03-0	[22-06-0]
27	chinone	0-09-0	
28			
29			
30			
31	pethagores	3-00-0	
June 11	2 tambercame (ne)	3-00-0	3-04-0
	[Total]		[25-10-0]
19	1 tambercame	1-16-0	
20	2 tambercame	1-15-0	
21	Jew of Malta	0-13-0	
22	focas	2-10-0	
22	troye (ne)	3-09-0	3-13-0
23	nutt	0-12-0	
24			
25	beager	0-19-0	1-01-0
26	1 tambercame	1-10-0	1-10-0
27	2 tambercame	1-00-0	1-01-0
28			
29			
30			
July 1	paradox (ne)	2-05-0	2-07-0
2	troye	1-04-0	1-05-0
3	fostes	0-14-0	
4	[Total]		[36-07-0]
5	focasse	1-02-0	1-03-0

6	sege of london	0-15-0	0-17-0
7	wisman	0-16-0	
8	2 tambercame	1-03-0	1-02-0
	[Total]		[39-09-0]

Henslowe's total £39-10-0 (f. 71v)

It is significant that by 25 May the players had repaid £22-06-0, or 12s. 8d. more than they had borrowed. Since income in May was more than adequate to cover the Company's expenses that month, the reason for borrowing from Henslowe must have been related to convenience (scheduling payments over a longer period) rather than to need.

A similar explanation may account for the undated advances recorded beneath the May loans. In two separate transactions, Henslowe lent Alleyn a total of £10-10-0 'to by a new sewte of a parell' and 'to fenesh vp the blacke veluet gowne' (f. 71v). The first of these loans at least must have been made shortly before 11 June when the players turned over £3-04-0 to Henslowe from the income of the première of 2 *Tamar Cham*. Box-office revenue dropped the following week when the Company gave only four performances, and no further repayments were made until the première of *Troy* on 22 June. Thereafter, fairly regular payments were turned over until 8 July when the players had paid Henslowe a total of £39-09-0 (incorrectly recorded as £39-10-0), or some £7-00-0 more than their debt. On 22 July the Privy Council issued an order to close the theatres, thereby ending the Spring season on the very day the Admiral's Men mounted their last new production, *The Tinker of Totnes*, on 24 July. Sometime later, Henslowe returned to Alleyn the £7-06-8 which he estimated he owed the Company (f. 71v).

The procedures worked out by Alleyn and Henslowe in the spring of 1596 are of particular interest in that they suggest how the relationship between the players and their landlord developed. Since Henslowe left relatively little room between the first advance and the first repayment, he obviously did not expect the accounts to continue. But what both parties probably regarded as a temporary loan seems to have evolved into something else. That the players continued to hand over money to Henslowe after they had repaid their debt must indicate that they saw some advantage in accumulating a reserve. Why they should have preferred to deposit this surplus with their landlord rather than in their own coffers is unclear. Nevertheless, what is apparent is that (deliberately or not) the Admiral's Men hit upon a system of financing production expenses by regularly setting aside some money from their half of the gallery income.

The next evidence of the actors' financial difficulties occurs on folios 22v–23. There Henslowe opened an account which he called 'A note of Suche money as I haue lent vnto thes meane': 'edward alleyn martyne slather Jeames donstall & Jewbey'. An initial group of four loans was for what appears to be pre-season expenses, such as bringing in new players ('to feache fleacher'), paying wages, and purchasing a new play ('hawodes bocke'). Below this group, Henslowe entered a further five advances which he marked off from the rest by a large bracket in the left margin. These items, totalling £9-00-0, are undated. By early December he had advanced the Company an additional £15-15-0 for a variety of production expenditures, such as 'coper lace', a 'headtier & a Rebata', a 'saten dublet wth syluer lace' and 'other thinges', almost all for the play *Vortigern*.

As in the previous season, the players began to repay their banker very shortly after the first loan. On 29 October they turned over £1-00-0 (although their gallery receipts that day had amounted to no more than fifteen shillings), and three days later they repaid a further £1-00-0 (out of receipts of £2-07-0). In November, however, the players missed a total of ten playing days, and Henslowe's entire weekly gallery takings on one occasion were only twelve shillings (Table IV.9). As a result, the sharers were unable to maintain their schedule of repayments, and by early December they were £22-15-0 in Henslowe's debt. Receipts in December picked up only slightly (in spite of three new productions before Christmas), and the Company was forced to return to Henslowe for funds for 'stewtley's hose' and to buy a play from 'mr porter'. Attempts to pay Henslowe £2-00-0 on 13 December were apparently unsuccessful (since the entry was cancelled), so by the end of the year the Admiral's Men had borrowed a total of £35-15-0 and made repayments of only £2-00-0.

In January 1597 the Company's fortunes began to change as weekly receipts rose to normal levels. Not only were the players able to stage four plays without recourse to Henslowe (*Nabuchodonizer*, *That Will Be Shall Be*, *Alexander and Lodowick*, and *A Woman Hard to Please*), but they began to pay off their debt. The pattern of these repayments suggests a change in the method employed. Instead of frequent small instalments from the gallery receipts, the players made large but irregular payments (mostly from the takings at a première). These sums (£7-00-0, £5-00-0, and £4-00-0) are all substantially greater than the gallery receipts on the corresponding days, and probably represent those takings plus a share of the house money. By the end of playing in Lent, the Company had managed to repay a total of £20-00-0, leaving them £15-15-0 in arrears at Easter.

After a two-week rest, the players began a partial schedule on 3 March 1597. During March, they borrowed an additional £8-09-0 to purchase a play and 'by sylckes & other thinges for guido'. On 25 March Henslowe advanced Alleyn a further £5-14-0 to bring the Company's debt to an even £30-00-0. Why the actors began borrowing again after a period of eight weeks during which they were self-sufficient is suggested by the performance schedule for March. Acting began on the third of the month, but, as was usual during Lent, the Company did not perform every day. Because of this, income was curtailed, and it is not surprising that they were forced to seek help to pay production expenses for the 'ne' play they mounted in this period.

The summer of 1597 was a crucially important one for the Admiral's Men and marks a new stage in the Company's relationship with Philip Henslowe. After the prohibition on playing by the Privy Council and the failure of Francis Langley to renew his licence for the Swan Playhouse, the principal actors from Admiral's and Pembroke's Men combined to form a reorganized Admiral's Company at the Rose. This new troupe was under the leadership of Robert Shaa (Alleyn having retired from acting about this time), and it is not unlikely that the changes in Henslowe's accounts reflect Shaa's style of management.

On 23 October Henslowe began a new account which he set up as a personal loan to Robert Shaa. Shaa, of course, was only acting as a representative of the Company which Henslowe described as 'my lorde admeralls men & my lord of penbrockes' (f. 37). Between 23 October and 1 December, Shaa received a total of £6-19-0 to spend on playbooks and costumes. Evidence that the players originally intended to repay these advances by a series of direct payments similar to those made by Alleyn the previous season is to be found on folio 37v, where Henslowe has noted receipt of 'pte of payment' on 1 December. It is worth noting that this payment is quite separate from the weekly sums Henslowe had been receiving 'of' the two companies since 21 October. Furthermore, whereas the latter sum was received on a Saturday, the single payment of the loan was made on a Thursday, possibly just after a particularly profitable performance. It seems fairly clear from these entries that, in Henslowe's mind at any rate, the sums were being collected for very different purposes. Apparently Henslowe expected further lump sum repayments, for he left room to record them on folio 37v, but none was forthcoming, and eventually he cancelled the 1 December entry, possibly when other arrangements for retiring the debt were made.

In terms of the total amount borrowed, the 1597–98 season is very similar to that of a year earlier (£2-02-0 per week compared to £2-04-0). The strangest aspect of these new loans, however, is that the actors seem to have made no effort to repay them. When Henslowe drew up a reckoning after 8 March 1598, the sharers acknowledged that they owed him £46-07-3 (f. 44v) which, added to the outstanding balance of £30-00-0, meant an accumulated deficit of £76-07-3. Income was significantly lower than in the prosperous days of 1594–95 (Table IV.5), but it was no less than in the previous year, when the actors managed to repay Henslowe £20-00-0 in four months.

LITERARY MANAGEMENT

Under Alleyn's management, the Admiral's Men had spent relatively little of the money they borrowed on playscripts. During Spring–Summer 1596, Henslowe recorded no loans specifically for plays, and the following season the Company spent only £7-10-0 (out of a total of £35-15-0 borrowed) for scripts (Table IV.9). This pattern was completely reversed by the amalgamated Pembroke's–Admiral's men under Shaa. Shaa and his associates spent almost three-quarters of the money they borrowed on new plays. A major problem facing the players in the autumn of 1597, therefore, was that of working out a satisfactory method of approving these growing expenses.

As the number of individuals receiving advances increased, so did the difficulty of ensuring that they were acting on behalf of the Company. It was customary for individuals approaching Henslowe for money to present some kind of authorization to show that a particular expenditure had been approved. A few such authorizations have survived (Mss I, 26, 31–6), but normally the only clue we have to the nature of the approval given is in the diary entry itself. These entries follow a standard form – 'layd owt vnto Robarte shawe to by a boocke for the companey' (f. 43v). This particular entry probably indicates that Shaa himself collected the money and, since he was a sharer, also tacitly approved the expenditure. Only rarely, however, are transactions so straightforward. Frequently playwrights approached Henslowe directly and received money for work submitted ('layd owt . . . for a boocke called mother Read cape to antony monday & drayton' – f. 43v), or for the promise of work to be completed later ('lent vnto Bengemen Johnson . . . vpon a boocke wch he showed the plotte vnto the company wch he promysed to dd vnto the company at cryssmas next' – f. 43v). The danger inherent in a system which permitted writers to borrow money without authority on scripts that had not yet been completed is evident from two entries made towards the end of June. On folio 46v Henslowe recorded a balancing of his account with Chettle with the note 'all his pte of boockes to this place are payde wch weare dew vnto him & he Reastes be syddes in my Deatte the some of xxx s[hillings]'. Apparently Chettle had managed to elicit £1-10-0 from Henslowe on the promise of providing work which was never delivered. (Or Henslowe was mixing personal and company accounts.) Clearly, if the actors were not to be continually charged for non-existent scripts, some more effective means of control was necessary.

During 1598 literary expenditures reached their highest peak (averaging £4-03-0 per week), and unspecified advances outnumbered properly authorized loans by three to one (Table V.2). Beginning in December of that year, however, requests for payments were much more consistently approved by one of the leading sharers. This tighter control over expenses appears to have had an effect on literary management. In the two years between December 1598 and the time the Company left the Rose to move to the Fortune, three-quarters of the payments to authors were authorized. The contrast between the procedures used to purchase scripts before and after December 1598 is even more marked if we compare the number of play titles approved in each period. Of the forty-six titles mentioned in the diary in the early period, twenty-five were paid for without a recorded approval from one of the sharers. In the second period, the Company purchased forty-eight plays for which Henslowe recorded specific authorization for all but seven.

Another striking feature of the literary expenses recorded in the diary after December 1598 is the sharp increase in the number of partial payments. Before that date, such payments constituted only about one-fifth of the total; after, they amounted to almost half. This suggests that the Company may have begun to discourage writers from completing unpromising scripts, or it may indicate that they began to put more emphasis on doctoring plays already in hand.

The stricter supervision of literary expenditures reflected in the Company's accounts in 1599 makes possible the identification of policy-makers among the share-holders. Following the reorganization, Robert Shaa, Thomas Downton, and Samuel Rowley emerged as the three players most consistently involved in dealing with the dramatists. In the early months, responsibility for decision-making seems to have been shared fairly evenly between the two senior men. During the ten months immediately following reorganization. Downton's name is more frequently found authorizing payments to writers, but during the Fall–Winter season of 1599–1600, Shaa's influence becomes predominant. After the move to the Fortune in the autumn of 1600, there is a dramatic shift of responsibility as Downton's name virtually disappears from the accounts of literary payments, and Shaa and Rowley between them make most of the authorizations. Another significant change of authority occurs following Shaa's departure from the Company (probably during Lent in 1602), when Thomas Downton again emerges as the individual responsible for most decisions.

Further insight into the players' literary management is provided by an inventory of playbooks drawn up sometime during the summer or early autumn of 1598. Once part of the Henslowe–Alleyn papers, the original manuscript has been lost and is now known only in the transcribed form published by Malone in his 1790 edition of Shakespeare. Described as 'A Note of all suche bookes as belong to the Stocke, and such as I have bought since the 3d of March 1598' (HD: 323) the document presents several interesting puzzles. Not the least of these is the identity of the author. The phrase 'I have bought' sounds suspiciously like Henslowe, and if indeed he is the compiler of the list then the words probably mean no more than 'have lent the actors to buy'. The fact that one of the plays on the list *Vayvode*, belonged to Edward Alleyn in January 1599 raises the possibility that he may have been the 'I' in question. By whomever compiled, however, the inventory is most probably (like the companion inventories of properties and costumes) a list belonging to the players. Its composite nature is indicated by the play titles, which can be divided into five categories. These include: unknown plays (*Black Joan, Sturgeflattery*); old Pembroke's plays (*Hardicanute, Bourbon, Friar Spendleton*); an old Admiral's play (*Comedy of Humours*); and five plays purchased from Martin Slater (1 and 2 *Hercules, Phocas, Pythagoras*, and *Alexander and Lodowick*). The remaining seventeen books are works purchased by the Admiral's Men between 21 October 1597 and 29 August 1598.

When the inventory is compared with the loan accounts and with other playhouse inventories, several startling anomalies emerge. Perhaps the most striking of these is how incomplete the list appears to be. Henslowe's records show that during the first two weeks of the Fall–Winter (1597–98) season, the amalgamated Company produced *Jeronimo, Comedy of Humours, Dr Faustus, Hardicanute, Friar Spendleton* and *Bourbon* (f. 27v). And yet the Company apparently did not own books for *Jeronimo* and *Dr Faustus*. Since the plays could hardly be staged without a prompt-book, the logical conclusion is that these volumes must have been stored separately (possibly because they belonged to one of the sharers).

A related problem is the absence from the list of several plays for which the players had presumably paid. This group includes a total of fourteen plays. Nine of these (*Love Prevented, Funeral of Richard, Ill of a Woman, A Woman's Tragedy, 1 Hannibal & Hermes, Valentine & Orsen, 1 Brute, Hot Anger Soon Cold*, and *Chance Medley*) were almost certainly completed, while the remainder may never have been finished (Haughton's book, Benjamin's plot, *The Miller*, *Pierce of Exton* and *Catline*). How can we account for this discrepancy? One possibility is that Admiral's and Pembroke's Men retained their separate identities and that the missing plays belonged to Pembroke's. Such an hypothesis ignores the presence of several of Pembroke's plays in the stock, however, and the fact that the distinction between the two companies which Henslowe began to make in his diary was abandoned by the beginning of 1598. A more cogent explanation – that the 'stocke' included only prompt-books – is suggested by the fact that all but two of the fourteen works for which the actors borrowed money to pay production expenses are included in the inventory. (One of the exceptions, *1 Brute*, was produced after the inventory was drawn up.) This suggests that the plays purchased but not listed had not yet been annotated for the stage, and that such plays were perhaps not considered to be part of the stock.

Another subject the inventories illuminate is that of the relationship between produced and unproduced plays. It might be assumed that only plays paid for 'in full' and included in the diary production accounts ever reached the stage. But the records call that assumption into question. The inclusion of *A Woman Will Have Her Will* in the inventory suggests that the work was produced in spite of the fact that the diary records payments of only £1-00-0 for the piece. Even more persuasive evidence is provided by the case of *1 Brute* for which Chettle and Day received £3-14-0 'in earnest' between 30 July and 16 September 1598, and the actors paid £1-04-0 in production expenses on 12 December.

In the years for which we have detailed records, the players mounted new plays at the rate of about two a month but acquired them somewhat faster. This would suggest that in normal conditions a company could gradually accumulate a surplus of scripts from which to choose their new productions. The records of the Pembroke's–Admiral's Company from October 1597 to May 1598, however, indicate that the actors produced most of the plays they purchased. Furthermore, in mid-May they resorted to the unusual tactic of buying a block of five old plays from Martin Slater. All of this suggests that the seasons immediately following the amalgamation of Pembroke's and Admiral's Men were unusual, and that the players may have been struggling to build up their stock after the break-up of the Company in 1597.

PRODUCTION MANAGEMENT

From the beginning, the actors seem to have exercised tighter control over production expenses than they did over expenditures on playbooks. This, at least, is the implication of the figures in Table V.3. There it is evident that specified advances outnumbered unauthorized expenditures in all but five seasons. The consistency of the pattern at the Rose makes more noticeable the change when the Company moved to the Fortune. There for the first three seasons the practice was altered. For the first time, unauthorized advances began to outnumber those approved by a named sharer. This became most extreme in the Fall–Winter season of 1601–2 when unauthorized payments were in the majority by two-and-one-half times. This change coincided with Downton's withdrawal from production management, and was reversed when he returned in 1602–3, so it may reflect his personal influence. Another difference in the production management is the greater participation of theatre craftsmen. Tailors and tiremen had received money from Henslowe at the Rose, but after 1600 they played a more prominent role.

The production expenditures recorded in the diary enable us to see more clearly how the players financed their plays. One of the most interesting seasons was Fall–Winter 1598–99 (Table IV.13). During that period, expenditures rose very rapidly to an unprecedented average of £6-14-9 per week with budgets for individual productions three or four times what they had been. These figures reflect several special circumstances. To begin with, they include a number of rather large payments which were not directly related to production. For example, some of the sharers borrowed £35-00-0 to come to an agreement with their former landlord, Francis Langley, and the Company purchased several expensive costumes to add to the stock. The season also saw a number of unusual expenditures for the purchase of musical instruments and the discharge of Chettle and Dekker from prison. Even when these allowances are made, however, the rate of spending on production remains unusually high. It is possible that this increase does not represent a change in production expenses so much as a change in the percentage of those costs going through Henslowe's accounts. When the players agreed to turn over to Henslowe the receipts from their half of the galleries beginning 29 July 1598, they may also have decided to pay a smaller proportion of their regular running expenses from their own revenue.

That the actors sometimes paid for and staged plays without borrowing money from Henslowe is a possibility which has already been suggested. Considerable evidence of the practice is to be found in the production accounts. Suspicion is raised by certain anomalies such as the production costs of £1-04-0 for 1 *Brute* in a season when every other play cost more than £10-00-0 to mount. It seems extremely likely that additional money was spent on this production, but that it came out of the players' pockets directly. Further evidence of the independent financing of productions is provided by the consolidated weekly accounts (Table IV.13). There we see that the Company performed regularly for thirty weeks. During comparable seasons in earlier years, Strange's and Admiral's Men produced a new play every two weeks or so. If the Admiral's Men had followed their earlier practice, then they would have mounted twelve to fifteen new productions rather than the seven for which they borrowed funds from Henslowe. All the evidence seems to point to one conclusion – that Henslowe's diary does not give us a complete record of all new plays staged by the players after 1597.

Still further insight into the players' production methods is provided by a series of playhouse inventories of costumes and properties compiled during March 1598 (HD: 317–25). The first thing that strikes one about the lists of costumes is their size. If we follow the distinction implied in the documents themselves between the more expensive costumes for leading roles and the 'Clownes, Hermetes and divers other sewtes', then the Company maintained a surprisingly small stock. The 13 March inventory lists 13 doublets, 10 suits, 4 jerkins, 8 gowns, 5 coats, 8 pairs of hose, 13 cloaks and 6 venetians. For secondary characters there are some 20 suits, 20 gowns, 25 capes, and 23 coats (but only 6 trousers, 5 jerkins, 2 doublets, and 8 pairs of hose). Noteworthy too is the almost total absence of shirts, shoes, and stockings, and the comparatively meagre supply of female garments such as bodices (3), farthingales (4), head tiers (6), and rebatoes (stiff collars) (4). The size of the inventory corresponds fairly closely to the list of costumes in Alleyn's hand which is probably a schedule of the Company's stock about 1602. It itemizes 14 cloaks, 13 gowns, 15 antik suits, 16 jerkins and doublets, 10 pairs of hose, and 6 venetians (Ms I, 30). What the size of these inventories suggests is that the actors were responsible for supplying many of their own costumes (a practice that continued in the British theatre into the twentieth century). This helps to explain Henslowe's occasional confusion between company and personal loans, and to account for entries such as the loan to William Birde 'to bye a payer of sylke stockens to playe the gwisse in' (f. 38v).

The obvious question that arises in connection with these inventories is what happened to the costumes and other 'divers things' purchased on a fairly regular basis for new productions? There are two possibilities. One is that the sharers periodically divided the stock among themselves and sold it off or pawned it to raise money. The other is that they gave part of their stock to Henslowe as security against their loan. There is no evidence either way, but the relatively small size of the costume stock (and Henslowe's pawn accounts) suggests that clothing was a readily marketable commodity in which there was an active second hand trade. There may, therefore, have been a fairly rapid turnover of lavish costumes that could be identified with a particular role or play. The stock would then consist mostly of nondescript costumes which could be used by the minor characters interchangeably in various productions. These would be supplemented from the sharers' personal wardrobes, and by the costumes it might be possible to make in the two-week rehearsal period before an opening.

The situation with respect to properties was very different. There would be no great market for such items, and one would expect that they would be less desirable to a sharer or creditor than playbooks or costumes. It is not surprising, therefore, that specialized items such as Tamburlaine's bridle, the cauldron for *The Jew of Malta*, the wheel and frame for *The Siege of London*, or the trees with golden apples from *Fortunatus* should remain in the playhouse for years. Many large properties such as the 'frame for the heading' in *Black Joan* seem to be closely identified with a single production, probably because the play in question could not be produced without them.

The property inventory provides us with our most concrete evidence of the players' staging practices. Most significant, perhaps, are the many scenic devices that were apparently employed regularly on the Rose stage. The Company was equipped with not one but two mossy banks, no less than three trees, as many tombs, and one Hell mouth. All this suggests a stage more cluttered than is sometimes imagined. In addition, there are a number of mysterious items such as the 'sittie of Rome, ii stepells, a clothe of the Sone & Mone, Belendon stable, and a payer of stayers for Fayeton' which would seem to indicate the use of painted cloths on the stage and possibly an external staircase to the upper level.

Almost as surprising as the presence of so many large properties is the inexplicable absence of some small ones. There are, for example, no chairs or benches in the inventory, nor any tables, trenchers, or mugs for the numerous banquet and tavern scenes in Elizabethan drama. The seventeen foils (while certainly more than the four or five mentioned by the chorus in *Henry V*), seem an absolute minimum to present believable battle scenes. There are none of the letters and purses regularly required in plays of the period, nor is any mention made of books, writing materials, and other objects needed for 'study' scenes. It would seem that the inventory is only a partial list of the Company's resources. Many of these smaller items were probably kept backstage or supplied by the actors.

The light thrown by Henslowe's diary on the activities of the players is fitful and indirect. The entries are written from the landlord's point of view and inevitably reflect his interests and limited perspective. Henslowe's phrasing is far from consistent or 'scientific' so that his entries sometimes imply a degree of authority he can scarcely have exercised. In spite of these drawbacks, the diary remains our most reliable picture of the Elizabethan theatre and of the activities of all those associated with it.

4 · THE PLAYWRIGHTS

NONE OF THE ACTIVITIES reflected in Henslowe's diary and discussed in the previous pages would have been possible without the contribution of the dramatists who supplied the plays. The establishment of permanent theatres and resident acting companies in London was of great significance to writers, because it created a new, easily accessible market. In the eyes of many, however, playwriting was scarcely less vicious than the theatre it served. Playhouses were widely believed to be haunts of iniquity, sites of riot, and both the final and efficient causes of plague. Moreover, at a time when publishers concerned themselves almost exclusively with works of religion or popular ballads and broadsheets, plays were hardly considered to be literature at all. This prejudice was reinforced by the reputation of playwrights such as Marlowe and Greene, who gave fuel by their conduct to rumour and scandalous speculation. Young men with talent and ambition contemplating a literary career at the beginning of the 1590s were caught, therefore, in a perplexing dilemma. On the one hand, those associated with the Court held literature to be a gentlemanly pastime, but were less than generous in inviting new writers into their ranks. On the other, the players offered attractive pecuniary inducements, but these could be yielded to only at a cost in pride or reputation. Henslowe's records begin, therefore, at a period of transition. The first generation of playwrights, men such as Marlowe, Kyd, Greene, Peele and Shakespeare, born in the decade 1555–66 and maturing in the 1580s, had demonstrated that playwriting could be a viable, even successful, career. Younger authors like Thomas Heywood, Ben Jonson, John Marston, or Thomas Dekker coming to London in the early 1590s and hoping to make a reputation with their pens found in the public theatres a unique opportunity. Not only did writing for the stage provide the first real possibility of literary professionalism, but the increasing support of the theatre by the Court meant that the profession was beginning to acquire a moderate respectability.

Henslowe's diary provides a wealth of information about the new professional playwrights, but, as we have come to realize, that information is partial and sometimes ambiguous. Indeed, it has been frequently argued that the diary is unrepresentative, and that the 'financial arrangements obtaining in the groups of companies under Henslowe's control were the exception rather than the rule' (Greg 1904: II, 113). Quite apart from the erroneous impression conveyed by the phrase 'under Henslowe's control', this interpretation of the facts is completely without foundation (Bentley 1971: 65). The truth is that we know practically nothing about how other companies were financed (no other account books having survived), and while it is true that the Chamberlain's Men owned their playhouse, there is no reason to suppose that the laws of theatre economics operated differently at the Globe than they did at the Rose, or that 'methods . . . forced on [the Admiral's Men] by their want of capital' (Greg 1904: II, 113) would be in any way unique. Until new evidence is forthcoming we must conclude that the working conditions of dramatists writing for the Admiral's Men were probably typical of the time.

Before examining the evidence of the diary in detail, it will be useful to consider the illuminating correspondence between Robert Daborne and Henslowe in the years 1613–14 (Ms I, 70–98). The letters date from the period when Philip Henslowe and Jacob Meade were connected with the Lady Elizabeth's Men at the Hope Theatre. As we have seen, Henslowe's relationship with this Company differed in certain respects from his association with the Admiral's Men in the late 1590s. Furthermore, Daborne's dealings seem to have been with Henslowe himself, rather than with the players. Consequently, the parallels between Daborne's situation and that of the Rose playwrights is far from exact. Nevertheless the letters illustrate a number of practices which throw light on the diary extracts.

The correspondence reveals that Daborne consistently delivered his manuscript in parts, and that he was paid according to an agreed-upon schedule. In the case of *Machiavelli and the Devil*, for example, he was to receive £6 as a first instalment 'in earnest (possibly for the first act), £4 upon the delivery of three acts, and £10 upon the completion of the last scene (Ms I, 70). It was understood that the playwright would submit copy that was 'fayr written' (that is not his rough draft), and that he would read his work to Henslowe and Alleyn for their approval as well as to the 'general company' so they could decide whether or not to buy it (Ms I, 75).

Daborne wrote *Machiavelli* on his own, but he occasionally enlisted the help of other dramatists. In June 1613 he gave Cyril Tourneur an act of *The Arraignment of London* to write, presumably to hasten the completion of the play. At another time he collaborated with Nathan Field and Philip Massinger, and apparently spent 'a great deale of time in conference about [the] plott' (Ms I, 100). We could wish that Daborne had been more descriptive of that conference, but from his comments and entries in Henslowe's diary we can get a general idea of the process by which a play evolved from manuscript to performance.

Normally the conception for a play originated with the playwright, but there were times when a dramatist worked on ideas that were given to him. Daborne, for example, offered to dramatize 'any other book' of Henslowe's that he would be allowed to read (Ms I, 73). Dekker and others claimed in a deposition drawn up in the seventeenth century that they wrote a play entitled *Keep the Widow Waking* at the suggestion of Ralph Savage, book-keeper to the King's Men (Sisson 1936: 161). In some cases the outline of the story would be set down in an 'author plot' giving basic information, such as the sequence of the scenes (Ms I, 26) or details of the setting (Adams 1946: 25). No complete author plot from a public theatre of the time has survived, but we know that Jonson showed such a plot to the Company (f. 43v) and that Chapman wrote a tragedy from Jonson's outline (f. 51v).

An author plot might control the general shape of the drama, but clearly there was plenty of scope for elaboration of the initial ideas in the process of composition. A few printed texts and some sixteenth-century manuscripts such as *The Book of Sir Thomas More* illustrate how speeches and scenes were modified as the playwright or playwrights worked on them. Daborne could not resist improving a scene even though the actors' parts had been prepared and distributed (Ms I, 81).

What is of considerable interest to modern readers is how the playwright (or in many cases playwrights) developed the germ incorporated in the story idea or the plot outline into the finished play. Did the dramatist listen to suggestions from the actors? How much was he influenced by his knowledge of the acting company, or by current theatrical fashions? When he worked with other dramatists, how was the writing shared? Did the collaborators consult at every stage of the composition, or did they write independently from a shared plot outline? Was there a senior writer in charge of the project, or were decisions made in committee? How were the playwrights paid? Was money given out only for goods received, or were the playwrights (like Daborne) able to extract advances on promises and hard-luck stories?

Prior to October 1596 Henslowe's accounts tell us virtually nothing about these matters. The performance records maintained from 1592–7 list titles, but are silent on the question of authorship. When the players began to borrow money for playbooks and production expenses, however, Henslowe's records of these loans become more detailed. Information about authors, dates, and fees paid enable us to begin to piece together a picture of how the playwrights worked. As usual, however, this process of reconstruction must be carried out with caution. Only very rarely are Henslowe's records complete and unambiguous.

In general, the players borrowed money for three different purposes: to make a lump sum payment for a completed play, to make an instalment payment for part of a play, or to give a playwright an advance for work to be delivered at a future date. At first Henslowe did not distinguish clearly among these different purposes. 'Lent vnto Robarte shawe . . . to by a boocke for the company' (f. 37) seems clear enough, but the amount paid out (£2) is puzzling. It is well below the regular fee for a new work so it is impossible to know if the play in question, *The Cobbler*, is an old work, or whether Henslowe is simply being asked for the final instalment of a larger payment. The landlord's usual phrase 'layd owt' causes even more problems. 'Layd owt . . . for A boocke' (f. 37) suggests purchase, but 'Layd owt . . . toward his boocke' (f. 37) implies only partial payment. 'Lent vnto Bengemen Johnsone . . . vpon a Bocke . . . wch he showed the plotte vnto the company' (f. 37v) suggests a very different sort of transaction. Henslowe himself (or the players) may have become aware of the inherent ambiguity of his terminology for he seems to have made an effort to be somewhat more precise. In January 1598 he made 'the laste payment of the Boocke of Mother Readcape' (f. 44v). Thereafter he fairly regularly distinguished between 'part' and 'full' payments until May 1598, when he introduced a new term, 'in earneste' (f. 45v). It might appear at first that this implies a further distinction between a payment and an advance, but it is not at all clear that Henslowe is consistent in his use of the term. At any rate, by the spring of 1598, Henslowe's terminology had become established, and in the great majority of cases it is possible to determine whether a particular payment represents the whole or only a fraction of the total, and whether or not a play has been completed.

The majority but not all: occasionally plays we would infer from the payment records had remained unfinished appear from other evidence to have been produced. One source of such outside evidence is the production accounts. *The Conquest of West Indies* was never paid 'in full', and yet the fact that the Company borrowed money to buy costumes (f. 94) suggests pretty conclusively that the work was completed. Table III shows other examples of apparently unfinished plays which were subsequently produced, including *Jephtha* (f. 105v) and *Judas* (f. 95). *Troilus and Cressida* is another play which was credited with only partial payments (f. 54v), but a surviving plot of the play indicates it was staged. Similarly, Haughton was paid only £1 for *A Woman Will Have Her Will* (f. 44v), but the title appears in an inventory of playbooks, and, of course, the work was published in 1616 as *Englishmen for My Money*. All of these examples show that Henslowe's records do not always give us the full picture.

A similar uncertainty surrounds the diary's attributions of authorship. Henslowe usually designated the playwright (or playwrights) to whom a particular payment was being made. But in the case of partial payments, we cannot always assume that the named dramatists were the only collaborators involved. For example, payments for 1 *Cardinal Wolsey* went to Chettle; Chettle, Munday, and Drayton; and finally to Chettle, Munday, Drayton, and Wentworth Smith (ff. 93, 94, 94v). Table III.a shows numerous instances where important information about collaborators is revealed in late instalment payments. What this means is that we cannot be certain that the diary's information about unfinished plays is complete. Although all the recorded payments go to a single author, we cannot rule out the possibility that the work is an unfinished collaboration. Even full payments may be misleading. The receipt for £8 for 2 *Henry Richmond* signed by Robert Wilson (f. 65) would suggest that the play was his alone. The letter of authorization approving this payment, however (one of the few such letters to survive), refers to 'their booke' which implies that the play in question is a collaboration (Ms I, 26). One consequence of this unfortunate ambiguity in the records is that we cannot be as confident as we would like to be about patterns of authorship among the playwrights working for the Admiral's Men.

This is particularly disappointing when it comes to a discussion of collaboration. One of the more surprising features of the dramatic activity at the Rose is the very high incidence of multiple authorship. Just how widespread the practice was is evident in the following list where we see that collaborated plays (C) were never less than 25% of the total plays negotiated for, and that the proportion of finished collaborated plays (FC) to the total of all finished plays (FT) was very much higher. These figures show that collaborated plays accounted for 60 per cent of the plays completed in Fall–Winter 1598, and an astonishing 82 per cent in Spring–Summer 1598.

Although these statistics suggest that the syndicates may have been more successful

Season	F	O	I	A	Tot.	C	%	FT	FC	%
F-W 1597/98	5	2	3	–	8	2	25	5	2	40
S-S 1598	11	5	5	–	16	10	62	11	9	82
F-W 1598/99	15	3	9	2	24	10	41	15	9	60
S-S 1599	6	–	10	–	16	5	31	6	3	50
F-W 1599/00	8	–	8	1	16	6	37	8	3	37
S-S 1600	7	–	4	–	11	4	36	7	4	57

than individual authors in bringing their enterprises to completion, they demonstrate little else. We would like to know much more about these writing teams. Who determined which playwright or playwrights would dramatize a particular story? Was the association of collaborators arranged by the actors who commissioned the play, as Lawrence suggests (1927: 341), or did the playwriting syndicates evolve for other reasons? What were the conditions that made collaboration such a prominent feature at the Rose? Perhaps all we can do is to look at the patterns of collaboration and the sequence of payments to see if we can discern any clues as to the playwrights' methods of work. As Schoenbaum has pointed out (1966: 226), a play might be divided in a variety of ways: the allocation of scenes might be entirely mechanical (for example by act); one author might supply the plot and another carry out its execution; one writer might take the main action, another the underplot; or one playwright might undertake farcical scenes while another wrote the serious episodes. There is evidence that all of these methods were used. Amateur dramatists in the Inns of Court divided their labours by acts (Rabkin 1976: 8), and Lawrence and Bentley (1971) assume this to have been the usual method among the professionals as well. Both Chapman and Chettle wrote plays based on others' ideas, and the practice was likely widespread. Middleton and Rowley almost certainly divided *The Changeling* along plot lines (Hoy 1976: 5).

Most of these theories assume a more or less orderly collaboration between two dramatists, and some of the payments in the diary might reflect such a practice. But frequently the entries show no such order, and it is likely that in some cases collaboration was more complicated than these theories allow. One unknown is the means by which continuity or consistency was ensured when four or five different hands were contributing to a single piece. Evidence taken in a court of law in the seventeenth century shows that collaborators worked fairly closely with one another. It was affirmed that Thomas Dekker 'wrote two sheetes of paper conteyning the first Act of a Play called The Late Murder in White Chappell, or Keepe the Widow waking, and a speech in the Last Scene of the Last Act of the Boy who had killed his mother' (Sisson 1936: 110). What is surprising about this account is Dekker's contribution of that single speech. This kind of close association between collaborators is at odds with the picture of independent composition of acts, scenes, or plots often put forward as the usual method. But it corresponds quite closely with the one surviving example of a dramatic collaboration, the manuscript book of *Sir Thomas More*.

Daborne's references to collaboration in his correspondence are relevant here. He mentions that he had 'given Cyrill Tourneur an act of ye Arreignment of london to write' (Ms I, 78) which suggests that Daborne himself oversaw the allocation of acts and decided upon his collaborators. On the other hand, his collaboration with Nathan Field, the leading actor of the company, must have been of a different kind. It is impossible to derive many firm conclusions from the diary entries, but the tables of playwrights' income (Table V) show some interesting patterns. For example, it appears that the syndicates often operated on the same seasonal basis as the players. A group of writers associated with one another on several projects during a particular season will go their separate ways, disappear, or realign themselves when playing ceases. For example, Dekker and Drayton collaborated on seven plays in Spring–Summer 1599, after which Drayton temporarily disappeared (possibly lured away by the new boys' companies?). Sometimes the groupings appear to have been fluid, at others fairly static. In Fall–Winter 1599–1600 seven playwrights – Chettle, Dekker, Drayton, Hathway, Haughton, Day and Munday (with the assistance in one play of Wilson) – among them did all the writing for the entire season. The dramatists appear to have been grouped into two 'syndicates'. Drayton and Munday collaborated with Hathway and Wilson; Chettle and Dekker worked with Day and Haughton, who seem to have formed some sort of a partnership. The groups functioned independently – Hathway always collaborating with Drayton and Munday, Haughton only writing with Chettle, Dekker, or Day.

However organized, the playwrights worked with considerable speed. Henslowe's accounts indicate that plays were normally finished in four to six weeks. Drayton promised to complete a book in a 'fortnyght' (f. 49); Chettle and Day promised to deliver *Henry I* in twenty days (f. 45); Jonson hoped to work his plot into finished form in the same time (f. 37v).

Carol Chillington (1979) thinks that the patterns of payment to authors indicate that there were three basic ways in which playwrights collaborated. Some syndicates were organized from the play's inception, and the collaborating writers collected money from Henslowe together. Haughton and Day shared all payments for 2 *Blind Beggar* (f. 85v, 86), as did Hathway and Rankins for *Hannibal* (f. 71), Drayton and Dekker for *Conan Prince of Cornwall* (f. 51). These may be examples of writers participating equally at every stage of composition. Other syndicates appear to develop as the play goes along (as Daborne brought in Tourneur part way through the composition of *The Arraignment of London*). The study of playwrights' income shows that frequently collaborators collected fees individually, or shared the total income unequally. This suggests that in such cases there was less consultation, and the writers were not working as a unit. A third pattern is noticeable in those cases where the whole syndicate is mentioned in the initial payment, after which instalments are paid to individuals. This may reflect a system whereby the plot is devised by the group, but individual dramatists write their own scenes.

Although it is unlikely that collaborating playwrights would be as concerned as individual dramatists with questions of artistic unity, it would nevertheless be necessary for them to work out some method of co-ordination. Daborne's letters, the relative experience of different members of some syndicates, and common sense all suggest that some kind of hierarchy existed. The possible nature of such a hierarchy is hinted at in Ben Jonson's prologue to *Volpone* where he affirms:

> 'Tis known, five weeks fully penned it
> From his own hand, without coadjutor,
> Novice, journeyman, or tutor.

Jonson does not define his terms, of course, nor can we be certain that they were ones the players would have used, but he does imply a chain of command in the theatre from which he seems pleased to have escaped. It is worth adopting Jonson's terminology to see if the diary entries are consistent with a hypothetical system of apprenticeship by which playwrights moved through the stages of novice and journeyman to author.

As we have seen, a number of playwrights mentioned appear first as protégés or associates of more established authors. Mr Pett, who may have collaborated with William Haughton on *Strange News Out of Poland* (f. 69), is otherwise unknown. So is Will Boyle, whose play *Jugurth* was sold to the Admiral's Men by William Birde (f. 67v). John Day's first play, *The Conquest of Brute* (f. 49) may have been revised and expanded into a two-part work by Henry Chettle (ff. 49, 51). Frequently authors received less than the usual £6 fee for their first play. Heywood was paid £1-10 for his book in 1596 (f. 23); Porter got £5 and £4 (f. 22v); Haughton received ten shillings (f. 43v); Hathway £5 for *King Arthur* (f. 45v); Rankins £3 for *Mulmutius Dunwallow* (f. 50v). The figures may be incomplete, but cumulatively they suggest that some kind of scale of payment may have been in effect.

To what extent, then, did senior dramatists act as 'tutors' of their younger or less experienced colleagues? Undoubtedly in some cases a play or dramatic idea was simply paid for and given to another writer to alter or finish. This is apparently what happened to Jonson's plot which Chapman worked up into a tragedy. It also seems to have been the fate of Haughton's *Judas* completed by Birde and Rowley (f. 95), and possibly Robinson's *Felmalenco* (f. 107). Thomas Nashe implies that his work on *The Isle of Dogs* was finished by the actors 'without [his] consent, or the least guesse of [his] drift or scope' (1599: sig. B), but this may have been special pleading. On the other hand, there is evidence that in some cases both players and playwrights encouraged young writers in whom they saw promise. The career of a young dramatist such as Day is suggestive.

John Day, son of a Norfolk husbandman, became a sizar at Cambridge in 1592. His academic pursuits may not have been all-consuming, however, for in less than a year he had been expelled for stealing a book, and made his way to London to earn his living as a writer. By the summer of 1598, when he was just twenty-four, he sold *The Conquest of Brute* to the Admiral's Men for £2 (f. 49). Whether it was incomplete or deemed unsatisfactory, the play was given to Chettle, who revised and possibly expanded it. Day next appears in the diary in November 1599, when he and Haughton were paid £5 for *The Tragedy of Cox* (ff. 65–65v). During that Fall–Winter season Day wrote regularly for the Company, collaborating with Haughton on *Thomas*

Merry (f. 65v), and with Dekker and Haughton on *The Spanish Moor's Tragedy* (f. 67v). He also began *An Italian Tragedy* (f. 67) which probably remained incomplete. Altogether during the season he earned about £6-10-0. The following spring and summer he worked in association with Chettle, Dekker, and Haughton, collaborating on three plays, and earning about £8-00-0. When the Company moved to the Fortune, Day was one of the few dramatists to remain actively associated with it. Between February and May 1601 he had a hand in four plays, mostly with William Haughton, for which he was paid some £7-05-0. Thereafter he contributed regularly to Admiral's, finally 'by hime sellfe' (f. 105), and when Worcester's moved into the Rose in 1602 he wrote for both companies, realizing an income of close to £14 from the two sources.

Day's career illustrates how a young writer might 'break in' to the theatre and move up from novice to 'coadjutor'. Evidence that this progress was sometimes achieved with the help of a senior, more experienced, writer is provided by the example of Henry Chettle. Chettle was born about 1560, the son of Robert Chettle, dyer, of London. He was apprenticed to a printer in 1579, and became a stationer himself in 1584. Between 1588 and 1591 he was in partnership with the printers John Danter and William Hoskins, and seems to have continued his association with the trade until as late as 1596 (ES III: 263). It is not known when he began writing for the stage. His connection with playwrights, however, began at least as early as 1592 when he 'edited' *Groat's-worth of Wit* in which the embittered Greene attacked Shakespeare, and warned several of his fellow writers to beware of the players. In his epistle to *Kind Heart's Dream*, Chettle disclaimed any acquaintance with the playwrights Greene alluded to, so it may be doubted that he was closely connected with the theatre at that time. On the other hand, it has been suggested (Sanders 1933: 402) that the confessional parts of *Groat's-worth of Wit* are actually by Chettle – a suggestion recently reinforced by computer analysis (Marder 1970: 42) – in which case his knowledge of theatrical politics may have been more intimate than he was inclined to admit.

Clearly as a young apprentice coming of age in the London of the early 1580s Chettle could hardly have been unaffected by the excitement and controversy surrounding the nascent professional drama. It is altogether probable, therefore, but impossible to prove, that Chettle began writing for the stage in the mid-nineties, a few years before Francis Meres listed him among the best English playwrights for comedy. It is not until the Fall–Winter season of 1597–98, however, that we have positive evidence of Chettle's dramatic activity. In Henslowe's records of the newly amalgamated Admiral's–Pembroke's Men we find him collaborating with Anthony Munday in February and March on a second part of *Robin Hood*. He may also have contributed to Part One (probably written between 5 January and 15 February 1598), but successive editors and critics have failed to find in it unequivocal traces of his work. Altogether Chettle's role in this first season is relatively minor, compared say to that of Dekker or Munday, and he earned less than £3-00-0 in five months.

In the Spring–Summer season, however, Chettle suddenly became the most prolific and highly paid of the dramatists working for Shaa and Downton. He began in close association with Drayton, Dekker, and Wilson and shortly after 13 March he received about £2-10 for his share of *Henry I* (f. 45). By 30 March he had collected some £1-10 for work on *Earl Goodwin*, and a wek later received ten shillings for his part in *Pierce of Exton*. Between 2 and 6 May he began work on *Black Bateman of the North*, but left it so that he could contribute to a sequel to *Earl Goodwin*, for which he was paid on 6 May. He finished his part of *Black Bateman* by 22 May, and wrote more for 2 *Earl Goodwin* by 10 June. At this point his close association with Drayton, Dekker, and Wilson ended. At first he began working with Anthony Munday on *The Funeral of Richard Coeur de Lion* (probably a sequel to the two *Robin Hood* plays), but since subsequent payments went to Munday, Drayton, and Wilson, he appears to have left the project. He then proceeded to work on a sequel to *Black Bateman* with Henry Porter, for which he collected about £3-10 by 8 July. The play was probably continued by Wilson, for by 14 July Chettle had somehow written *A Woman's Tragedy*, for which he collected £5-00-0 on the same day that he picked up a final instalment of fifteen shillings for 2 *Black Bateman*. His unflagging efforts during this season netted Chettle about £18-15-0.

From these accounts it would appear that a busy professional dramatist had to have both speed and flexibility. Chettle often moved on to other projects before the play he had contributed to was finished, so that he was probably not always involved in all parts of a work. Furthermore, he was apparently able to alternate or combine projects, interrupting one to work on another. In the six-month Fall–Winter season of 1598–99 Chettle's activities became even more diverse. By 18 August he had completed *Hot Anger Soon Cold* with Henry Porter and Ben Jonson. This is Jonson's first appearance in the diary since the previous year, when his plot was taken over by George Chapman. Porter and Chettle had just finished collaborating on 2 *Black Bateman* so it is possible that Jonson was brought in as 'coadjutor' in a relatively subordinate role. Whatever his contribution, it was not preserved by the author when he published his collected works, and it marks the only appearance of the dramatist in the diary that season. On 26 August Chettle collected five shillings for his contribution to *Cataline*, a play begun by Robert Wilson (f. 49v), and three days later he was paid £1 for *Vayvode* (f. 49v). In fact, this latter play must have been an old one belonging to Edward Alleyn, for the Admiral's Men purchased it from their former leading actor in January 1599 (f. 53). The work was very likely being rehearsed in August, for costumes were purchased between 21 and 25 August. The most likely explanation of Chettle's involvement is that he was called in to make some revisions just before the play opened.

Chettle's next project also looks like one suggested by the actors. Between 8 and 16 September, he collected £1-14-0 for 'A Boocke called Brute' (f. 50), probably a revision of Day's *Conquest of Brute with the First Finding of Bath* (f. 49). That the play was performed with some success is suggested by the fact that Chettle began work on a sequel which he finished by himself by 22 October (f. 51v). The time he took to write the play (some thirty-eight days) was longer than typical and, along with other evidence from the diary, suggests that Chettle may have been having personal problems about this time. One indication of such problems (whether as symptom or cause it is impossible to say) is his need to borrow money.

The earliest allusion to Chettle's borrowing was on 24 June, when Henslowe entered a loan of ten shillings in the Company accounts, but noted below it that Chettle 'Reastes be syddes in my Deatte' £1-10-0 (f. 46v). There is insufficient information in the diary to enable us to sort out completely the complicated relationships between Chettle, on the one hand, and the players and their landlord–banker on the other. This first loan was made at a time when Chettle was working on *Funeral of Richard* and collecting frequent small sums (f. 46v). By 16 September the playwright's indebtedness had grown to £8-09-0, and the diary entry recording this fact makes it clear that the money was owed to the Company (f. 50). Like the earlier entry, too, it specifies that everything owing to the playwright for parts of books had been paid. This implies some possible uncertainty on the part of one or both parties as to when payments were advances for plays and when they were loans (a confusion sometimes reflected in the entries themselves). It also implies that money changed hands on occasion without Chettle actually delivering a manuscript. Had Henslowe been in the habit of giving out cash only for papers received, it would presumably have been unnecessary to specify that Chettle had no more instalments coming to him. By 22 October Chettle had increased his liability to £9-09-0, but he acknowledged the fact in a promissory note to Henslowe which was witnessed by Robert Shaa (f. 62). What this implies is that Henslowe was to collect the money for the Company, which he began to do towards the end of the season, by crediting the unpaid balance of Chettle's fee for *Polyphemus* and *The Spencers* to the playwright's debt (f. 61).

Chettle's need for money may have been no more than a consequence of the fact that his purse (like Roberto's in Greene's *Groat's-worth of Wit*) 'Like the sea sometime sweld, [and] anon . . . fell to a low ebbe.' But Henslowe treated Chettle's loans in a special way. Whereas advances to other playwrights were usually protected by signed receipts or bonds, Chettle's loans were often noted casually in the margin of the diary (ff. 51v, 65, 91). Nor is there evidence of an attempt to total these amounts or balance them against repayments. This informality suggests to me that Chettle had a closer, possibly a more personal, relationship with Henslowe and the players than many of the other playwrights. It does not, as some commentators have maintained, reflect a deliberate policy on the part of Henslowe to keep the playwright indebted to him.

The players do seem to have tried to bind their dramatists to them from time to time, eliciting promises from both Porter (f. 54) and Chettle (f. 105) to write for no other company, but such schemes seem to have been fruitless. The parallel records for Admiral's and Worcester's Men in 1602–03 enable us to catch a glimpse of how the playwrights moved from one management to another. From August 1602 to March 1603 most of the Admiral's dramatists were also contributing to the repertoire of Worcester's Men. While Heywood, Dekker, and Smith did most of their work for one company, several playwrights, such as Chettle, Hathway, and Day divided their time fairly equally between the two organizations. If we assume that collaborators shared their income equally (by no means a self-evident conclusion), then it is possible to estimate each playwright's earnings during this particular 31-week period. These can be summarized as follows:

	CE	DA	DE	HY	HE	MI	SM
Wors.	7-10	5-15	10-05	6-15	23-10	1-00	25-05
Adms.	7-00	8-00	3-00	5-00	3-00	6-05	2-00

What this table suggests is that the majority of the playwrights mentioned in the diary were independent agents selling their talents wherever they could. In the period under discussion, for example, Day, Hathway, and Smith moved freely from one theatre to another. On 17 November 1602 they sold *Merry as May Be* to Downton and Juby at the Fortune (f. 108). By 24 November, Day and Hathway delivered the first sheets of *Black Dog of Newgate* to John Duke at the Rose (f. 118). On 26 November, Christopher Beeston and Robert Pallant of Worcester's borrowed £2 to pay Day, Hathway, Smith and an unnamed poet for the same play. A month later the work was completed and the authors collected the remainder of their fee (f. 118v). By 7 January, Hathway and Smith were writing *The Unfortunate General* for Beeston and Duke. Day was involved by January, and the work was finished three days later (f. 199v). Within five days the company had begun preparations to stage the play. Work on a second part of *Black Dog* began on 29 January on the approval of John Duke, conveyed to Henslowe by John Lowin (f. 119v). This sequel was finished on 3 February and twelve days later a company tireman collected money from Henslowe to buy material for costumes. About that time, however, objections from the actors (or perhaps more probably the censor) necessitated changes in the script. These were begun on 21 February and continued until 26 February at a total cost of £2 (f. 120). Between 1 and 7 March, Day and Hathway sold *Boss of Billingsgate* to the Admiral's Men and were paid £6 on the authorization of Edward Juby (ff. 109–109v). About the same time (7–12 March), Wentworth Smith sold *The Italian Tragedy* to Worcester's Men on the approval of Thomas Blackwood and John Lowin (ff. 120–120v). This is almost certainly the *Italian Tragedy* Day had tried to sell to Shaa in January 1599, when he was first beginning his career (f. 67). In all likelihood the work remained unfinished at that time and now Day contributed his foul papers to the common cause of the syndicate.

The activities of Day, Hathway, and Smith illustrate the fluidity of relations between playwrights and actors. During the first part of the season, Smith collaborated with Heywood on *Albere Galles* (f. 115v) and *Marshal Osric* (f. 116), wrote *Two Brothers* (f. 116v) by himself, and joined the group of Chettle, Dekker, Heywood, and Webster writing *1 Lady Jane* (f. 117). This pattern suggests a close association with Heywood and Worcester's Men. As we have seen, however, by November he had teamed up with Hathway and Day and was contributing to the Admiral's repertoire. The dramatists, for the most part, appear to have been in fairly great demand. It would be surprising if they did not occasionally exploit their position to their own advantage.

There was one way, however (and perhaps only one) by which a playwright might gain some influence over his employers. This was to become a sharer in a company and thereby acquire a role in company management. Of all the dramatists mentioned in the diary only one seems to have worked his way into this position. Thomas Heywood may have been writing for Admiral's Men as early as 1594 (Greg 1904: II, 284), and certainly sold a 'bocke' to the Company in 1596 (f. 23). In March 1598 he bound himself to Henslowe as a 'covenante searvante' (f. 231) to 'play' in no other theatre but the Rose. He sold two plays to the Company in the following year, *War Without Blows* (ff. 52v–53) and *Joan as Good as My Lady* (f. 53v), both of which he appears to have written by himself. He may have joined Derby's Men sometime in 1599 and written *Edward IV* for them, but by 1602 he was a sharer in Lord Worcester's Men at the Rose. He played a prominent role in Worcester's Men, authorizing expenditures for both playbooks and costumes, and collaborating on five plays including *Albere Galles* (f. 115v). *Marshal Osric* (f. 116v), 1 *Lady Jane* (f. 117), *Christmas Comes but Once a Year* (f. 117v), and an unnamed work (f. 119). He also wrote additions for *Cutting Dick* (f. 116), and composed *Blind Eats Many a Fly* (f. 118), and *A Woman Killed With Kindness* (f. 120) alone.

One would imagine that in his position as playwright and sharer, Heywood might have assumed particular responsibility for the supervision of literary expenditures. But such an assumption is not borne out by the evidence. Heywood was certainly active in authorizing literary expenditures, giving altogether eleven approvals during the season. But in every case these approvals were for plays on which he himself was working. The records do not suggest that Heywood was active in seeking out new dramatists (Middleton was introduced by John Duke), nor does he seem to have taken much interest in the work of Day, Hathway, and Smith who among them contributed four plays to the season. Another surprising feature of Heywood's position with Worcester's Men was that it did not prevent him from writing for the Admiral's Company. Between 17 December and 7 January, he and Chettle sold *The London Florentine* to Admiral's for £6-10-0. If Heywood had any influence over Worcester's literary policy in the choice of scripts, selection of playwrights, or scheduling of productions, the diary gives no idea of how that influence was exerted.

It remains to consider the playwrights' income. Full as they are, the players' literary accounts do not always provide us with all we need to know to estimate how much the dramatists earned. Not infrequently the entries are incomplete. Sometimes the names of the authors are not mentioned (2 *Robin Hood* f. 44v; *Page of Plymouth* f. 64), or are entered later in questionable circumstances (Porter f. 46). In other cases, the information is ambiguous or difficult to interpret. For example, money is frequently collected by a third party (Porter for Chettle f. 47; Drayton for Munday f. 49; Chettle for Wilson f. 49v; Bradshaw for Dekker and Drayton f. 51) and it is not clear whether or not the sum is to be divided. At other times, two collaborators are mentioned although the payment seems to be to one only (*Spencers* f. 44); or a collaborator is mentioned but unnamed (the 'other Jentellman' f. 64).

When all names, titles, and amounts are included in an entry, however, it is still often impossible to be certain how the money was divided. In some instances the total is not easily divisible (fifty shillings to Drayton, Wilson and Dekker f. 49). But even when such division can be made, it is not safe to assume that it should be apportioned equally. Very occasionally Henslowe specifies how a sum is to be allocated (Drayton thirty shillings, Wilson ten shillings, Munday twenty-five shillings, f. 49), and in these cases the distribution is never even. There is no way of knowing if Henslowe was always aware of how the money he was paying out was to be shared. Very probably he was not. On the other hand, it may be that the few times he specified the division were exceptional deviations from the normal practice of sharing a fee equally.

It has been estimated that during the last part of the sixteenth century a schoolmaster earned between £12 and £20 annually which probably did not include other perquisites such as board or lodging. A workman made sixpence a day with food, and tenpence without. Wages at this latter rate for a six-day week over a full year would amount to between £12 and £13. At the other end of the social scale, Thomas Lodge estimated that a gentleman could live comfortably on £40 a year. Allowing for inflation, therefore, we might suppose that in 1600 an income of £15 a year would have been considered equivalent to a working-class wage, and that to live like a 'gentleman' would require two or three times that amount. Against this background we might conclude that professional dramatists were reasonably well paid for their efforts. Chettle's earnings varied from £18-15-0 in 1597–8 to £25-05-0 in 1601–2. This income was certainly adequate (better by far than he could have hoped to win by his pen in any other field). But it may have seemed inadequate to an ambitious individual surrounded on all sides by displays of ostentatious wealth. Chettle's constant borrowing, his hectic writing schedule, and possibly his periods of imprisonment, all betoken a man spending beyond his means. This is not at all the same as a man living in poverty, but from the perspective of the victim it may be no less painful.

The evidence of Henslowe's diary suggests that conditions in the theatre (at least as they affected the playwrights) probably did not differ much at the beginning of the seventeenth century from how Daborne found them in 1613–14. Except for the few most industrious writers, the theatre did not provide an 'assured way to get money'. The life was certainly not the leisured contemplation of the muse that gentlemen undergraduates might have supposed. On the other hand, it was probably no harder than the life of an actor. For those with the necessary energy and facility it provided a reasonable, though not extravagant, livelihood. But there is little doubt that it failed to supply the non-material rewards of prestige or immortality sometimes associated with the literary life. Those the ambitious playwright had to find elsewhere.

5 · THE PLAYS

EADERS whose interest in the Elizabethan drama is focused primarily on plays usually find Henslowe's diary a disappointment. The pedestrian prose, erratic spelling, chaotic organization, and (especially) the confusing figures seem as remote as it is possible to be from the passion and poetry of the Elizabethan drama. What, such readers wonder, do these endless lists and dry accounts have to do with the work of Shakespeare or Marlowe? While understandable, such an attitude ignores (or under-emphasizes) the fact that Elizabethan plays (like those of other ages) are rooted in the theatrical conditions of their time, and have developed as they have, at least in part, in response to those conditions. To understand Shakespeare and his contemporaries fully, therefore, we must try to imagine their works in their original theatrical context. As a guide to that context, Henslowe's diary is indispensable.

Henslowe did not prepare his diary for theatre historians, however, and to understand his records it is necessary to recast them. Information that Henslowe recorded chronologically needs to be reconciled with the actors' playing seasons; expenses have to be set off against income; details relating to individual plays must be collated, and a distinction made between expenditures of different kinds. This abstracting and summarizing of information in the accounts has been done in the series of tables appended to this volume, where interested readers are urged to check out the claims made in the discursive commentary. What follows is an explanation of the rationale of those tables and an attempt to suggest some of the things they tell us about the plays in Henslowe's theatres.

TABULATING THE ACCOUNTS

The diary contains a bewildering variety of information including the titles of plays, the names of players, playwrights, and craftsmen, and a wealth of detail about properties and costumes. This information can be correlated to show anything from the box-office receipts of individual plays, to the income of particular playwrights, or the production schedule of an acting company. In the interest of economy, the appended tables have been limited to five – a list of plays, an abstract of the daily income receipts, a condensation of the loan records, a compilation of all income and expense accounts, and a final series of summaries. These five tables include most of the theatrical information in the diary, and can be used as a basis for further correlation if required.

What is most striking about the titles mentioned in Henslowe's diary (Table I) is how few of them can be identified with extant plays. In part this is because fully

90 per cent of the works have perished. But difficulties of identification are compounded by Henslowe's methods. Sometimes he simply designates a work by its author – 'a boocke by yonge harton' (f. 43v); Ben Jonson's 'plotte' (f. 43v); 'mr chapman . . . for his tragedie' (f. 52v); 'mr maxton in earneste of A Boocke' (f. 64v) – or the circumstances – 'A comodey for the corte' (f. 49); 'for the playe wch harey chettell Layd vnto hime to pane [pawn]' (f. 109v). Occasionally, such entries have been corrected by the insertion of the title at a later time (or in a different hand). But the impression conveyed by many of these entries is that Henslowe was not vitally concerned with the contents of the playbooks for which he was lending money. In many cases, indeed, he may have been completely ignorant of their nature. This raises vexing problems concerning the true identity of many of the scripts passing through his playhouses.

Without any means of verifying the identification of titles in the diary, the reader must constantly remind himself that familiar titles may refer to source plays or earlier versions of extant texts. Take, for example, the question of 'Shakespearian' titles in the diary. Of the seven works mentioned – *King Lear* (39), *Hamlet* (43), *Henry V* (82), *Troilus and Cressida* (172), *Henry VI* (11), *Titus Andronicus* (37), and *The Taming of a Shrew* (44), only the last three conform to the orthodox notions concerning Shakespearian chronology. Consequently, it is probable (although not, by the nature of the evidence, absolutely certain) that *Hamlet* and *Troilus* are lost plays which Shakespeare may have known, and that *Henry V* and *King Lear* refer to the old Queen's Men's plays preserved as *The Famous Victories of Henry V*, and *King Leir*. Until the complicated relationship between *a Shrew* and *the Shrew* is fully understood, it is impossible to know if Henslowe's title refers to a source play or to Shakespeare's version of the story. Similar uncertainties surround both *Henry VI* and *Titus Andronicus*, described as 'ne' (new?) plays on 3 March 1592 (f. 7), and 23 January 1594 (f. 8v) respectively. Commentators who feel that *Titus* must have been written earlier suggest that perhaps the performance by Sussex's Men was a revision. Of course, all such speculation is completely unverifiable.

In addition to the probability that familiar titles do not refer to the plays we know, there is the certainty that some extant plays lie concealed behind unrecognizable names. Some obvious examples include *Jeronimo* (16) for *The Spanish Tragedy*, *The Guise* (26) for *The Massacre at Paris*, 1 and 2 *Robin Hood* (125, 127) for *The Downfall* and *Death of Robert, Earl of Huntington*, *Woman Will Have Her Will* (126) for *Englishmen for My Money*, *Lady Jane* (270) for *Sir Thomas Wyatt*, and *The Comedy of Humours* (106) for *An Humorous Day's Mirth*. This last identification hinges on the appearance of two items ('Verones sonnes hose' and 'Labesyas [Labesha's] clocke') in a surviving playhouse inventory (HD 318, 321). On the assumption that similar evidence for other plays has disappeared, commentators have suggested possible identifications of other Henslowe titles. Of these, *Longshanks* (75) for *Edward I*, and *The Devil and His Dame* (204) for *Grim the Collier of Croyden* are two of the least fanciful. In no case, however, is any kind of external verification provided (or, of course) possible. So it is wise, in identifying extant plays (by italics in Table I) to err on the side of prudence.

If the diary can tell us little about individual plays, it does reveal much about how plays in general were written and prepared for the stage. Some of this information is contained in the accounts in which Henslowe recorded income from particular performances. Starting in 1592, titles and receipts appear chronologically in the diary with the entries of one week frequently marked off by a line at the beginning of the series. From these records it is possible to compile a performance calendar (Table II) showing a company's playing schedule over an entire season. In drawing up such a schedule, however, it is necessary to deal with Henslowe's dating. The problem can be illustrated by looking at the accounts for January 1593 (ff. 9–8v). In that month, according to Henslowe's dates, the company missed several mid-week performances (2, 11, 26, 27, 29 January), played on one Sunday (14 January), and apparently gave double performances on 30 and 31 January. This can be represented as follows:

Su	Mo	Tu	We	Th	Fr	Sa
	1		3	4	5*	6
	8	9	10		12	13
14	15	16	17	18	19	20
	22	23	24	25		
		30*	31			
	30	31				

On the face of it, this schedule is extremely improbable, and it is easier to believe that Henslowe mistook the date than that the Company produced two plays on the same day. In his Commentary, Greg adjusted Henslowe's dates and suggested that in the present example, Strange's Men performed regularly six days a week, and did not play on Sunday. Greg's schedule is as follows:

Su	Mo	Tu	We	Th	Fr	Sa
		2	3	4	5*	6
	8	9	10	11	12	13
	15	16	17	18	19	20
	22	23	24	25	26*	27
	29		31			

The revision seems eminently reasonable and solves a number of problems, such as the Sunday performance and the 'double features'. It does not, however, explain why, if Henslowe's lines indicate a break between weekly groups of playing dates, there should be lines against both 6 and 8 January. Nor is it clear why Greg should accept Henslowe's dating on 31 January, but revise 30 (Tuesday) to 29 (Monday).

Because questions concerning Henslowe's dating cannot be solved unequivocally, it has been thought wise to leave the matter open. The Performance Calendar (Table II) therefore provides two alternatives. The left-hand calendar shows Henslowe's dating with the underlined figures designating the first title in each new group, and an asterisk indicating a 'ne' play. The right-hand calendar shows the playing schedule as Greg has revised it to avoid Sunday performances. This second calendar shows the date of performance (by location), the title of the play (by number) above the line, and the income recorded by Henslowe (in pounds, shillings and pence) below the line.

In this right-hand calendar it is possible to look at the record of a particular play and compare it with those of other works performed in the same season. For example, each play can be given a 'profile' made up of the dates of first and last performances, the number of times it was played in the season, the range in box-office income, the total amount taken in, and the average receipts per performance. Just how this might be done for a particular season is shown in the table.

FALL–WINTER 1592–93

No.	Title	Dates	P	High	Low	Total	Average
Current							
1	Friar Bacon	10–30/1	3	1-04-0	0-12-0	2-16-0	0-18-8
2	Muly Mollocco	29/12–20/1	3	3-10-0	1-00-0	5-10-0	1-16-8
5	Sir John	4–31/1	3	0-12-0	0-09-0	1-13-0	0-11-0
7	Jew of Malta	1/1–1/2	3	2-16-0	1-15-0	7-11-0	2-10-4
11	Henry VI	6–31/1	2	2-06-0	1-06-0	3-12-0	1-16-0
16	Jeronimo	30/12–22/1	3	3-08-0	1-00-0	5-10-0	1-16-8
20	Titus & Vesp.	6–25/1	3	3-12-0	1-10-0	5-12-0	1-17-4
21	2 Tamar Cham	19/1	1	1-16-0		1-16-0	1-16-0
23	Knack (Knave)	31/12–24/1	4	1-10-0	1-04-0	5-07-0	1-06-9
	Totals 9		25			39-12-0	1-11-8
Revivals							
25	Cosmo	12–23/1	2	2-04-0	1-10-0	3-14-0	1-17-0
	Totals 1		2			3-14-0	1-17-0
'Ne' Plays							
24	Jealous Com.	5/1	1	2-04-0		2-04-0	2-04-0
26	Guise	30/1	1	3-14-0		3-14-0	3-14-0
	Totals 2		2			5-18-0	2-19-0
	GRAND TOTALS 12		29			48-19-0	1-13-8

In such a table, works in the current repertoire can be compared with revivals or 'ne' plays to show the kind of information the players themselves might have considered in making decisions about their programme.

In the spring of 1596 Henslowe began to lend the players money for various production expenses and to record these transactions in his diary. The landlord's meticulous descriptions of his advances include details about properties and costumes; they list the names of playwrights and the titles of plays; frequently they include the names of individuals who have authorized payments or received money; and, of course, they usually record the date upon which the loan was made. From these details it is possible to draw up a summary of the players' theatrical expenses (Table III) from which one may deduce a great deal about how they acquired and staged their plays. The compiling of such a table, however, involves some difficulties. First there is the problem of separating the more or less continuous accounts into seasons. The difficulty here is that Henslowe's reckonings do not always coincide with the seasons reflected in the records of income. For example, playing was continuous from 24 July 1598 (f. 48), to 24 February 1599 (f. 48v) and this whole period should logically be described as the Fall–Winter 1598–99 season. However, Henslowe drew up a balance on 29 July 1598 (f. 48), one week into this 'season'. In order to accommodate Henslowe's figures, the break between the Spring–Summer 1598 season (Table III.5) and the Fall–Winter 1598–99 season (Table III.6) has been set at 30 July. Similarly a division of the season from 6 October 1599 (f. 48v), to 9 February 1600 (f. 67v), has been made at 13 October (Tables III.8, III.9) to coincide with Henslowe's balance on that day (f. 64v).

A second problem involves the division of Henslowe's undifferentiated entries into 'literary' and 'production' accounts. In order to focus on the players' relationship to their writers, payments related to individual plays have been brought together and the information contained in them summarized in Table III.a. Only the sums borrowed in the period specified are included, so many play titles appear in more than one season. Entries in the table are set out as follows:

Fol.	No.	Title	Dates	Approved	Authors	Status	Total
44	125	1 *Robin Hood*	15/2	U	Mu	F? (P)	5-00-0

The folio page on which the earliest entry appears is followed by the number of the play assigned in the chronological list (Table I) and its title. The dates of its first and last entries are recorded by day and month (the year being obvious from the season). If the advance was approved, that information is conveyed by the initials of the sharer or, if no approval was noted, that is shown by a U (unapproved). The author (or authors) are indicated by initials, along with the status of the payment (F/full, I/in earnest) and that of the plays (O/old, A/altered). If there is evidence that a play was subsequently produced, it is shown by the symbol P.

Not surprisingly, perhaps, money borrowed for production expenses was used for a far wider range of purposes than the sums taken to pay playwrights. Henslowe's entries record a variety of expenses from entertainment or transportation costs, to licence fees, craftsmen's wages, payments for cloth or copper lace, and occasionally legal expenses. Sometimes special emergencies, such as the arrest of a player or the injury of a spectator, involved the actors in unforeseen expenditures. The entries recording these expenses suggest how dramatic manuscripts were handled once a decision to produce them was made. These records are summarized in Table III.b as follows:

Fol.	No.	Details	Dates	Approved	S-Total	U-Total	C-Total
45		Good cheer	25/3	U		0-05-0	
	125	*Robin Hood*	28/3	U	0-14-0		
		Costumes	7/4	U		1-00-0	

Not all of these expenses can be attributed to particular plays, so it is useful to distinguish between 'specified' advances (S-Total) which were lent for the production of a named play, and 'unspecified' loans (U-Total) for undetermined or alternative purposes. In the example above, for example, the players borrowed five shillings on

25 March for 'good cheer' (probably drink during a playreading). Three days later they got fourteen shillings to pay for licences for parts 1 and 2 of *Robin Hood*, the only evidence (apart from costumes listed in a playhouse inventory) that the plays were produced. The £1-00-0 borrowed on 7 April for costumes may well have been for the same work, but since Henslowe does not tell us we cannot be sure.

By bringing together all the information referring to those plays which were actually produced, it is possible to get a clearer idea of a company's production procedures. In the summer of 1599, for example, the Admiral's Men mounted two plays – *Page of Plymouth* (180), and *Polyphemus* (168). Payments for the first were made to Jonson and Dekker between 10 August and 2 September (ff. 63v–64), and to Chettle for the second on 27 February (f. 53v). On 12 September the Company borrowed money 'to bye wemen gownes' for *Page* (f. 64), so presumably they were already rehearsing the piece they had purchased just ten days before. By contrast, the second play had been in their possession for some seven months before they borrowed eight shillings to pay the 'little tailor' for divers things for the production of *Polyphemus* (f. 64v).

A more extensive overview of a company's activities is provided by the Consolidated Weekly Accounts (Table IV) which bring together the players' various transactions with Henslowe on a weekly basis. The income accounts, representing a percentage of the total gallery income, are laid out in such a way as to reflect a company's success from week to week and from season to season. This table also shows at a glance a company's playing schedule, how frequently new plays were staged, and how these premières affected the gallery receipts. When Henslowe begins to record loans to the players, these advances can be compared with weekly income, and (when payments are recorded) with the actor's ability to pay back their loan. This provides a running balance and shows a company's growing debt.

THE PLAYS IN THE PLAYHOUSE

The tabulation of Henslowe's accounts allows us to form a much clearer picture of the players' financial health from week to week, and to observe how the companies allocated their fluctuating revenue. How we interpret these figures, of course, will depend on our own preconceptions, and our knowledge of theatre practice drawn from other sources. To assess what the diary can tell us about the plays, therefore, it is necessary to review what we believe to have been the practice of Elizabethan companies in preparing a script for production.

The manuscript delivered to the players was rarely a finished product. Like the properties and costumes the actors acquired, a script had to meet certain theatrical specifications. When a doublet did not fit it was altered. When a dramatic manuscript proved unsatisfactory, all the evidence suggests that it was changed. Elizabethan notions of copyright protected printers and stationers; they did nothing for authors. While most of the changes made to a dramatist's work were probably minor, nevertheless the progress of a script through the theatre from rehearsal to production involved continual modifications.

Playhouse alterations could be of several kinds. Some were merely annotations indicating a need for special effects (*Captives*, lines 651, 867, 2395), designating the number of supernumeraries, eliminating small roles, or perhaps even ruling out discovery scenes (Greg 1950: 33, note 3). Others were changes in the text itself to reduce the playing time, or to eliminate literary or overly rhetorical passages (Hart 1942: 121). That plays were cut in this way we know from the comments of authors such as Jonson, Webster, and Brome who asserted that the published versions of their works were longer than those presented in the theatre. Furthermore, certain manuscript plays such as *Edmond Ironsides* (lines 1390, 1694) and *Thomas of Woodstock* (f. 167v) show signs that scenes or characters have been omitted in transcription or performance.

Once the prompter or book-holder had adapted the dramatist's vision to the realities of the company's resources, he would make a transcription of the manuscript to serve as the production prompt-book, sometimes annotating it still further to facilitate its use in the playhouse. Stage directions were sometimes underlined or rewritten, warning cues put in the margin, and actors' names inserted. Occasionally, parts of the text would be transcribed to another page for the convenience of the prompter (Greg 1925: 156). The resulting prompt-book was the foundation upon which a production would be built, but it had to be supplemented by two other kinds of stage documents. First there were the actors' parts – long rolls of parchment containing the speeches of a single character along with brief two- or three-word cues. Since these parts gave no indication of the length of time between speeches, or of the scene in which they appeared, it was necessary to prepare a scene-by-scene outline of the play to help the actors identify their entrances. This 'plot' was pasted to a board, and hung backstage where it could be consulted by prompter and players during performance.

The play which finally reached the stage differed in several respects, therefore, from the manuscript which left the playwright's hands. Still further changes might be introduced during its life in the theatre. Even in the early performances, it is unlikely that the actors reproduced the text of the prompt-book exactly. Actors do not have infallible memories even when they are supplied with reliable scripts, and study of the one surviving part from the period suggests that the scribes who prepared them could be very careless (van Damm 1929). The fact that the plays were performed infrequently in repertoire with many other works led to a different kind of corruption, whereby speeches or images from one play would be transferred by the actor's faulty memory to another. Even more radical changes might be introduced during the run of the piece, particularly if it had a long stage life. Popular works from the 1580s, such as *The Jew of Malta* or *The Spanish Tragedy*, were still being performed in the third decade of the seventeenth century, by which time they might have been frequently revised.

Henslowe's diary tells us disappointingly little about the early stages of script preparation and rehearsal. Nevertheless, a comparison of literary and production expenses does enable us to work out a rudimentary schedule. The length of time between the final payment 'in full' to the playwright and payment for a licence, or for the first production expense, is a reflection of the time (and possibly the care) taken in the first stage of the theatrical life of a work. What is surprising about these figures is the haste with which plays were often rushed into production. In a great many cases, pre-rehearsal preparations took only about two weeks. A period of a fortnight to study, annotate, transcribe, license, and prepare parts for a play is not long, and suggests perhaps a certain slapdash efficiency. But what are we to make of cases such as 1 *Civil Wars of France* (f. 50v), *Fortunatus* (f. 66), or *Jephtha* (ff. 105v–106v) when the prompt-books were prepared and presumably rehearsals begun in nine, six, and three days respectively? The figures are only indicative, of course, but they do under-line a basic fact of the Elizabethan repertory system – that everything moved much more quickly than in a modern classical theatre, and the attention to detail we expect in contemporary productions was almost certainly impossible.

The reasons for these instances of exceptional haste can only be guessed. In one case, payments to Chettle for *Vayvode* actually postdated expenditures for production (f. 49v). This play was probably an old work belonging to Edward Alleyn which the company had made arrangements to produce, and which they subsequently purchased from Alleyn in January 1599. Chettle's contribution was probably a prologue or alter-ation requested by the actors after rehearsals had begun.

Another example of hasty production is 2 *Two Angry Women* paid for 'in full' on 12 February 1599 (f. 53v), almost two weeks after the first loan for production costs (f. 53). Unless the final payment to Porter was unaccountably delayed, the company had begun rehearsing before the play had been completed. The next most rapid staging was that of 1 *Civil Wars*, mounted in about nine days. The play was completed by Dekker and Day on 29 September 1598, just twenty-five days after 2 *Hannibal & Hermes* by the same authors (f. 50, 50v). The actors put it into production in spite of the fact that they had other plays on hand, including 1 *Brute* which they subsequently produced. *Civil Wars* must have been popular, since a sequel was paid for by 3 November 1598 and put into rehearsal immediately.

The speed with which these plays were mounted raises interesting questions about how the actors planned their programme. What governed the choice of such plays? Why were they put ahead of other scripts which had been paid for and apparently never produced? Generally speaking, the players had to make three kinds of decision with respect to their repertoire. In each new season they would have to choose a cer-tain number of plays from those already rehearsed for their current programme, select the new plays to be produced, and decide whether or not to revive old plays from previous years. It is hard to imagine that such decisions would not be based, at least in part, on an awareness of a play's popularity with the audience. We do not know if the players themselves kept a record of each play's income, but a table such as that compiled above for the Strange's Fall–Winter season of 1592–93 enables us to see how closely programming decisions reflect financial success.

The season in question began late (29 December) after a six-month break. Of the plays that had been performed during the spring, nine were carried over into the new season. These included five from the current repertoire (*Bacon, Mollocco, Mandeville, Jew of Malta,* and *The Spanish Tragedy*), and four of the five 'ne' plays. In some cases these choices are easily understandable. *The Spanish Tragedy*, *Muly Mollocco* and *The Jew of Malta* were the three most popular old plays from the previous season, having been performed thirteen, eleven, and ten times respectively, and having averaged £1-17-0, £1-12-8, and £2-03-7 at the box office. The inclusion of *Friar Bacon* and *Sir John Mandeville*, however, is more puzzling. Neither work had been particularly popular. *Friar Bacon* averaged £0-14-1 for four performances and *Sir John* £1-05-8 for five, both below the seasonal average of £1-10-1. Here it is likely that other factors, such as the wishes of the leading actor, may have overridden purely economic considerations. Neither work did particularly well in the new season, averaging only £0-18-8 and eleven shillings, far below the average. Another curious feature of the programme is the omission of *The Tanner of Denmark*, which had been given its first (and only) performance on 23 or 26 May. The dropping of this work from the repertoire after only one appearance is the more puzzling in view of the fact that Henslowe recorded the second highest daily takings of the season at its première.

During this brief six-week Fall–Winter season the players produced two 'ne' plays and staged one revival. *The Jealous Comedy* opened just seven playing days after the beginning of the season, so it is probable that rehearsals had begun before playing commenced. The second 'ne' play, *The Massacre at Paris*, opened on 28 or 30 January, eighteen playing days after the première of *The Jealous Comedy*. There is some doubt that this performance in fact represents the first production of Marlowe's play. Attendance reflected in Henslowe's receipts was high, but not significantly higher than that recorded at other premières.

Another curious feature of this season is the revival of a previously unrecorded play, *Cosmo*, for two performances in January. There is no way of knowing when the play had last been performed or how much rehearsal was required to ready it for the stage. It was first given on 11 or 12 January, just five playing days after the première of *The Jealous Comedy*, so there would have been ample time to make the necessary preparations. *Cosmo* was relatively successful, but it is puzzling why the players should have scheduled an old play rather than repeating the one they had just opened.

Close scrutiny of Henslowe's income figures for the years 1592–7 enables us to observe certain differences between seasons and companies. For example, in 1592 Strange's Men performed no less than fifteen different works in the first seventeen playing days (Table II.1). Since much, if not all, of their time during this period was likely to have been taken up with rehearsals of *Henry VI* (a new play which they opened just eleven playing days after the beginning of the season), all of these works must have been mounted with little or no preparation. What is unusual is the small number of repeated performances (only two in the first seventeen days). Furthermore, fully one-third of the works presented during this period were not staged again. Indeed, if we eliminate the three most popular plays (*Muly Mollocco*, *The Jew of Malta*, and *Jeronimo*), then the Company gave forty-one performances of fifteen plays for an average of less than three performances each. This is in sharp contrast to the Admiral's Men's first season in 1594, when that Company relied on a relatively small number of current works, giving 103 performances of thirteen plays. By 1595 the

Admiral's Men had a wider selection of plays in their repertoire, and gave a more varied programme (twenty plays in ten weeks compared to only thirty plays in a season more than four times as long) with relatively fewer performances of each play. These figures imply that both Strange's in 1592 and Admiral's in 1595 had a substantial number of works that they could mount with little rehearsal, and that they gave the public a wide selection. In 1594 the players apparently had a smaller repertoire ready to perform (possibly because their stock of playbooks had been divided when the companies split up during the period of plague), and as a result they were forced to offer them more frequently. The fact that the income in 1594 was not materially affected by the longer runs of individual plays may be explained by the public's thirst for dramatic entertainment after the long prohibition of playing during most of 1593.

Perhaps the most difficult decisions the actors had to make were those relating to the selection of new plays. The normal period for the preparation of a new work seems to have been about two weeks, but there were many deviations from this pattern. Sometimes openings were delayed. The period of more than a month between *Henry VI* and *Titus and Vespasian* (Table II.1) may have been to avoid Easter week. The opening of a new play in either the week before or the week after Easter might not have significantly altered the receipts of those periods, which were traditionally the lowest and highest of the season. Two weeks later, however, the première caused an increase in the average weekly income. At other times, the failure to produce new plays may have been caused by troubles in the company. In the Fall–Winter season of 1596–97, the Admiral's Men gave only seventeen performances in the first nine weeks. This no doubt contributed to the delay in mounting the first new play, which was not premièred until the sixth week of the season. Sometimes, preparations for new plays appear to have been rushed. When the Admiral's Men did begin presenting premières in December 1596, they did so at the hectic rate of almost one a week for a period of some seven weeks (Table II.9).

Closely related to the staging of new plays was the problem of programming revivals. It is not always possible to identify such revivals, or to determine how much time and money was spent in their preparation. Sometimes Henslowe's records do not go back far enough to establish the previous performance history of plays such as *Muly Mollocco* or *Jeronimo*, which may have been revivals in the first Strange's season. At other times, the absence of production expense accounts makes it impossible to know if the players prepared alterations, or ordered new costumes for the staging of old works between 1592 and 1596. In the first Admiral's season, *The Jew of Malta* (performed by Strange's in 1592–93, and by Sussex's in 1594) was played on 14 May, just one month after it had appeared in the Sussex–Queen's repertoire on 3 April. In the same season, the company revived *Guise* (last acted by Strange's in 1593) as well as 1 and 2 *Tamburlaine* and *Dr Faustus*, which were also old plays by that time. In the Fall–Winter season of 1595–96, *The Jew of Malta* (last performed in December 1594), was staged five days after the première of a new play; *The Siege of London* (last presented in March 1595) appeared three days after a new production; and *The Welshman* (previously unrecorded) was mounted the day following a première. This ability of the Elizabethan players to revive works which had remained unperformed for months (or even years) is an aspect of their work that seems particularly astonishing.

The ratio of revivals to new plays may indicate something about the quality or success of a season. In 1594 the Admiral's Men presented a large number of revivals of works that had first appeared in the 1580s (Table II.5). This group is difficult to define exactly because in several cases the origin of a work is unknown. The two parts of *Tamburlaine* were performed by the earlier Admiral's Men before 1590, when the first part was published. *Dr Faustus* was probably acted by an unknown company before the worsening plague put an end to London playing in January 1593. *Mahomet*, *The Siege of London*, and *Long Meg* may also have been special revivals and were possibly vehicles for the Company's leading actor, Edward Alleyn. Whatever their nature, all of these 'revivals' attracted larger-than-average crowds to their performances, and collectively did better business than the new plays presented that season.

Some light on the process of revision is also shed by Henslowe's accounts. In the years from 1596 to 1603 about a dozen works were altered or 'mended' by the companies in Henslowe's theatres. Some of these revisions were for special occasions. For example, Thomas Dekker was paid £2-00-0 to alter his play *Phaeton* for Court (ff. 70v–71). The sum is about one-third of the fee paid for a new play, so it is likely that the changes were substantial. On the other hand, the 'prologue & a epiloge' which Dekker supplied for 'ponesciones pillet' (Pontius Pilate?), while also probably for a Court performance, did not likely affect the text of the old play itself (f. 96). *Tasso's Melancholy* performed as a 'ne' play by the Admiral's Men in 1595, was restaged at the Fortune in 1602, at which time Dekker was paid for two sets of alterations (ff. 96, 108). Here we have fairly clear evidence of progressive revision which may very well have necessitated the alteration or transcription of the prompt-book.

By far the majority of payments for revisions recorded in Henslowe's diary are to single authors for changes in other men's work. In some cases we do not know the names of the original authors, so it is possible (but unlikely) that Dekker, for example, had a hand in writing *Fortunatus*, *Pontius Pilate*, or *Tasso's Melancholy*, all of which he revised. But it was Chettle who was paid to revise Munday's 1 *Robin Hood* (f. 52); and Dekker who mended *Sir John Oldcastle* by Munday, Drayton, and Hathway (f. 115). Jonson's revisions of *The Spanish Tragedy* (f. 94), Middleton's alterations of Greene's *Friar Bacon* (f. 108v), and Rowley and Bird's changes in *Dr Faustus* are special cases, since the original authors, Kyd, Greene, and Marlowe, were all dead. But Dekker's revisions of his own *Phaeton* some three years after it was first produced seems to be an exceptional case.

The question of collaborative revision is more complex. There is one series of entries in the diary which indicates that the process was not unknown. Early in 1602 Hathway, Day, and Smith collaborated on a second part of *Black Dog of Newgate* for Worcester's Men, for which they were paid £7-00-0 in full on 3 February (f. 119v). The Company purchased costumes by 15 February, and were presumably planning to stage the play shortly thereafter. Between 21 and 26 February, however, they paid the three playwrights an extra £2-00-0 for 'adicyones' (f. 120). This looks suspiciously like last-minute changes necessitated by some unforeseen emergency – possibly objections by the censor. In this case the revisions were part of the original collaborative effort so all of the writers participated. It may or may not be significant that the revision was undertaken for Worcester's, not for Admiral's Men, and that it appears to have been done in a rush (since preparations for production were already under way). From the evidence of Henslowe's diary, however, we would have to say that the kind of collaborative revision evident in the manuscript play *Sir Thomas More* is apparently not contrary to contemporary practice.

Since the acting companies were primarily self-dependent, commercial organizations, their health (and indeed their survival) depended on their ability to limit their expenses to what they could afford. A particularly startling feature of the picture the diary reveals, therefore, is the apparent extravagance of the staging. Compared to £5-00-0 or £8-00-0 paid out for a play, the actors would spend £20-00-0, £30-00-0, or even more on production. These figures may be unusual, and it is true that other plays appear to have been staged at minimal or even no cost. But the relatively large proportion of unassignable production expenses, and evidence that the players occasionally paid production costs from their own pockets suggest that considerable attention was paid to the physical aspect of production. It is interesting, in this respect, to compare the players' spending on plays and production in the seasons for which we have records. These expenses, expressed as weekly averages, can be summarized as follows:

Season	Literary	Production	Ratio
F–W 1597–8	1-07-9	0-14-5	2:1
S–S 1598	4-03-0	1-17-0	2:1
F–W 1598–99	3-14-8	6-14-9	1:2
S–S 1599	1-08-4	3-13-3	1:2
S 1599	1-16-1	0-13-9	2:1
F–W 1599–1600	3-19-9	2-03-9	2:1
S–S 1600	2-03-5	3-07-7	2:3
Move to Fortune			
F–W 1600–01	0-14-5	1-00-3	2:3
S–S 1601	2-01-6	3-09-3	2:3
F–W 1601–02	2-01-8	3-04-4	2:3
S–S–F–W 1602–03	2-06-11	1-00-3	?

In this, as in so many other examples, however, the information provided by the diary is ambiguous. The true explanation of the apparently higher production costs in certain seasons may never be known. Similarly, the exact identity of plays such as 'harey the vj' must remain a mystery, as must details about the players' organization and their dealings with dramatists and craftsmen. In the final analysis it could be argued that the diary reveals nothing, or at best merely reflects each reader's preconceptions. That may be true. But it is all the more reason why the document should be returned to again and again. The discursive commentary which makes up the bulk of this volume is intended to raise rather than to answer questions. The tables are for readers interested in pursuing certain questions further than they have been followed in the commentary. Together they may stimulate an interest in the theatrical context of the Elizabethan drama and lead readers back to the diary itself.

6 · TABLES AND SUMMARIES

INFORMATION in the diary has been tabulated in the following pages in a form that, it is hoped, will prove useful to readers wishing to question certain conclusions in earlier chapters, or to follow up other lines of enquiry. The chronological list of the plays (Table I) establishes a number for each work mentioned in the diary which is occasionally used as the sole means of identifying a play. This means of identification has been resorted to in the Performance Calendar (Table II) where it was impossible to spell out the titles in full. Consequently, readers consulting the calendar will need to make frequent reference to the list of titles.

As explained in the text, the Performance Calendar, which is based on the 1592–7 income accounts, is arranged to show both the dating recorded in the diary (the calendar on the left-hand side), and an adjustment of those dates that has been suggested by W. W. Greg (the calendar on the right). In the former the dates of performance recorded by Henslowe are shown; the beginning of the playing week is underlined, and the dates of the 'ne' performances are indicated by an asterisk. The right-hand calendar shows the date of performance (by location), the title of the play (by number above the line), and the income recorded by Henslowe (in pounds, shillings, and pence below the line). Following Greg's theory, the dates in the right-hand calendar have been adjusted to avoid Sunday performances, and the weekly totals (based on those adjusted dates) have been recorded in a separate column to provide a basis for comparison with weekly figures in later years.

The loan accounts which Henslowe maintained between 1596–1603 have been separated into literary and production expenses which are shown on facing pages. On the left, because they usually preceed the production costs, are all advances relating to plays and playwrights with the exception of payments for licences, which are considered a production expense. Facing them are the loans for costumes, properties and other miscellaneous expenses involved in running the company. All expenses are divided into seasons (although in the case of payments to authors such a division is relatively arbitrary). This division enables a reader to see at a glance how the companies allocated their funds from year to year.

In the record of literary expenses (Table III.a) payments relating to individual plays are brought together and the information contained in the various entries summarized. Dates of the first and last payments are recorded along with the names of the sharers who approved the loans, and those of the authors receiving the money. Whether the sums represent full or partial payment, and whether those payments were made for an old play or for alterations is recorded to indicate the play's status. If there is evidence that the play was subsequently produced, this too is reported. Finally, the total amount paid for the work (in that particular season) is specified in the last column.

The production expenses on the facing pages (Table III.b) are arranged somewhat differently. In those cases where advances were for a particular play, they are entered in a 'specified total' column. Payments which cannot be linked to a particular production, and advances for non-dramatic activities such as loans, entertainment, or wages are listed in an 'unspecified total' column.

Information from both income and loan accounts is brought together in Table IV, and both weekly and seasonal totals recorded. This table consolidates all the theatrical accounts to show the players' financial dealings week by week, and season by season. From 1596, the weekly income is compared with weekly expenses (including repayments to Henslowe), and a running balance is maintained. Where the titles of 'ne' plays are known, they are listed in the column headed 'Details' in the week when the première occurred. After 1597, when the daily performance records cease, the titles of new productions are derived from the loan accounts, and the date of the première is suggested by the insertion of the title in square brackets.

One final summary (Table V) compiles all the seasonal totals to show how the various companies fared year by year.

TABLE 1. A CHRONOLOGICAL LIST OF PLAY TITLES MENTIONED IN THE DIARY

1	*Friar Bacon*	52	*1 Tamburlaine*
2	Muly Mollocco	53	Palamon and Arcite
3	Orlando	54	Love of an English Lady
4	Don Horatio	55	*Dr Faustus*
5	Sir John Mandeville	56	Grecian Comedy
6	Henry of Cornwall	57	French Doctor
7	*Jew of Malta*	58	*Knack to Know an Honest Man*
8	Clorys and Orgasto	59	1 Caesar and Pompey
9	Pope Joan	60	Diocletian
10	Machiavel	61	Warlamchester
11	*Henry VI*	62	Wise Man of West Chester
12	Bendo and Richardo	63	Set at Maw
13	Four Plays in One	64	*2 Tamburlaine*
14	*Looking-Glass for London*	65	Siege of London
15	Zenobia	66	Antony and Vallia
16	*Jeronimo (Spanish Tragedy)*	67	French Comedy
17	Constantine	68	Long Meg of Westminster
18	Jerusalem	69	Mack
19	Brandimer	70	Seleo and Olympio
20	Titus and Vespasian	71	1 Hercules
21	2 Tamar Cham	72	2 Hercules
22	Tanner of Denmark	73	Seven Days of the Week
23	*Knack to Know a Knave*	74	2 Caesar and Pompey
24	Jealous Comedy	75	Longshanks
25	Cosmo	76	Crack me this Nut
26	*Guise (Massacre at Paris)*	77	New World's Tragedy
27	God Speed the Plough	78	Disguises
28	Huon of Bordeaux	79	Wonder of a Woman
29	*George a Green*	80	Barnardo and Fiammetta
30	Buckingham	81	Toy to Please Chaste Ladies
31	Richard the Confessor	82	*Henry V*
32	William the Conqueror	83	Welshman
33	Friar Francis	84	Chinon of England
34	Abraham and Lot	85	Pythagoras
35	Fair Maid of Italy	86	2 Seven Days of the Week
36	King Lud	87	*1 Fortunatus*
37	*Titus Andronicus*	88	*Blind Beggar of Alexandria*
38	Ranger's Comedy	89	Julian the Apostate
39	*King Lear*	90	1 Tamar Cham
40	Cutlack	91	Phocas
41	Hester and Ahasuerus	92	Troy
42	Bellendon	93	Paradox
43	Hamlet	94	Tinker of Totness
44	*Taming of a Shrew*	95	Vortigern
45	Galiaso	96	*Stukeley*
46	Philipo and Hippolito	97	Nebuchadnezzar
47	Godfrey of Boulogne	98	That Will Be Shall Be
48	Merchant of Emden	99	Alexander and Lodowick
49	Tasso's Melancholy	100	Woman Hard to Please
50	Mahomet	101	Osric
51	Venetian Comedy	102	Guido

103	Five Plays in One	156	Conan, Prince of Cornwall
104	Time's Triumph	157	(Chapman's Playbook)
105	Uther Pendragon	158	2 Civil Wars of France
106	*Comedy of Humours*	159	3 Civil Wars of France
107	Henry I	160	Tis No Deceit
108	Frederick and Basilea	161	War Without Blows
109	Hengist	162	Two Merry Women of Abington
110	Martin Swart	163	William Longsword
111	Witch of Islington	164	Intro to Civil Wars of France
112	Sturgeflattery	165	World Runs on Wheels
113	Hardicanute	166	Joan as Good as My Lady
114	Friar Spendleton	167	Friar Fox
115	Bourbon	168	Polyphemus
116	The Cobbler	169	Two Merry Women of Abington
117	(Book of Yong Harton)	170	The Spencers
118	Branholt	171	Four Kings
119	(Benjamin's Plot)	172	Troilus and Cressida
120	Alice Pierce	173	Orestes
121	Black Joan	174	Agamemnon
122	Mother Redcap	175	All Fools
123	Dido	176	*Gentle Craft* (*Shoemaker's Holiday*)
124	Phaeton	177	Pastoral Tragedy
125	*1 Robin Hood*	178	Stepmother's Tragedy
126	*Woman Will Have Her Will*	179	Bear a Brain
127	*2 Robin Hood*	180	Page of Plymouth
128	The Miller	181	Poor Man's Paradise
129	Triplicity of Cuckolds	182	Robert II, King of Scots
130	Henry I and Prince of Wales	183	(Play by Marston)
131	1 Earl Goodwin	184	Tristram of Lyonesse
132	Pierce of Exton	185	*1 Sir John Oldcastle*
133	King Arthur	186	2 Sir John Oldcastle
134	1 Black Bateman	187	*Patient Grissell*
135	2 Earl Goodwin	188	Tragedy of John Cox
136	Love Prevented	189	2 Henry of Richmond
137	Funeral of Richard	190	Tragedy of Merry
138	Ill of a Woman	191	Orphan's Tragedy
139	2 Black Bateman	192	Arcadian Virgin
140	Madman's Morris	193	Italian Tragedy
141	Woman's Tragedy	194	Owen Tudor
142	1 Hannibal and Hermes	195	Truth's Supplication
143	Valentine and Orsen	196	Jugurtha
144	Pierce of Winchester	197	Spanish Moor's Tragedy
145	1 Brutus	198	Damon and Pythias
146	(A Comedy for the Court)	199	Seven Wise Masters
147	Hot Anger Soon Cold	200	Ferrex and Porrex
148	Chance Medley	201	English Fugitives
149	Cataline	202	Cupid and Psyche
150	Vayvode	203	Wooing of Death
151	2 Hannibal	204	Devil and His Dame
152	1 Civil Wars of France	205	Strange News Out of Poland
153	Fount of New Fashion	206	*1 Blind Beggar of Bethnal Green*
154	Mulmutius Dunwallow	207	Judas
155	Brute Greenshield	208	1 Fair Constance of Rome

209	2 Fair Constance of Rome	245	Mortimer
210	Fortune's Tennis	246	Earl Hertford
211	Robin Hood's Pennyworths	247	Joshua
212	Hannibal and Scipio	248	Randal, Earl of Chester
213	Scogen and Skelton	249	As Merry as May Be
214	2 Blind Beggar of Bethnal Green	250	Set at Tennis
215	Conquest of Spain	251	1 London Florentine
216	All is Not Gold that Glisters	252	Prologue and Epilogue for Court
217	Conquest of West Indies	253	Hoffman
218	King Sebastian	254	Singer's Voluntary
219	Six Yeomen of the West	255	Four Sons of Aymon
220	3 Blind Beggar of Bethnal Green	256	Boss of Billingsgate
221	1 Cardinal Wolsey	257	Siege of Dunkirk
222	Earl of Gloucester	258	(Play of Chettle)
223	Friar Rush and the Proud Woman	259	2 London Florentine
224	2 Tom Dough	260	*Patient Man & Honest Whore*
225	Life of Cardinal Wolsey	261	Like Unto Like
226	1 Six Clothiers	262	Roderick
227	2 Six Clothiers	263	(Chettle's Tragedy)
228	Too Good to be True	264	Albere Galles
229	Spanish Fig	265	Marshal Osric
230	Prologue to Pontius Pilate	266	Cutting Dick
231	Malcolm King of Scots	267	Byron
232	Love Parts Friendship	268	Two (Three) Brothers
233	Bristol Tragedy	269	(Play by Middleton)
234	Jephthah	270	1 Lady Jane
235	Tobias	271	*2 Lady Jane*
236	Caesar's Fall	272	Christmas Comes But Once a Year
237	Richard Crookback	273	1 Black Dog of Newgate
238	Danish Tragedy	274	Blind Eats Many a Fly
239	Widow's Charm	275	Unfortunate General
240	Medicine for a Curst Wife	276	(Play by Chettle and Heywood)
241	Samson	277	2 Black Dog of Newgate
242	Philip of Spain	278	*A Woman Killed With Kindness*
243	Play of William Cartwright	279	Italian Tragedy
244	Felmelanco	280	Shore

NOTE: *Italic titles* extant

II.1 Spring-Summer 1592 (Strange's)

February 1592

Fol	Su	Mo	Tu	We	Th	Fr	Sa
7							<u>19</u>
	20	21		23	24	25	26
	<u>28</u>	29					

February 1592

	Sunday	Monday	Tuesdy	Wedsdy	Thusdy	Friday	Satday	Total
						18	1 / 0-17-3	0-17-3
20		2 / 1-09-0	3 / 0-16-6	4 / 0-13-6	5 / 0-12 6	6 / 1-12-0	7 / 2-10-0	7-13-6
27		8 / 0-18-0	2 / 1-14-0					

March 1592

Su	Mo	Tu	We	Th	Fr	Sa
		1	2	3*	4	
<u>6</u>	7	8	9	10	11	
<u>13</u>	14		16	17	18	
<u>20</u>	21	22	23		25	
<u>27</u>	28	29	30	31		

March 1592

	Sunday	Monday	Tuesdy	Wedsdy	Thusdy	Friday	Satday	Total
				9 / 0-15-0	10 / 0-14-0	11* / 3-06-8	12 / 0-16-0	8-13-8
5		13 / 1-11-6	11 / 3-00-0	14 / 0-07-0	15 / 1-02-6	7 / 2-16-0	11 / 2-07-6	11-04-6
12		4 / 1-09-0	16 / 4-11-0	15	6 / 1-11-6	2 / 1-08-6	7 / 1-19-0	9-19-0
19		16 / 1-18-0	17 / 0-12-0	18 / 0-18-0	6 / 0-13-6	24	1 / - 15 6	4-17-0
26E		14 / 2-15-0	11 / 3-08-0	2 / 3-02-0	4 / 1-19-0	16 / 3-00-0		

APRIL 1592

Fol	Su	Mo	Tu	We	Th	Fr	Sa
							1
	<u>3</u>	4	5	6	7	8	
7v	<u>10</u>	11*	12	13	14	15	
	<u>17</u>	18	19	20	21	22	
	<u>24</u>	25	26	27	28*	29	
	30						

APRIL 1592

	Sunday	Monday	Tuesdy	Wedsdy	Thusdy	Friday	Satday	Total
							5 / 1-10-0	15-14-0
2		10 / 1-02-0	7 / 2-03-0	11 / 2-01-0	19 / 1-02-0	16 / 1-06-0	2 / 1-03-0	8-17-0
9		4 / 1-08-0	20* / 3-04-0	12 / 1-03-0	11 / 1-06-0	16 / 1-13-0	5 / 1-06-0	10-00-0
16		2 / 1-10-0	7 / 2-08-6	14 / 1-04-0	20 / 2-16-0	11 / 1-13-0	4 / 0-17-0	10-08-6
23		16 / 1-08-0	18 / 2-06-0	1 / 1-04-0	2 / 1-06-0	21* / 3-04-0	6 / 1-06-0	10-14-0
30								

MAY 1592

Su	Mo	Tu	We	Th	Fr	Sa
		2	3	4	5	6
7	8/8	9	10	11	<u>13</u>	

MAY 1592

	Sunday	Monday	Tuesdy	Wedsdy	Thusdy	Friday	Satday	Total
		2 / 2-18-0	16 / 1-14-0	20 / 2-17-6	11 / 2-16-0	7 / 2-01-0	1 / 0-14-0	13-00-6
7		19 / 1-04-0	11 / 1-02-0	20 / 1-10-0	16 / 1-06-0	21 / 1-17-0	7 / 1-14-0	8-13-0

MAY 1592

Fol	Su	Mo	Tu	We	Th	Fr	Sa
	14	15	16	17	18	_19_	20
	21	22	23*	24	_25_	26	27
		29	30	31			

MAY 1592

	Sunday	Monday	Tuesdy	Wedsdy	Thusdy	Friday	Satday	Total
14	16 / 3-04-0	11 / 2-10-0	20 / 3-00-0	5 / 2-00-0	2 / 1-16-6	6 / 1-06-0		13-16-6
21	11 / 1-10-0	7 / 2-14-0	4 / 1-08-0	16 / 1-07-0	22* / 3-13-6	20 / 1-10-0		12-02-6
28	11 / 1-04-0	21 / 1-16-6	16 / 1-03-0					

JUNE 1592

Fol	Su	Mo	Tu	We	Th	Fr	Sa
8		_5_	6	7	8	9	10*
	_12_	**13**	14	15	16		
	_18_	19	20	21	22		

JUNE 1592

	Sunday	Monday	Tuesdy	Wedsdy	Thusdy	Friday	Satday	Total
				10 / 1-06-0	7 / 1-13-0	2 / 1-03-0		8-05-6
4	12 / 1-12-0	20 / 2-02-0	14 / 1-09-0	21 / 2-00-0	16 / 1-08-0	23* / 3-12-0		12-03-0
11	11 / 1-12-0	2 / 1-00-0	7 / 1-18-0	23 / 2-12-0	5 / 1-00-0	17		8-02-0
18	16 / 1-04-0	11 / 1-11-0	4 / 0-15-0	21 / 1-12-0	23 / 1-07-0	24		6-09-0
							Total	181-10-5

II.2 Fall-Winter 1592-93 (Strange's)

DECEMBER 1592

Su	Mo	Tu	We	Th	Fr	Sa
					_29_	30
31						

DECEMBER 1592

	Sunday	Monday	Tuesdy	Wedsdy	Thusdy	Friday	Satday	Total
			27	28	2 / 3-10-0	16 / 3-08-0		6-18-0
31								

JANUARY 1593

Fol	Su	Mo	Tu	We	Th	Fr	Sa
	1		3	4	5*	_6_	
	_8_	9	10		12	13	
	14	_15_	16	17	18	19	20
	_22_	23	24	25			
8v		30*31					
		_30_ 31					

JANUARY 1593

	Sunday	Monday	Tuesdy	Wedsdy	Thusdy	Friday	Satday	Total
	23 / 1-10-0	7 / 2-16-0	23 / 1-09-0	5 / 0-12-0	24* / 2-04-0	20 / 2-12-0		11-03-0
7	16 / 1-02-0	2 / 1-00-0	1 / 1-04-0	25 / 2-04-0	5 / 0-09-0	23 / 1-04-0		7-03-0
14	20 / 1-10-0	11 / 2-06-0	1 / 1-00-0	7 / 3-00-0	21 / 1-16-0	2 / 1-00-0		10-12-0
23	16 / 1-00-0	25 / 1-10-0	23 / 1-04-0	20 / 1-10-0	26* / 3-14-0	5 / 0-12-0		9-10-0
28	1 / 0-12-0	30	11 / 1-06-0					

FEBRUARY 1593

Fol	Su	Mo	Tu	We	Th	Fr	Sa
8v						1	

FEBRUARY 1593

Sunday	Monday	Tuesdy	Wedsdy	Thusdy	Friday	Satday	Total
				$\frac{7}{1\text{-}15\text{-}0}$	2	3	3-13-0
						Total	48-19-0

II.3 Fall Winter 1593-94 (Sussex's)

DECEMBER 1593

Su	Mo	Tu	We	Th	Fr	Sa
				27	28	29
30	31					

DECEMBER 1593

Sunday	Monday	Tuesdy	Wedsdy	Thusdy	Friday	Satday	Total
25	$\frac{27}{3\text{-}01\text{-}0}$	$\frac{28}{3\text{-}10\text{-}0}$	$\frac{29}{3\text{-}10\text{-}0}$	$\frac{30}{2\text{-}11\text{-}0}$			12-12-0
30	$\frac{31}{1\text{-}18\text{-}0}$						

JANUARY 1594

Su	Mo	Tu	We	Th	Fr	Sa
		1	2	3	4	5
	7	8	9	10	11	12
	14	15	16	17	18	
20	21	22	23*			
27	28			31		

JANUARY 1594

Sunday	Monday	Tuesdy	Wedsdy	Thusdy	Friday	Satday	Total
	$\frac{30}{2\text{-}18\text{-}0}$	$\frac{29}{0\text{-}18\text{-}0}$	$\frac{28}{0\text{-}14\text{-}0}$	$\frac{32}{1\text{-}02\text{-}0}$	$\frac{27}{0\text{-}11\text{-}0}$		8-01-0
6	$\frac{33}{3\text{-}01\text{-}0}$	$\frac{29}{1\text{-}03\text{-}0}$	$\frac{34}{2\text{-}12\text{-}0}$	$\frac{30}{1\text{-}02\text{-}0}$	$\frac{28}{0\text{-}05\text{-}0}$	$\frac{35}{0\text{-}09\text{-}0}$	8-12-0
13	$\frac{33}{1\text{-}16\text{-}0}$	$\frac{29}{1\text{-}00\text{-}0}$	$\frac{31}{0\text{-}11\text{-}0}$	$\frac{34}{1\text{-}10\text{-}0}$	$\frac{36}{1\text{-}02\text{-}0}$	19	5-19-0
20	$\frac{33}{1\text{-}10\text{-}0}$	$\frac{35}{1\text{-}02\text{-}0}$	$\frac{29}{1\text{-}05\text{-}0}$	$\frac{37*}{3\text{-}08\text{-}0}$	25	26	7-05-0
27	$\frac{30}{0\text{-}18\text{-}0}$	$\frac{37}{2\text{-}00\text{-}0}$	30	$\frac{34}{0\text{-}12\text{-}0}$			

FEBRUARY 1594

Su	Mo	Tu	We	Th	Fr	Sa
4		6				

FEBRUARY 1594

Sunday	Monday	Tuesdy	Wedsdy	Thusdy	Friday	Satday	Total
					1	2	3-10-0
3	$\frac{7}{2\text{-}10\text{-}0}$	5	$\frac{37}{2\text{-}00\text{-}0}$	7	8	9	4-10-0
						Total	50-09-0

II.4 SPRING 1594 (SUSSEX'S AND QUEEN'S)

	APRIL 1594								APRIL 1594							
Fol	Su	Mo	Tu	We	Th	Fr	Sa		Sunday	Monday	Tuesdy	Wedsdy	Thusdy	Friday	Satday	Total
9		1	2	3	4	5	6	E		1 2-03-0	38 3-00-0	7 3-00-0	35 1-03-0	1 1-00-0	39 1-18-0	12-04-0
		7	8					7		7 1-16-0	39 1-16-0	10	11	12	13	3-12-0
															Total	15-16-0

II.4b SPRING 1594 (ADMIRAL'S)

MAY 1594								MAY 1594							
Su	Mo	Tu	We	Th	Fr	Sa		Sunday	Monday	Tuesdy	Wedsdy	Thusdy	Friday	Satday	Total
		14	15	16				12	13	7 2-08-0	38 1-13-0	40 2-02-0	17	18	6-03-0

II.4c SPRING 1594 (ADMIRAL's & CHAMBERLAIN'S)

JUNE 1594								JUNE 1594							
Su	Mo	Tu	We	Th	Fr	Sa		Sunday	Monday	Tuesdy	Wedsdy	Thusdy	Friday	Satday	Total
	3	4	5	6		8*		2	3	4	41 0-08-0	7 0-10-0	37 0-12-0	40 0-11-0	2-01-0
	9	10	11-12	13		15		9	42* 0-17-0	43 0-08-0	41 0-05-0	44 0-09-0	37 0-07-0	7 0-04-0	2-10-0
														Total	4-11-0

II.5 SPRING-SUMMER-FALL-WINTER 1594-95 (ADMIRAL'S)

JUNE 1594								JUNE 1594							
Su	Mo	Tu	We	Th	Fr	Sa		Sunday	Monday	Tuesdy	Wedsdy	Thusdy	Friday	Satday	Total
	17	18	19	20		22		16	42 3-04-0	18	40 1-15-0	38 1-02-0	26 2-14-0	42 1-10-0	10-05-0

PERFORMANCE CALENDAR

JUNE 1594

Fol	Su Mo Tu We Th Fr Sa
9	23 24 25 26*27
9v	30

	Sunday	Monday	Tuesdy	Wedsdy	Thusdy	Friday	Satday	Total
23	38 / 2-19-0	7 / 1-03-0	40 / 1-05-0	26 / 1-16-0	45* / 3-04-0	40 / 1-16-0		12-03-0
30								

JULY 1594

Su Mo Tu We Th Fr Sa
2 3 4 5 6
8 9*10 11 12 13
15 16 17 18 19*20
22 23 24 25 26 27
29 30*31

	Sunday	Monday	Tuesdy	Wedsdy	Thusdy	Friday	Satday	Total
		7 / 2-01-0	42 / 2-02-6	26 / 1-11-0	40 / 1-04-0	38 / 0-18-0	42 / 1-14-0	9-10-6
7		26 / 1-07-0	46* / 3-02-0	7 / 1-07-0	42 / 1-07-0	45 / 2-06-0	46 / 2-00-0	11-09-0
14		40 / 1-15-0	26 / 1-11-0	38 / 0-15-0	46 / 1-13-0	47* / 3-11-0	42 / 1-07-0	10-12-0
21		7 / 1-11-0	45 / 1-11-0	46 / 1-10-0	42 / 2-08-0	47 / 2-07-0	26 / 1-02-0	10-09-0
28		40 / 1-09-0	48* / 3-08-0	42 / 1-07-0				

AUGUST 1594

Su Mo Tu We Th Fr Sa
1   3
nd 5 6 7/7 8/8 10
11*12 13 14 15 17
18 19 20 21 22 24
25*26 27 28 29

(Fol 10 at "25*26 27 28 29")

	Sunday	Monday	Tuesdy	Wedsdy	Thusdy	Friday	Satday	Total
					38 / 0-13-6	46 / 1-10-0	45 / 1-03-6	9-11-0
4		7 / 1-07-0	47 / 1-17-0	46 / 1-09-0	26 / 1-03-6	7 / 0-17-6	40 / 0-13-6	7-07-6
11		42 / 1-13-0	49* / 3-04-0	45 / 0-18-0	47 / 1-09-0	50 / 3-05-0	46 / 1-01-0	11-10-0
18		26 / 1-00-0	49 / 2-07-0	42 / 1-01-0	38 / 0-14-6	45 / 1-01-6	40 / 1-03-6	7-07-6
25		46 / 1-08-0	51* / 2-10-6	47 / 1-07-6	50 / 2-00-0	52 / 3-11-0	42 / 1-00-6	11-17-6

SEPTEMBER 1594

Su Mo Tu We Th Fr Sa
2 3 4 5 6 7
8 9 10 11 12 13
15 16 17*18 19 20 21

	Sunday	Monday	Tuesdy	Wedsdy	Thusdy	Friday	Satday	Total
1	7 / 1-03-6	49 / 2-06-0	46 / 1-02-0	51 / 1-16-6	40 / 0-11-0	26 / 0-17-6		7-16-6
8	47 / 2-00-0	50 / 1-15-0	45 / 1-05-0	42 / 1-04-6	52 / 2-05-0	46 / 1-00-0		9-09-6
15	51 / 1-16-6	38 / 0-15-0	53* / 2-11-0	49 / 1-07-6	46 / 0-14-6	47 / 1-10-0		8-14-6

SEPTEMBER 1594

Vol	Su	Mo	Tu	We	Th	Fr	Sa
10	22	23	24*	25	26		28
	29	30					

SEPTEMBER 1594

	Sunday	Monday	Tuesdy	Wedsdy	Thusdy	Friday	Satday	Total
22	50 / 1-08-0	51 / 1-05-0	42 / 0-16-6	54* / 2-07-0	26 / 0-14-0	40 / 0-13-0		7-03-0
29	52 / 1-11-0							

OCTOBER 1594

Su	Mo	Tu	We	Th	Fr	Sa
			2	3	4	
6	7	8	9		11	
13	14	15	16	17	18	
20	21	22*	23	24	25	
27	28	29	30			

(Vol: 10v)

OCTOBER 1594

	Sunday	Monday	Tuesdy	Wedsdy	Thusdy	Friday	Satday	Total
			45 / 0-17-0	55 / 3-12-0	38 / 0-10-0	51 / 0-17-0	56 / 1-06-0	8-13-0
6	47 / 1-00-0	46 / 0-12-0	49 / 1-07-0	55 / 2-04-0	11	51 / 0-16-0		5-19-0
13	42 / 1-02-0	50 / 1-06-0	52 / 1-08-0	53 / 1-07-0	52 / 2-00-0	57 / 1-02-0		8-05-0
20	7 / 0-13-0	55 / 1-13-0	58* / 2-00-0	49 / 1-03-0	54 / 1-03-0	45 / 0-11-0		1-03-0
27	53 / 2-07-0	57 / 0-15-0	58 / 2-07-0	47 / 0-15-0				

NOVEMBER 1594

Su	Mo	Tu	We	Th	Fr	Sa
					1	2
4	5	5	7	8*	9	
11	12	13	14	15	16*	
18		20	21	22	23	
25	26	27	28	29	30	

NOVEMBER 1594

	Sunday	Monday	Tuesdy	Wedsdy	Thusdy	Friday	Satday	Total
						58 / 3-03-0	42 / 0-07-0	9-14-0
3	52 / 1-19-0	55 / 1-18-0	50 / 0-15-0	58 / 2-04-0	59* / 3-02-0	53 / 0-12-0		10-10-0
10	51 / 1-01-0	49 / 1-05-0	56 / 0-15-0	59 / 1-15-0	42 / 0-12-0	60* / 2-14-0		8-02-0
17	57 / 1-07-0	19	55 / 0-18-0	58 / 1-00-0	60 / 2-03-0	56 / 0-10-0		5-18-0
4	59 / 1-12-0	51 / 0-13-0	52 / 1-02-0	61 / 1-03-0	58 / 1-00-0	61 / 1-18-0		7-08-0

DECEMBER 1594

Su	Mo	Tu	We	Th	Fr	Sa
1	2*	3	4		6	
8	9	10		12	13	14*
11		17		19	20	

DECEMBER 1594

	Sunday	Monday	Tuesdy	Wedsdy	Thusdy	Friday	Satday	Total
1	56 / 0-04-0	62* / 1-13-0	49 / 0-06-0	50 / 0-11-0	6	62 / 1-14-0		4-08-0
8	55 / 0-15-0	7 / 0-03-0	59 / 0-12-0	61 / 0-15-0	58 / 0-12-0	63* / 2-04-0		5-01-0
15	16	52 / 1-11-0	18	64 / 2-06-0	55 / 0-18-0	21		4-15-0

DECEMBER 1594

Fol	Su	Mo	Tu	We	Th	Fr	Sa
11				25	26	27	
	29	30					

DECEMBER 1594

Sunday	Monday	Tuesdy	Wedsdy	Thusdy	Friday	Satday	Total
22	23	24	25	56 / 2-06-0	65 / 3-03-0	55 / 2-12-0	8-01-0
29	62 / 3-02-0	52 / 1-02-0					

JANUARY 1595

Su	Mo	Tu	We	Th	Fr	Sa
		1	2	3	4	
7			9	10	11	
13	14	15		17	18	
19	21	22	23	24	25	
27	28	29	30	31		

JANUARY 1595

Sunday	Monday	Tuesdy	Wedsdy	Thusdy	Friday	Satday	Total
			64 / 3-02-0	63 / 1-04-0	57 / 1-01-0	66 / 0-11-0	10-02-0
5	6	58 / 1-02-0	8	55 / 1-02-0	56 / 1-08-0	49 / 1-00-0	4-12-0
12	58 / 1-13-0	65 / 1-08-0	62 / 3-00-0	63 / 1-05-0	59 / 1-05-0	38 / 0-15-0	9-06-0
19	20	49 / 1-16-0	65 / 1-12-0	62 / 3-06-0	55 / 1-04-0	56 / 0-15-0	8-13-0
26	52 / 1-10-0	63 / 1-07-0	64 / 2-07-0	57 / 0-18-0	56 / 1-08-0		

FEBRUARY 1595

Fol	Su	Mo	Tu	We	Th	Fr	Sa
							1
	3	4	5	6	7	8	
	10	11*12	13	14	15		
11v	17	18	19	20	21*22		
	24	25	26	27	28	29	

FEBRUARY 1595

Sunday	Monday	Tuesdy	Wedsdy	Thusdy	Friday	Satday	Total
					59 / 1-04-0		8-14-0
2	65 / 2-05-0	62 / 3-04-0	50 / 1-06-0	58 / 1-04-0	57 / 1-01-0	55 / 0-18-0	9-18-0
9	51 / 1-00-0	67* / 2-10-0	62 / 2-13-0	65 / 1-09-0	68 / 3-09-0	49 / 0-19-0	12-00-0
16	52 / 1-10-0	64 / 1-16-0	62 / 2-06-0	68 / 2-08-0	69* / 3-00-0	56 / 1-00-0	12-00-0
23	57 / 2-14-0	51 / 1-00-0	58 / 1-04-0	67 / 2-00-0	62 / 1-19-0		

MARCH 1595

Su	Mo	Tu	We	Th	Fr	Sa
3	4	5*	6			

MARCH 1595

Sunday	Monday	Tuesdy	Wedsdy	Thusdy	Friday	Satday	Total
					68 / 1-18-0		10-15-0
2	65 / 1-06-0	68 / 3-00-0	70* / 3-00-0	59 / 1-00-0	7	8	8-06-0

MARCH 1595

Fol	Su	Mo	Tu	We	Th	Fr	Sa
11v		10	11	12	13	14	

MARCH 1595

Sunday	Monday	Tuesdy	Wedsdy	Thusdy	Friday	Satday	Total
9	58 / 1-04-0	52 / 1-10-0	64 / 1-02-0	68 / 1-08-0	65 / 0-14-0	15	5-18-0

Total 339-07-0

II.6 SPRING-SUMMER, 1595 (ADMIRAL'S)

APRIL 1595

Su	Mo	Tu	We	Th	Fr	Sa
	21		23	24	25	26
27		29	30	31		

APRIL 1595

Sunday	Monday	Tuesdy	Wedsdy	Thusdy	Friday	Satday	Total
Easter 20	57 / 2-13-0	58 / 2-15-0	56 / 2-11-0	62 / 2-18-0	62 / 3-00-0	47 / 1-09-0	15-06-0
27	61 / 1-09-0	68 / 1-07-0	55 / 1-02-0				

MAY 1595

Su	Mo	Tu	We	Th	Fr	Sa
				1	2	3
5	6	7*	8	9	10	
12	13	14	15	16	17	
19	20	21	22	23*	24	
26	27	28	29	30	31	

(12v)

MAY 1595

Sunday	Monday	Tuesdy	Wedsdy	Thusdy	Friday	Satday	Total
				68 / 2-10-0	70 / 2-10-0	57 / 0-11-0	9-09-0
4	58 / 1-03-0	62 / 2-00-0	71* / 3-13-0	51 / 1-10-0	70 / 1-06-0	61 / 1-09-0	11-01-0
11	67 / 1-08-0	68 / 1-08-0	49 / 1-00-0	62 / 1-17-0	56 / 1-13-0	47 / 1-02-0	8-08-0
18	70 / 1-03-0	71 / 3-09-0	52 / 1-02-0	64 / 1-05-0	72* / 3-10-0	57 / 1-02-0	11-11-0
25	62 / 1-11-0	71 / 3-00-0	72 / 3-02-0	70 / 1-09-0	61 / 0-09-0	67 / 0-15-0	10-06-0

JUNE 1595

Su	Mo	Tu	We	Th	Fr	Sa
		3*	4	5	6	7
9	10	11	12	13	14	

JUNE 1595

Sunday	Monday	Tuesdy	Wedsdy	Thusdy	Friday	Satday	Total
1	2	73* / 3-10-0	62 / 1-02-0	55 / 0-17-0	73 / 2-04-0	70 / 0-15-0	8-08-0
Whit-sun 8	58 / 2-15-0	73 / 3-06-0	62 / 2-07-0	71 / 3-01-0	72 / 3-02-0	73 / 3-09-0	18-00-0

JUNE 1595

Fol	Su	Mo	Tu	We	Th	Fr	Sa
12v	16	17	18*	19	20	21	
		23	24	25	26		

JUNE 1595

	Sunday	Monday	Tuesdy	Wedsdy	Thusdy	Friday	Satday	Total
15	16 1-05-0	67 1-01-0	74* 2-15-0	68 1-02-0	66 1-00-0	58 0-13-0		7-16-0
22	73 3-05-0	67 1-10-0	59 1-02-0	74 1-00-0	27	28		6-17-0
						Total		107-02-0

II.7 FALL-WINTER 1595-96 (ADMIRAL'S)

AUGUST 1595

Su	Mo	Tu	We	Th	Fr	Sa
25	26	27	28	29*	30	

AUGUST 1595

	Sunday	Monday	Tuesdy	Wedsdy	Thusdy	Friday	Satday	Total
24	58 0-17-0	62 1-19-0	73 2-13-0	68 0-17-0	75* 2-00-0	65 0-18-0		9-04-0
31								

SEPTEMBER 1595

Su	Mo	Tu	We	Th	Fr	Sa
	1	2	3	4	5*	6
		9	10	11	12	13
nd	15	16	17*	18	19	20
22 22	23	24	25	26		
28	29	30				

(Fol 13)

SEPTEMBER 1595

	Sunday	Monday	Tuesdy	Wedsdy	Thusdy	Friday	Satday	Total
	71 3-04-0	72 3-00-0	73 2-12-0	70 0-18-0	76* 3-01-0	66 0-13-0		13-08-0
7	62 2-04-0	75 3-00-0	55 1-12-0	76 3-00-0	73 1-18-0	68 0-16-0		12-10-0
14	52 1-01-0	47 1-00-0	77* 3-05-0	58 0-17-0	57 0-16-0	65 0-17-0		7-16-0
21	73 2-04-0	71 1-11-0	72 1-03-0	76 2-02-0	77 1-18-0	55 0-13-0		9-11-0
28	76 3-06-0	62 0-15-0						

OCTOBER 1595

Su	Mo	Tu	We	Th	Fr	Sa
				2*	3	4
6 6	7	8	9	10		

OCTOBER 1595

	Sunday	Monday	Tuesdy	Wedsdy	Thusdy	Friday	Satday	Total
				75 1-12-0	78* 2-03-0	70 0-15-0	68 0-11-0	9-02-0
5	73 2-00-0	62 0-17-0	72 1-12-0	76 1-06-0	56 0-10-0	78 1-09-0		7-14-0

OCTOBER 1595

Fol	Su	Mo	Tu	We	Th	Fr	Sa
13	12	13	14	15*	16	17	
	19	20	21	22	23	24	25
	26	27	28*	29	30		

OCTOBER 1595

	Sunday	Monday	Tuesdy	Wedsdy	Thusdy	Friday	Satday	Total
12	71 / 1-09-0	72 / 1-05-0	73 / 0-17-0	79* / 2-13-0	78 / 0-10-0	73 / 1-08-0		8-02-0
19	62 / 0-17-0	76 / 1-01-0	75 / 1-10-0	77 / 1-13-0	79 / 1-03-0	76 / 1-03-0		7-07-0
26	71 / 1-12-0	66 / 1-07-0	78 / 0-19-0	80* / 2-02-0	73 / 0-13-0			

NOVEMBER 1595

Fol	Su	Mo	Tu	We	Th	Fr	Sa
	2	3	4	5	6	nd	
14	9	10		12	13	14*	15
			18	19	20	21	22
		24	25	26	27	28*	29
	31						

NOVEMBER 1595

	Sunday	Monday	Tuesdy	Wedsdy	Thusdy	Friday	Satday	Total
							78 / 1-09-0	8-02-0
2	72 / 1-08-0	77 / 1-09-0	79 / 1-07-0	76 / 1-04-0	80 / 0-17-0	62 / 1-00-0		7-05-0
9	75 / 1-13-0	78 / 0-15-0	52 / 0-18-0	64 / 1-12-0	81* / 2-11-0	73 / 0-18-0		8-07-0
16		17	76 / 1-04-0	80 / 0-06-0	79 / 1-00-0	81 / 1-01-0	70 / 0-04-6	3-15-6
23	71 / 1-00-0	72 / 0-16-0	75 / 0-18-0	77 / 0-18-0	82* / 3-06-0	83 / 0-07-0		7-05-0
30								

DECEMBER 1595

Su	Mo	Tu	We	Th	Fr	Sa
		2	3	4		6
	8		10		12	
14		16		18		
	22			25	26	
28	29	30				

DECEMBER 1595

	Sunday	Monday	Tuesdy	Wedsdy	Thusdy	Friday	Satday	Total
		81 / 0-12-0	82 / 1-15-0	80 / 0-07-0	79 / 0-14-0	5	76 / 0-15-0	4-03-0
7		82 / 2-03-0	9	75 / 1-10-0	11	77 / 1-11-6	13	5-04-6
14	73 / 1-04-0	82 / 1-09-0		17	71 / 0-13-0	19	20	3-06-0
21	77 / 1-00-0		23	24	25	79 / 3-02-0	80 / 2-18-0	7-00-0
28	82 / 2-16-0	75 / 1-12-0	62 / 1-02-0					

JANUARY 1596

Su	Mo	Tu	We	Th	Fr	Sa
				1	2	3*

JANUARY 1596

	Sunday	Monday	Tuesdy	Wedsdy	Thusdy	Friday	Satday	Total
					73 / 2-02-0	76 / 0-09-0	84* / 2-10-0	10-11-0

JANUARY 1596

Fol	Su	Mo	Tu	We	Th	Fr	Sa
14		5	6	7	8	9	10
		12	13	14	15	16*	nd
14v	18	19	20	21	22*	23	
	25	26	27	28	29	30	

JANUARY 1596

	Sunday	Monday	Tuesdy	Wedsdy	Thusdy	Friday	Satday	Total
4	82 / 1-06-0	71 / 3-00-0	58 / 1-00-0	77 / 0-18-0	7 / 2-16-0	81 / 0-18-0		9-18-0
11	84 / 2-10-0	65 / 0-15-0	76 / 1-03-0	79 / 1-07-0	85* / 3-01-0	62 / 0-18-0		9-14-0
18	7 / 1-18-0	82 / 1-00-0	80 / 0-11-0	84 / 1-13-0	86* / 3-00-0	85 / 1-16-0		9-18-0
25	77 / 0-14-0	86 / 1-04-0	84 / 1-01-0	85 / 1-10-0	7 / 1-05-0	79 / 0-11-0		6-05-0

FEBRUARY 1596

Su	Mo	Tu	We	Th	Fr	Sa
	2	3	4	5	6	7
	9	10	11	12*	13	
15	16	17	18	19	20	
22	23	24	25	26	27	

FEBRUARY 1596

	Sunday	Monday	Tuesdy	Wedsdy	Thusdy	Friday	Satday	Total
1	7 / 2-17-0	87 / 3-00-0	62 / 0-12-0	75 / 0-14-0	82 / 0-18-0	76 / 0-19-0		9-00-0
8	85 / 1-00-0	87 / 2-00-0	84 / 1-00-0	88* / 3-00-0	55 / 1-05-0		14	8-05-0
15	85 / 1-15-0	88 / 3-06-0	7 / 1-00-0	70 / 0-10-0	88 / 2-13-0	87 / 1-02-0		10-06-0
22	88 / 1-16-0	85 / 1-14-0	84 / 2-16-0	73 / 1-00-0	88 / 3-00-0	75 / 1-10-0		11-16-0

Total   224-15-0

II.8 SPRING-SUMMER 1596 (ADMIRAL'S)

APRIL 1596

Fol	Su	Mo	Tu	We	Th	Fr	Sa
15v		12	13	14	15	16	17
		19	20	21	22	23	24
		26	27	28	29*	30	

APRIL 1596

	Sunday	Monday	Tuesdy	Wedsdy	Thusdy	Friday	Satday	Total
Easter 11	80 / 1-10-0	81 / 1-19-0	87 / 0-18-0	88 / 2-00-0	58 / 0-11-0	62 / 1-10-0		8-08-0
18	55 / 0-12-0	7 / 1-00-0	75 / 0-14-0	85 / 0-18-0	84 / 1-00-0	82 / 0-15-0		4-19-0
25	88 / 2-00-0	77 / 1-09-0	75 / 1-00-0	89* / 2-07-0	62 / 0-10-0			

MAY 1596

Fol	Su	Mo	Tu	We	Th	Fr	Sa
15v							1
	2	3	4	5	6*	7	
	10	11	12	13	14		
	16	17	18	19*	20		22
	23	24	25	26	27		
21v	31						

MAY 1596

	Sunday	Monday	Tuesdy	Wedsdy	Thusdy	Friday	Satday	Total
							79 1-02-0	8-08-0
2	84 1-00-0	88 1-15-0	85 1-00-0	55 1-00-0	90* 2-07-0	76 0-18-0		8-00-0
9	89 1-06-0	87 0-18-0	90 2-05-0	88 2-00-0	7 1-04-0	15		7-13-0
16	84 1-13-0	90 2-06-0	88 2-09-0	91* 2-05-0	89 0-14-0	22		9-07-0
23	85 1-07-0	91 1-19-0	87 0-14-0	90 1-00-0	82 1-03-0	84 0-09-0		6-12-0
Whit- 30 sun	85 3-00-0							

JUNE 1596

Su	Mo	Tu	We	Th	Fr	Sa
	1	2	3	4	5	
7	8	9	10	11*	12	
14	15	16	17		19	
20	21	22 22	23		25	26
27						

JUNE 1596

	Sunday	Monday	Tuesdy	Wedsdy	Thusdy	Friday	Satday	Total
		84 0-03-0	75 3-00-0	88 2-01-0	91 1-11-0	90 1-08-0		11-03-0
6	76 1-08-0	62 1-00-0	81 0-18-0	90 1-08-0	21 3-00-0	55 0-17-0		8-11-0
13	65 1-10-0	85 1-03-0	91 1-00-0	82 1-07-0	18	19		5-00-0
20	90 1-16-0	21 1-15-0	7 0-13-0	91 2-10-0	92* 3-09-0	76 0-12-0		10-15-0
27	88 0-19-0	90 1-10-0	21 1-00-0					

JULY 1596

Su	Mo	Tu	We	Th	Fr	Sa
				1*	2	3
4	5 5	6	7 7	8 8	9	10
11	12		14	15	16	17
18*						

JULY 1596

	Sunday	Monday	Tuesdy	Wedsdy	Thusdy	Friday	Satday	Total
				93* 2-05-0	92 1-04-0	55 0-14-0		7-12-0
4	91 1-02-0	65 0-15-0	62 0-16-0	21 1-03-0	57 0-14-0	88 0-17-0		5-07-0
11	92 1-09-0	90 0-14-0	75 0-15-0	82 0-14-0	42 1-15-0	17		5-07-0
18	81 0-10-0	85 1-02-0	82 1-02-0	92 1-01-0	91 1-09-0	94* 3-00-0		8-04-0

Total 115-06-0

II.9   FALL-WINTER 1596-97(ADMIRAL'S)

OCTOBER 1596

Fol	Su	Mo	Tu	We	Th	Fr	Sa
25					27	28	29

OCTOBER 1596

Sunday	Monday	Tuesdy	Wedsdy	Thusdy	Friday	Satday	Total
24	25	26	84 2-12-0	55 1-07-0	57 0-15-0	30	4-14-0

NOVEMBER 1596

Su	Mo	Tu	We	Th	Fr	Sa
	1	2	3	4	5	6
	8	9	10	11	12	13
	15					

Fol
25v

| | | | | 25 | 26 | 27 |

NOVEMBER 1596

Sunday	Monday	Tuesdy	Wedsdy	Thusdy	Friday	Satday	Total
31	68 2-07-0	84 0-17-0	58 0-15-0	55 0-17-0	68 0-05-0	88 1-10-0	6-11-0
7	81 0-13-0	57 0-14-0	84 0-10-0	73 1-15-0	88 0-16-0	90 0-17-0	5-05-0
14	73 0-12-0	16	17	18	19	20	0-12-0
21	22	23	24	68 0-11-0	73 0-17-0	81 0-11-0	1-19-0
28	29	30					

DECEMBER 1596

Su	Mo	Tu	We	Th	Fr	Sa
		2			4*	
	8		10	11*		
12	14		16	17		
19*	21	22	23	24		
	27	28	29	30*31		

DECEMBER 1596

Sunday	Monday	Tuesdy	Wedsdy	Thusdy	Friday	Satday	Total
			1	88 1-00-0	3	95* 2-10-0	3-10-0
5	6	95 1-15-0	8	88 0-10-0	96* 2-00-0	73 0-09-0	4-14-0
12	96 2-00-0	14	95 1-15-0	55 0-09-0	17	97* 1-10-0	5-14-0
19	95 1-05-0	97 1-06-0	88 0-03-0	95 0-12-0	24	25	3-06-0
26	97 3-08-0	96 3-04-0	95 1-02-0	98* 2-10-0	73 0-06-0		

JANUARY 1597

Su	Mo	Tu	We	Th	Fr	Sa
	3	4	5	6	7	8

JANUARY 1597

Sunday	Monday	Tuesdy	Wedsdy	Thusdy	Friday	Satday	Total
						95 2-05-0	12-15-0
2	98 2-02-0	97 0-16-0	55 0-05-0	98 2-02-0	16 3-00-0	95 0-12-0	8-17-0

JANUARY 1597

Fol	Su	Mo	Tu	We	Th	Fr	Sa
25v		10	11	12	13	14*	15
		17	18	19	20	21	22
26		24	25	26	27*	28	29
		31					

JANUARY 1597

	Sunday	Monday	Tuesdy	Wedsdy	Thusdy	Friday	Satday	Total
9	96 / 1-08-0	16 / 2-00-0	97 / 0-13-0	98 / 1-02-0		99* / 2-15-0	88 / 0-09-0	8-07-0
16	16 / 1-00-0	98 / 0-15-0	97 / 0-10-0	96 / 0-11-0	95 / 0-12-0	16 / 0-19-0		4-07-0
23	98 / 0-17-0	88 / 0-19-0	97 / 0-09-0		100* / 2-11-0	68 / 0-07-0	100 / 2-03-0	7-06-0
30	16 / 1-04-0							

FEBRUARY 1597

Su	Mo	Tu	We	Th	Fr	Sa
		1	2	3	4	5
	7	8	9	10	11*	12

FEBRUARY 1597

	Sunday	Monday	Tuesdy	Wedsdy	Thusdy	Friday	Satday	Total
		100 / 1-05-0	98 / 1-18-0	101 / 1-09-0	100 / 1-08-0	95 / 1-09-0		8-13-0
6	101 / 0-14-0	100 / 1-09-0	16 / 0-17-0	96 / 0-18-0	99* / 3-05-0	99 / 1-14-0		8-17-0

Total 95-07-0

II.10 SPRING 1597 (ADMIRAL'S)

MARCH 1597

Fol	Su	Mo	Tu	We	Th	Fr	Sa
26					3		5
		7	8	9			12
		14	15				19*
	20	21	22				
		28	19	30	31		

MARCH 1597

	Sunday	Monday	Tuesdy	Wedsdy	Thusdy	Friday	Satday	Total
		1	2	98 / 0-09-0	4		99 / 1-15-0	2-04-0
6	100 / 1-05-0	16 / 1-01-0	99 / 1-16-0		10	11	95 / 0-18-0	5-00-0
13	88 / 0-18-0	96 / 1-05-0		16	17	18	102* / 2-00-0	4-03-0
20	99 / 0-17-0	97 / 0-05-0	102 / 1-04-0		24	25	26	2-06-0
Easter 27	100 / 1-11-0	99 / 2-01-0	102 / 2-17-0	42 / 1-15-0				

APRIL 1597

Fol	Su	Mo	Tu	We	Th	Fr	Sa
26						1	2
	4	5	6	7*	8	9	
26v	11	12	13	14	15	16	
	18*	19	20	21	22	23	
	25	26	27	28	29*	30	

APRIL 1597

	Sunday	Monday	Tuesdy	Wedsdy	Thusdy	Friday	Satday	Total
						88 / 0–05–0	95 / 0–04–0	8–13–0
3	102 / 1–08–0	99 / 1–02–0	98 / 0–07–0	103* / 2–01–0	100 / 0–05–0	9		5–03–0
10	42 / 1–00–0	99 / 0–14–0	104 / 1–05–0	96 / 0–17–0	103 / 1–08–0	100 / 0–05–0		5–09–0
17	67* / 2–00–0	42 / 0–09–0	103 / 0–19–0	16 / 0–17–0	67 / 1–02–0	102 / 0–16–0		6–03–0
24	103 / 1–13–0	67 / 1–02–0	99 / 1–02–0	42 / 1–00–0	105* / 2–14–0	98 / 0–14–0		8–05–0

MAY 1597

Su	Mo	Tu	We	Th	Fr	Sa
2	3	4	5	6	7	
9	10	11*	12		14	
16	17	18	19	20	21	
23	24	25	26	27	28	
30	31					

Fol 27

MAY 1597

	Sunday	Monday	Tuesdy	Wedsdy	Thusdy	Friday	Satday	Total
1	67 / 1–00–0	105 / 1–05–0	16 / 0–11–0	67 / 1–07–0	103 / 0–16–0	105 / 0–14–0		5–13–0
8	99 / 0–14–0	100 / 0–17–0	106* / 2–03–0	105 / 0–17–0	13	103 / 0–07–0		4–18–0
Whit- 15 sun	105 / 2–19–0	99 / 3–00–0	96 / 1–12–0	106 / 2–15–0	42 / 0–10–0	67 / 0–14–0		11–10–0
22	103 / 1–00–0	106 / 2–18–0	16 / 0–19–0	107* / 2–10–0	100 / 0–05–0	99 / 0–13–0		8–05–0
29	107 / 0–19–0	106 / 3–04–0						

JUNE 1597

Su	Mo	Tu	We	Th	Fr	Sa
		1	2	3*	4	
6	7	8	9	10	11	
13	14	15	16	17	18	
20	21	22	23	24	25	
27	28	29	30*			

JUNE 1597

	Sunday	Monday	Tuesdy	Wedsdy	Thusdy	Friday	Satday	Total
				67 / 0–13–0	105 / 0–16–0	108* / 2–02–0	106 / 3–06–0	11–00–0
5	98 / 0–10–0	106 / 3–10–0	107 / 0–12–0	108 / 1–00–0	103 / 0–11–0	106 / 2–18–0		9–01–0
12	105 / 1–00–0	107 / 0–14–0	42 / 0–13–0	67 / 0–07–0	106 / 2–10–0	108 / 0–11–0		5–15–0
19	16 / 0–14–0	106 / 3–00–0	109 / 0–06–0	67 / 0–08–0	107 / 0–14–0	42 / 0–07–0		5–09–0
26	96 / 0–14–0	103 / 1–00–0	99 / 1–02–0	110* / 2–08–0				

JULY 1597

Tol	Su	Mo	Tu	We	Th	Fr	Sa
27						1	2
		4	5	6	7	8	9
27v		12	13	14	15	16	
		18	19				
		27	28				

JULY 1597

Sunday	Monday	Tuesdy	Wedsdy	Thusdy	Friday	Satday	Total
					107 / 0-06-0	67 / 0-04-0	5-14-0
3	108 / 1-00-0	98 / 0-10-0	110 / 2-10-0	106 / 1-18-0	62 / 1-00-0	110 / 1-13-0	8-11-0
10	11	62 / 0-18-0	106 / 1-10-0	111 / 1-07-0	99 / 0-08-0	67 / 0-09-0	4-12-0
17	62 / 1-10-0	16 / 1-00-0	20	21	22	23	2-10-0
24	25	26	103 / 0-14-0	111 / 1-08-0	29	30	2-02-0
						Total	132-06-0

II.11   FALL-WINTER 1597 (ADMIRAL"S)

OCTOBER 1597

Su	Mo	Tu	We	Th	Fr	Sa
			11			
			19			

OCTOBER 1597

Sunday	Monday	Tuesdy	Wedsdy	Thusdy	Friday	Satday	Total
9	10	16 / 2-00-0	106 / 2-00-0	55	14	15	4-00-0
16	17	18	19	113 / 0-16-0	21	22	0-16-0
23	24	25	26	27	2 8	29	
30	114* / 2-00-0						

NOVEMBER 1597

Su	Mo	Tu	We	Th	Fr	Sa
		2	3	4	5	

NOVEMBER 1597

Sunday	Monday	Tuesdy	Wedsdy	Thusdy	Friday	Satday	Total
1	115 / 0-16-0	113 / 0-10-0	106 / 0-16-0	114 / 0-14-0			4-16-0
						Total	9-12-0

TABLE III

LITERARY AND PRODUCTION EXPENSES

KEY

Dates		**Authors**	
14/10	14 October	Ca	Chapman
		Ce	Chettle
Approvals		Da	Day
U	Unspecified authorization	De	Dekker
S	Specified authorization	Dr	Drayton
EA	Edward Alleyn	Hy	Hathway
RA	Richard Alleyn	Hn	Haughton
Be	Beeston	Hd	Heywood
Bi	Bird	Jo	Jonson
Bl	Blackwood	Mi	Middleton
Dn	Donston	Mu	Munday
Do	Downton	Po	Porter
Du	Duke	Ra	Rankin
Hd	Heywood	Sm	Smith
Je	Anthony Jeffes	We	Webster
Jo	Jones	Wi	Wilson
Ju	Juby		
Lo	Lowin	**Status**	
Ma	Massey	F	In Full
Pa	Pallant	I	In Earnest
Ro	Rowley	O	Old
Sh	Shaa	A	Alterations
Sl	Slater	P	Play produced
Sp	Spenser		
Th	Thare		
To	Towne		
Lt	Little Tailor		
DT	Dover the Tailor		
T	Tyreman		

101

III.2a FALL–WINTER (14 OCT. – 12 FEB.) 1596–97

Fol.	No.	Title	Dates	Approved	Authors	Status	Total
23		Hawodes Bocke	14/10	U	Hd	In?	1–10–0
		Totals (not in subsequent accounts)					1–10–0
		A Boocke	14/10	U		?	2–10–0
22v		Mr. Porter	16/12	U	Po	Fu?	5–00–0
						Total	7–10–0

III.3a SPRING–SUMMER (3 MAR. – 30 JULY) 1597

Fol.	No.	Title	Dates	Approved	Authors	Status	Total
22v		Mr. Porter	7/3	U	Po	?	4–00–0
						Total	4–00–0

PRODUCTION EXPENSES

III.1b SPRING-SUMMER 1596

Fol.	No.	Details	Dates	Approved	S-Total	U-Total	C-Total
71v		Lent Alleyn	2/5	EA		11-00-0	
		Lent Alleyn	10/5	EA		2-13-4	
		Lent Alleyn	13/5	EA		3-00-0	
		Lent Alleyn	15/5	EA		1-10-0	
		Lent Alleyn	16/5	EA		2-00-0	
		Lent Alleyn	25/5	EA		1-10-0	
		Lent Alleyn	n.d.	EA		7-10-0	
		Lent Alleyn	n.d.	EA		3-00-0	
				Totals		32-03-4	32-03-4

III.2b FALL-WINTER (14 OCT. – 12 FEB.) 1596 – 97

Fol.	No.	Details	Dates	Approved	S-Total	U-Total	C-Total
23		Feache Fleacher	?	Sl		0-06-0	
		Feache Brown	?	U		0-10-0	
		For Thomas Honte	?	EA		0-06-8	
				Totals		1-02-8	

NOT INCLUDED IN SUBSEQUENT ACCOUNTS

Fol.	No.	Details	Dates	Approved	S-Total	U-Total	C-Total
23		Loan	?	U		2-10-0	
		Loan	?	Sl		1-10-0	
		Loan	?	U		1-10-0	
		To Give Fleatcher	?	Sl,Dn,Ju		1-00-0	
22v	95	Vortigern	28-29/11	Sl,Dn	8-05-0		
		Things	3/12	U		3-10-0	
		Costumes	?	EA		4-00-0	
	96	Stukeley	8/12	U	3-00-0		
		Loan	11/12	Sl,Dn		2-00-0	
		Loan	14/12	Sl		1-00-0	
				Totals	11-05-0	17-00-0	28-05-0

III.3b SPRING-SUMMER (3 MAR. – 30 JULY) 1597

Fol.	No.	Details	Dates	Approved	S-Total	U-Total	C-Total
22v		The Carman	?	U		0-02-0	
	102	Guido	14/3	EA	4-09-0		
		Loan	25/3	EA		5-14-0	
				Totals	4-09-0	5-16-0	10-05-0

III.4a FALL-WINTER (21 OCT. - 8 MAR.) 1597-98

Fol.	No.	Title	Dates	Approved	Authors	Status	Total
43v	116	The Cobler	21/10	Sh,EA		Old?	2-00-0
	117	Book of Haughton	5/11	Sh,EA	Hn	In?	0-10-0
	119	Bengemen´s Plot	3/12	U	Jo	In?	1-00-0
	122	Mother Redcap	22/12-5/1	U	Dr,Mu	Full	6-00-0
44	124	Phaeton	15/1	U	De	F? (P)	4-00-0
	125	1 Robin Hood	15/2	U	Mu	F? (P)	5-00-0
44v	126	Woman Will Have	18/2	Sh	Hn	In	1-00-0
	127	2 Robin Hood	20/2-8/3	Sh,Do	Ce,Mu	F (P)	5-00-0
	128	The Miller	22/2	U	Lee	Old?	1-00-0
	129	Triplicity of Cuckolds	1/3	Sh,Do,Ju	De	Full?	5-00-0
						Total	30-10-0

III.5a SPRING-SUMMER (13 MAR. - 28 JULY) 1598

Fol.	No.	Title	Dates	Approved	Authors	Status	Total
45	130	Henry I	13-25/3	U	Ce,De,Dr	F (P)	6-05-0
	131	1 Earl Goodwin	25/3-30/3	U	Ce,De,Dr,Wi	F (P)	6-00-0
	132	Pierce of Exton	n.d.	U	Ce,De,Dr,Wi	I	2-00-0
45v	133	King Arthur	11-12/4	U	Hy	F	5-00-0
	134	1 Black Bateman	2-22/5	Do	Ce,De,Dr,Wi	F? (P)	7-00-0
45v	126	Woman Will Have	n.d.	Do	Hn	I	1-00-0
	135	2 Earl Goodwin	6/5-10/6	Do	Ce,De,Dr,Wi	F (P)	4-00-0
	71	1 Hercules	16/5	U		Old (P)	
	72	2 Hercules	16/5	U		Old	
	85	Pythagoras	16/5	U		Old	7-00-0
	91	Phocas	16/5	U		Old	
	99	Alexander & Lod.	16/5	U		Old (P)	
46	136	Love Prevented	30/5	Do	Po	F?	4-00-0
		Loan to Chapman	10/6	U			0-10-0
	137	Funeral of Richard	13-26/6	Bi	Ce,Dr,Mu,Wi	F?	5-15-0
46v	138	Ill of a Woman	16/5-15/6	Sh,Bi,Ju	Ca	I	4-00-0
		Loan to Chettle	24/6	U			0-10-0
47	139	2 Black Bateman	26/6-14/7	U	Ce,Wi,Po?	F	6-00-0
	140	Mad Man´s Morris	31/6-10/7	U	De,Dr,Wi	F (P)	6-00-0
47v	141	A Woman´s Tragedy	14/7	Sh	Ce	I?	5-00-0
	142	1 Hannibal & Hermes	17-28/7	U	De,Dr,Wi	F	6-10-0
	143	Valentine & Orsen	19/7	Sh,Ju	Hy,Mu	F	5-00-0
48	144	Pierce of Winchester	n.d.	U	De	I	0-10-0
						Total	83-00-0

PRODUCTION EXPENSES

III.4b FALL-WINTER (21 OCT. – 8 MAR.) 1597 –98

Fol.	No.	Details	Dates	Approved	S-Total	U-Total	C-Total
43v	118	Branholt	26/11	Sh	4–00–0		
		For Borne´s Gown	1/12	Sh		0–09–0	
	120	Alice Pierce	8–10/12	EA,Ju,Sh,Bi	2–02–7		
		For i j Gyges	12/12	U		0–06–8	
44	123	Dido	8/1	U	1–10–0		
		Licenses	n.d.	Dn		0–09–0	
	124	Phaeton	26–28/1	Do	5–00–0		
		Discharge Dekker	4/2	Dn	‾‾‾‾‾	2–00–0	
				Totals	12–12–7	3–04–8	15–17–3

III.5b SPRING-SUMMER (13 MAR. – 28 JULY) 1598

Fol.	No.	Details	Dates	Approved	S-Total	U-Total	C-Total
45	130	For Reading Henry I	n.d.	U		0–05–0	
		For the Carman	n.d.	U		0–03–0	
		Good Cheer	25/3	U		0–05–0	
	125	1 & 2 Robin Hood (Lic.)	28/3	U	0–14–0		
		Costume	7/4	U		1–00–0	
45v	131	1 Earl Goodwin	11/4	Do	1–04–0		
		Costumes	29/4	U		2–06–8	
		Costumes	9/5	U		7–00–0	
46	134	1 Black Bateman	13–14/6	Do	8–00–0		
46v	135	2 Earl Goodwin	26–27/6	Do	6–10–0		
47v		For a Picture	14/7	Bi		0–05–0	
	71	1 Hercules	16/7	Do	2–00–0		
		3 Licenses	24/7	U		1–01–0	
48	140	Mad Man´s Morris	25/7	Bi	4–13–4		
		A Woman´s Gown	28/7	U	‾‾‾‾‾	1–13–4	
				Totals	23–01–4	13–19–0	37–00–4

III.6a FALL-WINTER (30 JULY – 16 FEB.) 1598–99

Fol.	No.	Title	Dates	Approved	Authors	Status	Total
49	144	Pierce of Winchester	8/8–10/8	U	De,Dr,Wi	F (P)	5–00–0
	145	1 Brute	30/7–16/9	Si	Ce,Da	In (P)	3–14–0
	147	Hot Anger Soon Cold	18/8	U	Ce,Jo,Po	F	6–00–0
	148	Chance Medley	19–24/8	U	Ce?De?Dr,Mu,Wi	F	6–00–0
49v	149	Cataline	21–29/8	U	Ce,Wi	I	1–05–0
	150	Vayvode	29/8	Do	Ce	O? A? (P)	1–00–0
53	150	" bought from EA	21/1	U		O	2–00–0
50	151	2 Hannibal & Hermes	30/8–4/9	U	De,Dr	F	5–00–0
50v	152	1 Civil Wars	29/9	U	De,Dr	F? (P)	6–00–0
	153	Fount of New Fash.	1–12/10	U	Ca	F (P)	4–00–0
	154	Mulmutius Dun.	3/10	U	Ra	I?	3–00–0
51	155	2 Brute	12–22/10	U	Ce	F	6–00–0
	156	Conan	16–20/10	U	De,Dr	F?	6–00–0
51v	119	Play	23/10	Sh,Ju	Ca	I	?2–00–0
	157	Chapman's Tragedy	23/10–8/1	Sh,Ju	Ca	F	?7–00–0
	158	2 Civil Wars	3/11	U	De,Dr	F? (P)	6–00–0
52	159	3 Civil Wars	18/11–30/12	Sh	De,Dr	F?	6–00–0
	125	1 Robin Hood	18–25/11	Sh	Ce	O A	?0–15–0
	160	Tis No Deceit	25–28/11	Sh	Ce	I	?1–05–0
		Loan to Chapman	1/12	Sh			0–10–0
52v	161	War Without Blows	6/12–26/1	Sh	Hd	F	5–00–0
	162	2 Two Angry Women	22/12–12/2	Do	Po	F (P)	7–00–0
	163	William Longsword	20/1	Do	Dr	I	2–00–0
52v	164	Intro. Civil Wars	20/1	Ju	De	I	3–00–0
53	165	World Runs	22/1–13/2	Do	Ca	I	4–00–0
		Loan Porter	17/1	Bi,RA			1–00–0
53v	166	Joan as Good	10–12/2	Do	Hd	F	5–00–0
	167	Friar Fox	10/2	Do,Ro		F?	5–10–0
	168	Polyphemus	16/2	Ro	Ce	I	1–00–0
						Total	111–19–0

III.7a SPRING-SUMMER (26 FEB. – 9 JUNE) 1599

Fol.	No.	Title	Dates	Approved	Authors	Status	Total
53v	168	Polyphemus	27/2	Do	Ce	F (P)	2–10–0
	169	2 Two Merry Women	28/1	Sh,Do	Po	I	2–00–0
	170	The Spencers	4–22/3	Sh	Ce,Po	F (P)	6–00–0
54v		Loan Porter	7/4	Do			1–00–0
54v	172	Troilus & Cressida	7–16/4	Do	Ce,De	I	4–00–0
63	174	Agamemnon	26–30/5	Sh	Ce,De	F (P)	4–15–0
	165	World Runs	2/6	Sh	Ca	I	1–00–0
						Total	21–05–0

PRODUCTION EXPENSES

III.6b FALL-WINTER (30 JULY – 16 FEB.) 1598 – 99

Fol.	No.	Details	Dates	Approved	S-Total	U-Total	C-Total
49v	150	Vayvode	21–25/8	Sh,Do	17–05–0		
50		Agreement with Langley	19/9	U		35–00–0	
	144	Pierce of Winchester	23/9–12/10	Do	29–02–0		
50v		Costume	28/9	Ju		4–00–0	
		Costumes	1/10	U		1–00–0	
		Rich Clocke	4/10	U		19–00–0	
		Two Clockes	28/9	Do		12–10–0	
	152	1 Civil Wars	8–11/10	Do	10–00–0		
51v	153	Fount of New Fashion	8–14/11	Ju,Sh,Do	17–00–0		
		Bye a Sackebute	10/11	Do		2–00–0	
		Debt to Henslowe	4/11	U		2–00–0	
52	158	2 Civil Wars	19–24/11	Ju,Sh	20–00–0		
		Costumes	27/11	Sh		2–18–0	
		Costumes	28/11	U		4–00–0	
52v	145	1 Brute	12/12	Ro	1–04–0		
		Instruments	22/12	Jn		2–00–0	
		Discharge Chettle	17/1	Do		1–10–0	
53		Costumes	26/1	Do		2–15–0	
		Discharge Dekker	30/1	Do		3–10–0	
	162	2 Two Angry Women	31/1–12/2	Do	11–00–0		
		Costumes	1/2	Sh		4–10–0	
				Totals	105–11–0	96–13–0	202–04–0

III.7b SPRING-SUMMER (26 FEB. – 9 JUNE) 1599

Fol.	No.	Details	Dates	Approved	S-Total	U-Total	C-Total
54		Licenses	8–18/3	Do		1–08–0	
	171	Four Kings (Lic.)	n.d.	U	0–07–0		
	145	Greenshield (Lic.)	n.d.	U	0–07–0		
54v	99	Alexander & Lod.	31/3	Ju	5–00–0		
		To go to Corte	7/4	To,RA		0–10–0	
	170	The Spencers	9–16/4	Do	30–00–0		
		Costumes	11/4	U		0–10–0	
		Loan	17/4	Sh		1–10–0	
63		To the lace man	26/5	U		5–00–0	
	174	Agamemnon (Lic.)	3/6	U	0–07–0		
		The lace man	2–8/6/99	U		10–00–0	
				Totals	36–01–0	18–18–0	54–19–0

107

III.8a SUMMER (21 JUNE – 13 OCT.) 1599

Fol.	No.	Title	Dates	Approved	Authors	Status	Total
63	165	World Runs	21/6–2/7	Do,Bi,Ju	Ca	F	3–10–0
63v	176	Gentle Craft	15/7	Do,Ro	De	I?	3–00–0
	177	Pastoral Tragedy	17/7	Do	Ca	I	2–00–0
	179	Bear a Brain	1/8	Sh	De	F	2–00–0
		Loan to Dekker	1/8	Sh			1–00–0
	180	Page of Plymouth	10/8–2/9	Do,Bi,Ju	De,Jo	F (P)	8–00–0
	181	Poor Man´s Paradise	20–25/8	Do	Hn	I?	1–10–0
64	178	Stepmother´s Trag.	23–25/8	Do,Bi,Ju	Ce	I	2–00–0
	182	Robert II	3–27/9	Sh,Do,Ro,Bi	Ce,De,Jo	I	4–10–0
64v	183	Play by Marston	28/9	Bi	Ma	I	2–00–0
	184	Tristram	13/10	Do		I?	3–00–0
						Total	32–10–0

III.9a FALL-WINTER (14 OCT. – 16 FEB.) 1599 – 1600

Fol.	No.	Title	Dates	Approved	Authors	Status	Total
65	185	1 Oldcastle	16/10	Do	Dr,Hy,Mu,Wi	F?	?7–00–0
65	178	Stepmother´s Trag.	14/10	Sh	Ce	F	4–00–0
		Benefit Performance	n.d.	Ro			0–10–0
	186	2 Oldcastle	16/10–26/12	Do	Dr	F? (P)	?7–00–0
	187	Patient Grissel	n.d.–29/12	Sh,Ro	Ce,De,Hn	I? (P)	10–10–0
		Loan to Wilson	1/11	Sh			0–10–0
	188	Cox of Collumpton	1/14/11	Sh,Do	Da,Hn	F	5–00–0
	189	2 Henry Richmond	8/11	Sh	Wi	F	8–00–0
65v	87	Fortunatus	9–30/11	Sh,Do	De	F	6–00–0
		Advance to Chettle	10/11	Do			0–10–0
	190	Thomas Merry	21/11–6/12	Sh	Da,Hn	F (P)	5–00–0
	191	Orphan´s Tragedy	27/11	U	Ce	I	0–10–0
66	87	Fortunatus	1–12/12	Sh	De	A	3–00–0
66v	192	Arcadian Virgin	13–17/12	U	Ce,Hn	I	0–15–0
	193	Italian Tragedy	10/1	Sh	Da	I	2–00–0
	194	Owen Tudor	n.d.	Do	Dr,Hy,Mu,Wi	I	4–00–0
	195	Truth´s Supplication	18–30/1	To	De,Hn?	I	2–00–0
67v	196	Jugurtha	9/2	Bi	Boyle	I?	1–10–0
	197	Span. Moor´s Trag.	13/2	U	Da,De,Hn	I	3–00–0
	198	Damon & Pythias	16/2	U	Ce	I	1–00–0
						Total	71–15–0

PRODUCTION EXPENSES

III.8b SUMMER (21 JUNE – 13 OCT.) 1599

Fol.	No.	Details	Dates	Approved	S-Total	U-Total	C-Total
63v		Copper lace	5/7	Do		0–12–4	
		Musical instruments	13/7	Do		1–10–0	
64	180	Page of Plymouth	12/9	Ju,To	10–00–0		
64v	168	Polyphemus	4/10	U	0–08–0	_____	
				Totals	10–08–0	2–02–4	12–10–4

III.9b FALL-WINTER (14 OCT. – 16 FEB.) 1599 – 1600

Fol.	No.	Details	Dates	Approved	S-Total	U-Total	C-Total
66		Costumes	1/12	Do		10–00–0	
	87	Fortunatus	?	Do	10–00–0		
66v		Licenses	n.d.	–		0–14–0	
		To pay tailor	n.d.	Sh		1–05–0	
67		The lace man	9/1/00	Sh		5–00–0	
	190	Thomas Merry (Lic.)	n.d.	U	0–07–0		
	187	Patient Grissel	26/1	Sh	1–00–0		
		Lace man	28/1	Sh,Do		3–00–0	
67v		To by a drome	6/2	U		0–11–6	
		Instruments	7/2	Sh		1–02–0	
		Lace man	9/2	U		3–00–0	
		Coach man	9/2	U		3–00–0	
		Father Ogell	10/2	Do		0–10–0	
				Totals	11–07–0	28–02–6	39–09–6

109

III.10a SPRING–SUMMER (17 FEB. – 12 JULY) 1600

Fol.	No.	Title	Dates	Approved	Authors	Status	Total
67v	198	Damon & Pythias	10/3–6/5	Sh,Bi	Ce	F (P)	5–00–0
	199	Seven Wise Masters	1–8/3	Ro,Bi	Ce,Da,De,Hn	F (P)	6–00–0
68	200	Ferrex & Porrex	3/3–13/4	Sh	Hn	F (P)	4–15–0
68v	201	English Fugitives	16–24/4	U	Hn	I	1–10–0
	202	Cupid & Psyche	n.d.	Sh	Ce,Da,De	F (P)	6–00–0
69	203	Wooing of Death	27/4–14/5	U	Ce	I	1–00–0
		Loan to Chettle	6/5	RA			0–05–0
	205	Strange News	17/5	Sh	Hn,Pett	F (P)	6–00–0
	206	1 Blind Beggar B.G.	26/5	Sh	Ce,Da	F	5–10–0
69v	207	Judas	27/5	U	Hn	I (P)	0–10–0
	208	1 Fair Constance	3–14/6	Sh	De,Dr,Hy,Mu	F	5–09–0
		To Chettle & Day	19/6	Sh			0–10–0
	209	2 Fair Constance	20/6	Sh	De?Dr?Hy,Mu?	I	1–00–0
						Total	43–09–0

III.11a FALL–WINTER (6 SEPT. – 25 FEB.) 1600 – 1601

Fol.	No.	Title	Dates	Approved	Authors	Status	Total
70v	210	Fortune's Tennis	6/9	Sh	De	I?	1–00–0
70v	124	Phaeton	14–22/12	Ro	De	A (P)	2–00–0
	211	Robin Hood's Pen.	20/12–13/1	Ro,Bi	Hn	I?	4–00–0
71	212	Hannibal & Scipio	3–12/1	U	Hy,Ra	F	6–00–0
	213	Scogan & Skelton	23/1–25/2	Ro,To,EA	Hy,Ra	I	5–00–0
	214	2 Blind Beggar B.G.	29/1–10/2	Ro	Da,Hn	I	3–10–0
85v		Advance to Rankin	8/2	U			0–02–0
						Total	21–12–0

III.12a SPRING–SUMMER (8 MAR. – 13 JUNE) 1601

Fol.	No.	Title	Dates	Approved	Authors	Status	Total
86	213	Scogan & Skelton	8/3	U	Hy,Ra	F	0–18–0
	214	2 Blind Beggar B.G.	10/3–5/5	Ro	Da,Hn	F (P)	2–10–0
	215	Conquest of Spain	24/3–16/4	Ro	Hy,Ra	I	1–19–0
	216	All Is Not Gold	31/3–6/4	Ro	Ce	F	6–00–0
	217	Conquest W. Indies	4/4–21/5	Ro	Da,Hn,Sm	I	4–05–0
	218	King Sebastion	18/4–22/5	Ju,EA	Ce,De	F	6–00–0
	219	Six Yeomen	20/5–8/6	Ro	Da,Hn	F (P)	5–00–0
87	220	3 Blind Beggar B.G.	21/5	Ro	Da	I	0–10–0
87v	221	Life Cardinal W.	5/6	Ro	Ce	I	1–00–0
	222	Earl of Gloster	13/6	Do	Wadeson	I	1–00–0
						Total	29–02–0

PRODUCTION EXPENSES

III.10b SPRING–SUMMER (16 FEB. – 12 JULY) 1600

Fol.	No.	Details	Dates	Approved	S-Total	U-Total	C-Total
68		Discharge Haughton	10/3	Sh		0–10–0	
	186	2 Oldcastle	12/3	Sh	1–10–0		
		Stay printing Grissel	18/3	Sh		2–00–0	
	199	Seven Wise Masters	25/3–2/4	Sh	38–00–0		
68v		Costumes	2/4	Sh		2–00–0	
		Copper lace	n.d.	Sh		2–00–0	
		Silk man	13/4	Sh		2–00–0	
		To go to Winswarth	27/4	U		2–10–0	
69		For copper lace	6/5	Sh		0–08–0	
	200	Ferrex & Porrex (Lic.)	n.d.	U	0–07–0		
	198	Damon & Pythias (Lic.)	16/5	U	0–07–0		
69v	205	Strange News	25/5	Sh	3–00–0		
	202	Cupid & Psyche	5/6	Do	2–00–0		
		To pay E. Alleyn	n.d.	U	———	11–00–0	
				Totals	45–04–0	22–08–0	67–12–0

MOVE TO FORTUNE

III.11b FALL–WINTER (6 SEPT. – 25 FEB.) 1600 – 1601

Fol.	No.	Details	Dates	Approved	S-Total	U-Total	C-Total
70v		Costumes	14/8	Sh		3–00–0	
		Costumes	16/8	U		3–12–0	
		Lent to Shaa	29/8–12/9	Sh		7–08–0	
		To pay E. Alleyn	n.d.	U		1–12–0	
		Lent to company	11/11	U		4–00–0	
71		To pay tailor	20–23/12	U		1–19–0	
	124	Phaeton	2/1	Bi	1–00–0		
85v		To pay scrivener	6/3	U		1–07–6	
		For Bristoe´s wages	?	U		6–09–0	
				Totals	1–00–0	29–07–6	30–07–6

III.12b SPRING–SUMMER (8 MAR. – 13 JUNE) 1601

Fol.	No.	Details	Dates	Approved	S-Total	U-Total	C-Total
86v		Costumes	20/4/01	U		0–16–0	
	214	2 Blind Beggar B.G.	27/4/01	U (LT)	1–10–0		
	88	Blind Beggar Alex.	2–29/5	U (LT)	9–03–4		
		To get boy to hospital	n.d.	U		0–10–0	
87		Copper lace	8/5/01	U		0–05–0	
		Mercer	13/5/01	U		10–00–0	
	7	Jew of Malta	19–20/5	Ju,Sh	5–10–0		
87v		Mr. Heath (mercer)	5/6/01	U		14–15–0	
		Copper lace	6/6/01	U		6–00–0	
				Totals	16–03–4	32–06–7	48–09–11

111

III.13a FALL-WINTER (28 JUNE - 7 FEB.) 1601 - 1602

Fol.	No.	Title	Dates	Approved	Authors	Status	Total
92	217	Conquest W. Indies	5/8-1/9	Ro	Da,Hn	I (P)	2-10-0
	220	3 Blind Beggar B.G.	18-30/7	Ro	Da,Hn	F (P)	6-00-0
	221	1 Cardinal Wol.	28/6-18/8	Ro,EA	Ce	F (P)	5-00-0
91v	222	Earl of Gloster	n.d.	U	Wadeson	I?	0-10-0
	223	Friar Rush	4/7-29/11	Sh,Ro	Da,Hn	F	5-00-0
92	224	2 Tom Dough	30/7-11/9	Sh	Da,Hn	I	4-00-0
93	50	Mahomet	22/8	EA		O (P)	2-00-0
93v	62	Wiseman W. Chester	19/9	EA		O	2-00-0
	191	Orphan´s Trag.	24/9	Ro	Ce	I	0-10-0
94	16	Jeronimo	25/9	EA	Jo	A	2-00-0
	225	Rising Cardinal W.	24/8-12/11	Sh	Ce,Dr,Mu,Sm	F (P)	7-00-0
	226	1 Six Clothiers	12-22/10	Ro	Hy,Hn,Sm	I	5-00-0
94v	227	2 Six Clothiers	n.d.	Sh,Ro	Hy,Hn,Sm	I?	2-00-0
95	228	Too Good To Be True	14/11-7/1	Sh,To,EA	Ce,Hy,Sm	F	6-05-0
	95	Vortigern	20/11	EA		O	2-00-0
	207	Judas	20-24/12	Ro,Bi	Ro,Bi	F.	6-00-0
96	229	Spanish Fig	6/1	EA		I	3-00-0
96	230	Pontius Pilate	12/1	U	De	A	0-10-0
	49	Tasso´s Melancholy	16/1	U	De	A	1-00-0
	57	French Doctor	18/1	EA		O	2-00-0
	26	Guise	18/1	EA		O (P)	2-00-0
	76	Crack Me This Nut	18/1	EA		O (P)	2-00-0
104	223	Friar Rush	21/1	Sh	Ce	A	0-10-0
						Total	68-15-0

III.13b FALL-WINTER (28 JUNE – 7 FEB.) 1601 –02

Fol.	No.	Details	Dates	Approved	S-Total	U-Total	C-Total
91	219	Six Yeomen	1-6/7-01	Sh,Je	6-01-0		
		Copper lace	1-3/7/01	U		4-06-0	
91v		Copper lace	10-23/7/01	U		3-16-10	
92	50	Mahomet	2-4/8/01	U (DT)	3-12-4		
		Supper	3/8/01	U		1-00-0	
92v	221	Life of Cardinal W.	7-21/8/01	Ju,Sh	38-12-2		
		Copper lace	n.d.	U		0-05-6	
93		Dinner and jury	29/8/01	U		1-16-0	
	220	3 Blind Beggar B.G.	27/8-23/9/01	U (DT)	6-06-10		
93v	220	3 Blind Beggar (Lic.)	3/9	U	0-07-0		
	221	Wolsey (Lic.)	3/9	U	0-03-0		
		Tavern	21/9/01	U		3-12-9	
94	217	Conquest W. Indies	1/10-21/1/02	EA,Ju,Sh	14-07-9		
	26	Guise	3-26/11/01	Ju	7-14-6		
94v		Lent company	9/11/01	U		0-07-6	
95	76	Crack This Nut	4/12/01	U (LT)	0-05-0		
	71	Hercules	14-18/12/01	U (LT)	1-05-0		
95v		Properties	21-25/12/01	U (LT)		2-04-0	
		Lent to Shaa	26/12/01	Sh		0-17-3	
		Costume material	1-2/1/02	Sh		3-12-6	
	207	Judas	3/1/02	Je	1-10-0		
96		Costumes	n.d.	U		0-16-0	
104		To Spencer etc.	21/1/02	EA		1-08-0	
		Copper lace	25/1-7/2/02	EA		2-07-0	
				Totals	80-04-7	25-19-4	106-03-11

113

III.14a (23 FEB. – 12 MAR.) 1602 – 1603

Fol.	No.	Title	Dates	Approved	Authors	Status	Total
105		Lent to Chettle	25/3	Do,EA			3-00-0
	231	Malcolm King Scots	18/4	U	Massey	F? (P)	5-00-0
	232	Love Parts Friend	4/5	Do	Ce,Sm	F? (P)	6-00-0
	233	Bristol Tragedy	4-28/5	Ro,Ju,To	Da	F	5-00-0
105v	234	Jephtha	5/5	U	De,Mu	I (P)	5-00-0
	221	1 Cardinal Wol.	15/5	Do	Ce	A	1-00-0
	235	Tobias	16/5-27/6	Do	Ce	F	6-05-0
	236	Caesar's Fall	22-29/5	Do	De,Dr,Mi,Mu,We	F	8-00-0
106v	237	Richard Crookback	22/6	Bi,EA	Jo	I	?7-00-0
	16	Jeronimo	22/6	Bi,EA	Jo	A	?3-00-0
107	238	Danish Tragedy	7/7	Do	Ce	I	1-00-0
	239	Widow's Charm	9/7-11/9	Do,Bi,Ju	Mu?	I	1-10-0
	240	Medicine Curst Wife	19-31/7	Do,Ju	De	I	4-00-0
	241	Samson	29/7	Ro,Ju		F?	6-00-0
	242	Philip of Spain	8/8	EA		O	2-00-0
	75	Longshanks	8/8	EA		O	2-00-0
107v	243	William Cartwright	8/9	Bi,Ju,To	Hn	I?	2-10-0
	244	Felmelanco	9-27/9	Do,Je	Ce	F	6-00-0
108	247	Joshua	27/9	Ro	Ro	F	7-00-0
	21	2 Tamar Cham	2/10	EA		O	2-00-0
	248	Randal	21/10-9/11	Ju	Mi	F	6-00-0
	49	Tasso's Melancholy	3/11-4/12	Bi,EA	De	A	3-00-0
	249	Merry As May Be	5-17/11	Do,Ju	Da,Hy,Sm	F	8-00-0
108v	55	Dr. Faustus	22/11	Ro,Bi	Bi,Ro	A	4-00-0
	250	Set at Tennis	2/12	Ju	Mu	F	3-00-0
	1	Friar Bacon	14/12	Do	Mi	A	0-05-0
109		Prologue & Epilogue	29/12	Do	Ce	A	0-05-0
	251	London Florentine	17/12-7/1	Do	Ce,Hd	F	6-10-0
	253	Hoffman	29/12	Do	Ce	I	0-05-0
	254	Singer's Voluntary	13/1	U	Singer	F?	5-00-0
	255	Four Sons of Aymon	10/12	Sh		O?	2-00-0
	256	Boss of Billings.	1-12/3	Ju	Da,Hy	F	6-00-0
109v	257	Siege of Dunkirk	7/3	Ju	Massey	I	2-00-0
		For Play in Pawn	7/3	U	Ce	I?	1-00-0
	259	2 London Florentine	12/3	Do	Ce	I	1-00-0

Total   131-10-0

PRODUCTION EXPENSES

III.14b SPRING-SUMMER-FALL-WINTER (23 FEB. - 12 MAR.) 1602 - 03

Fol.	No.	Details	Dates	Approved	S-Total	U-Total	C-Total
105		Paid to Alleyn	23/2	EA		1-07-6	
		Costumes	21/4	EA		2-00-0	
	231	Malcolm	27/4	Do	1-10-0		
105v		Costumes	16/5	U		4-10-0	
		Wine at tavern	n.d.	U		0-02-0	
	225	2 Cardinal Wol.	18/5-2/6	Do	11-06-0		
106		Copper lace	31/5	Do		1-00-0	
	232	Love Parts Friendship	31/5	Do	2-10-0		
106v	234	Jephtha	8/5-5/7	Do	13-17-0		
107		Costumes	16/7	EA		1-10-0	
107v	245	Mortimer	10/9	Ju	6-18-0		
	246	Earl Hertford	n.d.	U	1-12-0		
108v		Mercer	18/12	U		8-18-0	
				Totals	37-13-0	19-07-6	57-00-6

WORCESTER´S MEN

III.15a <u>FALL-WINTER (17 AUG. - 12 MAR.) 1602 - 1603</u>

Fol.	No.	Title	Dates	Approved	Authors	Status	Total
115	185	Oldcastle	17/8-7/9	Th	De	A (P)	2-10-0
	263	A Tragedy	24/8-9/9	Du	Ce	I	?2-00-0
	240	Medicine for Wife	27/8-2/9	U	De	F	6-00-0
116		Bonus to Dekker	27/9	U			0-10-0
115v	264	Albere Galles	4/9	U	Hd,Sm	F	6-00-0
116	265	Marshall Osric	20-30/9	Hd	Hd,Sm	F (P)	6-00-0
	266	Cutting Dick	20/9	Hd	Hd	A	1-00-0
116v	268	Two Brothers	1-15/10	Du	Sm	F (P)	6-00-0
	269	A Play	3/10	Du	Mi	I	1-00-0
	270	1 Lady Jane	15-21/10	Th,Hd	Ce,De,Hd,Sm,We	F (P)	8-00-0
117v	271	2 Lady Jane	27/10	Du	De	I	0-05-0
	272	Christmas Comes	2-26/11	Du,Hd	Ce,De,Hd,We	F (P)	7-00-0
118	273	1 Black Dog	24/11-20/12	Du,Be,Pa	Da,Hy,Sm	F (P)	6-00-0
		To Smith	12/11	Lo			0-10-0
		To Chettle	12/11	Lo			0-03-0
	274	Blind Eats	24/11-7/1	Hd	Hd	F	6-00-0
	275	Unfortunate Gen.	7-19/1	Du,Be	Da,Hy,Sm	F (P)	7-00-0
119	276	A Play	14/1	Hd	Ce,Hd	I	2-00-0
119v	277	2 Black Dog	29/1-3/2	Du,Lo	Da,Hy,Sm	F (P)	7-00-0
120	278	Woman Killed	12/2-6/3	Hd	Hd	F (P)	6-00-0
	277	2 Black Dog	21-26/2	Du,Bl	Da,Hy,Sm	A	2-00-0
	279	Italian Tragedy	7-12/3	Lo,Bl	Sm	F	<u>6-00-0</u>

		Total	88-18-0

III.15b WORCESTER'S FALL-WINTER 1602 - 1603

Fol.	No.	Details	Dates	Approved	S-Total	U-Total	C-Total
115	185	Oldcastle etc.	21/8	Du,Th	15-00-0		
		Costumes & Props.	18/-27/8	Du,Bl		15-19-0	
		Tavern	21/8/02	U		0-09-0	
115v		Costumes & Props.	28/8-4/9	Du		11-07-4	
116		Costumes	10/9	Th		2-16-4	
116v		Wages	11/10	U		0-10-0	
		To pay Shaa	19/9	Bl		0-16-0	
		Targets	21-30/9	Th		2-00-0	
	267	Biron	25/9-3/10	Du	5-13-0		
116v		Properties	n.d.	U		0-01-2	
	268	Two Brothers	15-23/10	Th, (Ty)	3-09-0		
117		Costumes	22/10	U		20-00-0	
117v		Costumes	26/10	Be		1-00-0	
		Costumes	2-12/11	U		1-16-8	
	265	Marshal Osric	3/11	U	1-06-0		
	270	1 Lady Jane	6/11	Du	5-00-0		
118		Costumes from Shaa	6/12	U		17-00-0	
118	272	Christmas Comes	9/11-9/12	U	5-08-8		
118v		Costumes	18/12-1/1	Th,Du		2-09-0	
119	273	1 Black Dog	10-16/1	Du,Fr	1-02-0		
		Costumes	10-16/1	U		3-06-4	
119v	275	Unfortunate Gen.	24/1	Lo,Ca	2-10-0		
		Costumes	24/1-7/2	U		3-02-0	
120	277	2 Black Dog	15/2/	U	5-02-0		
	278	Woman Killed	5/2-7/3	Bl,Hd	7-03-0		
		Costumes	16/2-4/3	U		2-00-0	
120v		Clothes etc.	16/3	U		8-10-0	
				Totals	51-13-8	93-02-10	144-16-6

TABLE IV

CONSOLIDATED WEEKLY ACCOUNTS

IV.1 SPRING-SUMMER 1592 (STRANGE'S)

Fol.	Date	Details	Per.	Gallery	Fol.	Literary	Product.	Fol.	Total.	Fol.	Repay	Balance
7	Feb. 19		1	0-17-3								
	26		6	7-13-6								
	Mar. 4	Henry VI	6	8-13-8								
	11		6	11-04-6								
	18		5	9-19-0								
	25		5	4-17-0								
	Apr. 1	Easter Week	6	15-14-0								
	8		6	8-17-0								
7v	15	Titus & Vespasian	6	10-00-0								
	22		6	10-08-0								
	29	2 Tamar Cam	6	10-14-0								
	May 6		6	13-00-6								
	13		6	8-13-0								
	20	Whitsun Week	6	13-16-6								
	27	Tanner of Denmark	6	12-03-6								
8	June 3		6	8-05-6								
	10	Knack (Knave)	6	12-03-0								
	17		5	8-02-0								
	24		5	6-09-0								
		Totals	105	181-10-05								

IV.2 FALL-WINTER 1592-93 (STRANGE"S)

Fol.	Date	Details	Per.	Gallery	Fol.	Literary	Product.	Fol.	Total	Fol.	Repay	Balance
8	Dec. 30		2	6-18-0								
	Jan. 6	Jealous Comedy	6	11-03-0								
	13		6	7-03-0								
	20		6	10-12-0								
	27	Guise	6	9-10-0								
8v	Feb. 3		3	3-13-0								
		Totals	29	48-19-0								

IV.3 FALL-WINTER 1593-94 (SUSSEX'S)

Fol.	Date	Details	Per	Gallery	Fol.	Literary Product.	Fol.	Total	Fol.	Repay	Balance
8v	Dec. 29	Christmas Week	4	12-12-0							
	Jan. 1/5		6	8-01-0							
			6	8-12-0							

FALL-WINTER 1593 (SUSSEX'S)

Fol.	Date	Details	Per.	Income	Fol.	Literary Product.	Fol.	Total	Fol.	Repay	Balance
8v	Jan. 19		5	5-19-0							
	26	Titus Andronicus	4	7-05-0							
	Feb. 2		3	3-10-0							
	9		2	4-10-0							
		Totals	30	50-09-0							

IV.4 SPRING 1594 (SUSSEX & QUEEN'S)

Fol.	Date	Details	Per.	Income	Fol.	Literary Product.	Fol.	Total	Fol.	Repay	Balance
9	Apr. 6	Easter Week	6	12-04-0							
	13		2	3-12-0							
		Totals	8	15-16-0							
						(ADMIRAL'S)					
	May 18		2	6-03-0							
		Totals	3	6-03-0							
						(ADMIRAL'S & CHAMBERLAIN'S)					
	June 8		4	2-01-0							
	15		6	2-10-0							
		Totals	10	4-11-0							

IV.5 FALL-WINTER 1594-95 (ADMIRAL'S)

Fol.	Date		Details	Per.	Income	Fol.	Literary	Product.	Fol.	Total	Fol.	Repay	Balance
9	June	22		5	10-05-0								
		29	Galeaso	6	12-03-0								
9v	July	6		6	9-10-6								
		13	Phillipo & Hip.	6	11-09-0								
		20	Godfrey	6	10-12-0								
		27		6	10-09-0								
9v	Aug.	3	Merchant of E.	6	9-11-0								
		10		6	7-07-6								
		17	Tasso	6	11-10-0								
10		24		6	7-07-6								
		31	Venetian	6	11-17-6								
	Sept.	7		6	7-16-6								
		14		6	9-09-6								
	21	21	Palamon	6	8-14-6								
		28	Grecian Comedy	6	7-03-6								
	Oct.	5		6	8-13-0								
		12		5	5-19-0								
		19		6	8-05-0								
10v		26	Knack (Honest)	6	7-03-0								
	Nov.	2		6	9-14-0								
		9	Caesar & Pompey	6	10-10-0								
		16	Diocletian	6	8-02-0								
		23		5	5-18-0								
		30		6	7-08-0								
	Dec.	7	Wise Man	5	4-08-0								
		14	Set at Maw	6	5-01-0								
11		21		3	4-15-0								
		28		3	8-01-0								
	Jan.	4		3	10-02-0								
		11		4	4-12-0								
		18		6	9-06-0								
		25		5	8-13-0								
	Feb.	1		6	8-14-0								
		8		6	9-18-0								
		15	French Comedy	6	12-00-0								
		22	The Mack	6	12-00-0								
11v	Mar.	1		6	10-15-0								
		8	Seleo	4	8-06-0								
		15		5	5-18-0								
			Totals	218	339-07-0								
			Tots. Adm. & Ch.	228	343-18-0								

120

IV.6   SPRING-SUMMER 1595 (ADMIRAL'S)

Fol.	Date	Details	Per.	Income	Fol.	Literary	Product.	Fol.	Total	Fol.	Repay	Balance
11v	Apr. 26	Easter Week	6	15-06-0								
	May 3		6	9-09-0								
	10	1 Hercules	6	11-01-0								
	17		6	8-08-0								
12v	24	2 Hercules	6	11-11-0								
	31		6	10-06-0								
	Jun. 7	Seven Days	5	8-08-0								
	14	Whitsun Week	6	18-00-0								
	21	2 Caesar	6	7-16-0								
	28		4	6-17-0								
		Totals	57	107-02-0								

IV.7   FALL-WINTER 1595-96 (ADMIRAL'S)

Fol.	Date	Details	Per.	Income	Fol.	Literary	Product.	Fol.	Total	Fol.	Repay	Balance
12v	Aug. 30	Longshanks	6	9-04-0								
	Sept. 6	Crack Me Nut	6	13-08-0								
	13		6	12-10-0								
13	20	New World's Trag.	6	7-16-0								
	27		6	9-11-0								
	Oct. 4	Disguises	6	9-02-0								
	11		6	7-14-0								
	18	Wonder of a Wom.	6	8-02-0								
	25		6	7-07-0								
	Nov. 1	Barnardo	6	8-02-0								
	8		6	7-05-0								
14	15	Toy	6	8-07-0								
	22		5	3-15-6								
	29	Henry V	6	7-05-0								
	Dec. 6		5	4-03-0								
	13		3	5-04-6								
	20		3	3-06-0								
	27		3	7-00-0								
	Jan. 3	Chinon	6	10-11-0								
	10		6	9-18-0								

Fol.	Date	Details	Per.	Income	Fol.	Literary	Product.	Fol.	Total	Fol.	Repay	Balance
14	Jan. 17	Pythagoras	6	9-14-0								
14v	24	2 Seven Days	6	9-18-0								
	31		6	6-05-0								
	Feb. 7		6	9-00-0								
	14	Blind Beggar A.	5	8-05-0								
	21		6	10-06-0								
	28		6	11-16-0								
	Totals		150	224-15-0								

IV.8 SPRING-SUMMER 1596 (ADMIRAL'S)

Fol.	Date	Details	Per.	Income	Fol.	Literary	Product.	Fol.	Total	Fol.	Repay	Balance
15v	Apr. 17	Easter Week	6	8-08-0								
	24		6	4-19-0								
	May 1	Julian Apostate	6	8-08-0								
	8	1 Tamar Cham	6	8-00-0	71v							
	15		5	7-13-0			11-00-0					
	22	Phocas	5	9-07-0			7-03-4			71v	9-12-0	
	29		6	6-12-0			2-00-0				8-07-0	
21v	June 5	Whitsun Week	6	11-03-0			1-10-0	71v	21-13-4		4-07-0	
	12	2 Tamar Cham	6	8-11-0			7-10-0*					
	19		4	5-00-0						71v	3-04-0	
	26	Troy	6	10-15-0								
	July 3	Paradox	6	7-12-0			3-00-0*				6-04-0	
	10		5	5-07-0							4-13-0	
	17		5	5-07-0							3-02-0	
	24	Tinker of Totnes	6	8-04-0								
	Totals		85	115-06-0			32-03-4	71v	32-03-4	71v	39-09-0	(7-05-8)

* exact date unknown

IV.9   FALL-WINTER 1596-97 (ADMIRAL'S)

Fol.	Date	Details	Per.	Income	Fol.	Literary	Product	Fol.	Total	Fol.	Repay	Balance
	Oct. 16		3	4-14-0								
	23		6	6-11-0	23	1-10-0	0-16-0					0-00-0
25	30	Begin 27 Oct.	6	5-05-0			0-06-8	23	2-12-8	23	⎰2-12-8	
	Nov. 6		1	0-12-0		2-10-0	6-10-0				1-00-0	
	13		3	1-19-0							1-00-0	
	20		2	3-10-0								
25v	27		3	4-14-0								
	Dec. 4	Valteger	4	5-14-0			5-00-0					
	11	Stewtley	5	3-06-0			10-15-0					
	18		6	12-15-0								
	25	Nebuchadnezzar	6	8-17-0		5-00-0	5-00-0					
	Jan. 1	That Will Be	6	8-07-0			1-00-0					
	8		6	4-07-0							9-00-0	
	15	Alexander & Lod.	6	7-06-0*							5-00-0	
	22		6	8-13-0								
26	29	Woman Hard T.P.	6	8-17-0							4-00-0	
	Feb. 5											
	12											
		Totals	75	95-07-0		7-10-0	28-05-0	22v	35-15-0	23	20-00-0	15-15-0

* 5-column accounts begin

IV.10   SPRING-SUMMER 1592

Fol.	Date	Details	Per.	Income	Fol.	Literary	Product.	Fol.	Total	Fol.	Repay	Balance
	Feb. 19		2	2-04-0			0-02-0					
	26		4	5-00-0								
26	Mar. 5	Begin March 3	3	4-03-0								
	12		3	2-06-0	22v	4-00-0						
	19	Guido	6	8-13-0			4-09-0		8-11-0			
	26		5	5-03-0			5-14-0					
	Apr. 2	Easter Week	5	5-09-0								
	9	Five Plays	6	6-03-0								
26v	Apr. 16	**French Comedy**	6	8-05-0								
	23		6	5-13-0								
	30	**Uther Pendragon**	5	4-18-0								
	May 7		6	11-10-0								
	14	Comedy of Humours	6	8-05-0								
	21	Whitsun Week	6	11-00-0								
	28	Henry I	6	9-01-0								
27	June 4	Frederick & Bas.	6	5-15-0								
	11		6	5-09-0								
	18		6	5-14-0								
	25		6	8-11-0								
	July 2	Martin Swart	5	4-12-0								
27v	9		2	2-10-0								
	16		2	2-02-0								
	23											
	30											
		Totals	109	132-06-0	22v	4-00-0	10.05-0		14-05-0			

IV.11 FALL-WINTER 1597-98

Fol.	Date	Details	Per.	Income	Fol.	Literary	Product.	Fol.	Total	Fol.	Repay	Balance
27v	Oct. 15	Begin Oct. 11	3	4-00-1								
	22		?									
	29		1	0-16-0								
	Nov. 5	Friar Spendleton	5	4-16-0.								

Five-column accounts end

Fol.	Date	Details	Per.	Income	Fol.	Literary	Product.	Fol.	Total	Fol.	Repay	Balance
36v	Oct. 22			5-01-11*	43v	2-00-0						
	29			3-11-10								
	Nov. 5	Friar Spendleton		5-18-10		0-10-0						
	12			2-07-0								
	19			2-08-8								

* Weekly quarter gallery income

Fol.	Date	Details	Per.	Income	Fol.	Literary	Product.	Fol.	Total	Fol.	Repay	Balance
36v	Nov. 26	[Branholt]		2-04-0	43v		4-00-0					
	Dec. 3			2-04-0			0-09-0					
	10	[Alice Pierce]		1-06-0		1-00-0	2-02-7					
	17			2-09-0			0-06-8					
	24			--								
	31	Christmas Week		7-16-0		3-00-0						
	Jan. 7			1-10-0		0-05-0						
	14			2-10-0		2-15-0	1-10-0					
	21	[?]		3-09-0	44	4-00-0	0-09-0					
	28			1-08-9			5-00-0					
	Feb. 4	[Phaeton]		5-00-0			2-00-0					
	11			2-16-4								
	18			3-09-0								
	25	[Mother Redcap]		4-15-0	44v	6-00-0						
	Mar. 4	[Triangle of Cuckolds]		5-11-3		2-10-0						
	11					5-05-0						
						3-05-0						
		Totals		65-16-0	44v	30-10-0	15-17-3	44v	46-07-3			46-07-3

SPRING–SUMMER 1598

Fol.	Date	Details	Income	Fol.	Literary	Product.	Fol.	Total	Fol.	Repay	Balance
36v	Mar. 18			45							
35	25				2-00-0	0-13-0					
	Apr. –		1-06-0		8-05-0	0-14-0					
	8	[1 Robin Hood]	3-07-6		2-00-0	1-00-0					
	15		2-17-0	45v	2-00-0	1-04-0					
	22	Easter	6-03-6		5-00-0						
	29		2-12-6								
	May 5	[1 Earl Goodwin]	4-02-6		1-00-0	2-06-8					
	13	[2 Robin Hood]	5-02-0		2-00-0						
	20		4-06-0	46		7-00-0					
	27		3-04-6		9-00-0						
	June 3		2-12-6		7-00-0						
	10	Whitsun Week	5-16-7		4-00-0						
					3-10-0						
35	June 17	[1 Black Bateman]	3-16-0	46v	2-10-0	8-00-0					
	24	[2 Earl Goodwin]	5-07-0	47	3-15-0						
	July –		5-18-3		5-00-0	6-10-0					
	8		2-11-7		3-00-0						
	15		--	47v	10-00-0	0-05-0					
	22		--		9-00-0	2-00-0					

Henslowe begins to collect the "wholle gallereys" and to credit half to the players

Fol.	Date	Details	Income	Fol.	Literary	Product.	Fol.	Total	Fol.	Repay	Balance
35	June 29	[1 Hercules]	10-14-0*	48	3-10-0	7-17-8	48			10-14-0	
		Totals	59-03-5	48	83-00-0	37-00-4	48	120-00-4	48	10-14-0	109-06-4
		Grand totals						166-07-7			155-13-7

* Estimated other half gallery revenue

IV.13   FALL-WINTER 1598-99

Fol.	Date	Details	Income	Fol.	Literary	Product.	Fol.	Total	Fol.	Repay	Balance
48	Aug. 5		7-10-0*		2-00-0				48	7-10-0	
	12	[Mad Man's Morris]	9-09-0	49	5-00-0					9-09-0	
	19		8-12-0		10-05-0					8-12-0	
	26		8-02-0		2-10-0	17-05-0				8-02-0	
	Sept. 2	[Vayvode]	8-14-0	49v	4-00-0					8-14-0	
	9		9-03-0	50	3-19-0					9-03-0	
	16		6-18-0		0-05-0					6-18-0	
	23		8-02-0			45-00-0				8-02-0	
	30		5-14-0	50v	6-00-0	18-00-0				5-14-0	
	Oct. 7		6-03-0		6-00-0	32-10-0				6-03-0	
	14	[Pierce of Winchester]	7-15-0	51	1-10-0	15-02-0				7-15-0	
	21		10-14-0		9-00-0					10-14-0	
	28	[1 Civil Wars]	5-19-0	51v	5-10-0					5-19-0	
48v	Nov. 4		8-02-0		6-00-0				48v	8-02-0	
	11		5-03-0			7-00-0				5-03-0	
	18	[Fount of New Fashion]	6-16-0	52	1-10-0	14-00-0				6-16-0	
48v	Nov. 25		4-16-0	52	0-10-0	20-00-0			48v	4-16-0	
	Dec. 2	[2 Civil Wars]	6-16-0		1-10-0	6-18-0				6-16-0	
	9		7-16-0	52v	3-00-0					7-16-0	
	16		4-03-0			1-04-0				4-03-0	
	23		4-05-0			2-00-0				4-05-0	
	30	At Court 27 [1 Brute]	12-10-0		5-00-0					12-10-0	
	Jan. 6	At Court 6	7-17-0		5-00-0					7-17-0	
	13		8-11-0		3-00-0					8-11-0	
	20		8-13-0		3-00-0	1-10-0				8-13-0	
	27		7-06-0	53	6-00-0	2-15-0				7-06-0	
	Feb. 3		10-17-0		7-00-0	17-00-0				10-17-0	
	10	[2 Two Angry Women]	7-10-0	53v	8-10-0					10-17-0	
	17		7-10-0		6-00-0	2-00-0				7-10-0	
	24	At Court 18	15-03-0							15-03-0	
		Totals	236-09-0*	53v	111-19-0	202-04-0	53v	314-03-0	48v	236-09-0	77-14-0

* Income estimated equivalent to half-gallery repayments

127

IV.14 SPRING-SUMMER 1592

Fol.	Date	Details	Income	Fol.	Literary	Product.	Fol.	Total	Fol.	Repay	Balance
	Mar. 3		--		4-10-0						
	10		--	54	0-10-0						
	17		--			0-14-0					
48v	24		3-18-0*		5-10-0	1-01-0			48v	3-18-0	
	31		2-02-0	54v		5-07-0				2-02-0	
	Apr. 7		3-08-0		4-00-0	0-10-0				3-08-0	
	14	Easter Week	13-07-0			25-10-0				13-07-0	
	21	[The Spencers]	13-16-0		1-00-0	6-10-0				13-16-0	
	28	Gap in Records?	11-05-0							11-05-0	
	May 5	[Four Kings?]	8-10-0			--				8-10-0	
	12	[Brute]	9-00-0			--				9-00-0	
	19		11-11-0			--				11-11-0	
48v	May 26	Whitsun Week	10-08-0		1-10-0	5-00-0	63			10-08-0	
	June 2	[Agamemnon]	16-12-0		4-05-0	5-00-0				16-12-0	
	9		--			5-07-0					
		Totals	103-17-0*		21-05-0	54-19-0	63	76-04-0		103-17-0	(27-13-0)
		Grand totals						556-14-7	48v	351-00-0	205-14-7

* Estimated income equivalent to half gallery repayments

On folio 63 of his diary Henslowe estimates that he has advanced the actors a total of L586-12-7 or L29-18-0 more than is recorded in the surviving records. It may be that this figure includes money lent between April 23 and May 19 for which the accounts have been lost, or that it adds the L30-00-0 debt of the Admiral's Men from 25 March, 1597 (f. 22v).

IV.15 SUMMER 1599

Fol.	Date	Details	Income	Fol.	Literary	Product.	Fol.	Total	Fol.	Repay	Balance
	June 23			63	2-00-0						
	30										
	July 7			63v	1-10-0	0-12-4					
	14					1-10-0					
	21				5-00-0						
	28										
	Aug. 4				3-00-0						
	11				2-00-0						
	18										
	25			64	3-10-0						
	Sept. 1										
	8				8-00-0						
	15	[Page of Plymouth]			1-00-0	10-00-0					
	22				0-10-0						
	29			64v	3-00-0						
48v	Oct. 6	[Polyphemus]	5-03-0*	64v	3-00-0	0-08-0	64v	41-12-4	48v	5-03-0	
	13		2-00-0							2-00-0	
		Totals	7-03-0*		32-10-0	12-10-4		45-00-4		7-03-0	37-17-4
		Grand totals						601-14-11		358-03-0	243-11-11

When Henslowe balances his account with the players on 13 October 1599 (f. 64v)
his estimates of both the players' debt and his own advances seem to be just about
£30-00-0 too high.

IV.16　　FALL-WINTER 1599-1600

Fol.	Date	Details	Income	Fol.	Literary	Product.	Fol.	Total	Fol.	Repay	Balance
48v	Oct. 6	[Polyphemus]	5-03-0						48v	5-03-0	
	13		2-00-0	64v	3-00-0	0-08-0				2-00-0	
		Sub totals	7-03-0		3-00-0	0-08-0		3-08-0		7-03-0	(3-15-0)
		Balance forward						601-14-11		358-03-0	243-11-11
		Henslowe reckons the company's indebtedness as 274-00-0 (fol. 64v)									
62v	Oct. 20		4-03-0*	65	14-00-0		62v			4-03-0	
	27		3-14-0		1-00-0					3-14-0	
	Nov. 3		8-16-0		1-10-0					8-16-0	
	10		6-09-0	65v	12-00-0					6-09-0	
	17		2-17-0		3-00-0					2-17-0	
	24		7-04-0		3-10-0					7-04-0	
	Dec. 1		5-13-0	66	3-10-0	10-00-0				5-13-0	
	8		4-00-0		3-10-0					4-00-0	
	15	[Fortunatus]	2-17-0	66v	2-10-0	10-00-0				2-17-0	
	22		3-03-0		3-05-0					3-03-0	
	29	Christmas Week	10-08-0	67	10-10-0	1-19-0				10-08-0	
	Jan. 5		9-09-0							9-09-0	
	12	[Thomas Merry]	6-16-0		2-00-0	5-00-0				6-16-0	
	19		3-02-0		5-00-0	0-07-0				3-02-0	
	26		1-16-0			1-00-0				1-16-0	
	Feb. 2	[Patient Grissel]	7-14-0	67v	1-00-0	3-00-0				7-14-0	
	9		7-13-0		1-10-0	7-13-6				7-13-0	
	16				4-00-0	0-10-0					
		Totals	95-14-0*	67v	71-15-0	39-09-6		111-04-6	62v	95-14-0	15-10-6

IV.17   SPRING-SUMMER 1600

Fol.	Date	Details	Income	Fol.	Literary	Product.	Fol.	Total	Fol.	Repay	Balance
62v	Mar. 1		3-13-0*	67v	2-00-0				62v	3-13-0	
	8		6-00-0	68	4-00-0					6-00-0	
	15	[2 Oldcastle]	4-17-0		1-06-0	2-00-0				4-17-0	
	22		11-14-0		1-00-0	2-00-0				11-14-0	
	29	Easter Week	6-02-0		0-05-0	30-00-0				6-02-0	
	Apr. 5	[Seven Wise Masters]	5-10-0	68v	0-07-0	10-00-0				5-10-0	
	12		6-14-0		3-03-0	2-00-0				6-14-0	
	19		4-10-0		0-10-0	2-00-0				4-10-0	
	26		4-07-0		2-10-0					4-07-0	
	May 3	[Ferex & Porex]	4-15-0		3-14-0	2-10-0				4-15-0	
	10		12-04-0	69	4-05-0	0-15-0				12-04-0	
	17	Whitsun Week	4-07-0		7-10-0	0-07-0				4-07-0	
	24	[Damon & Pythias]	6-11-0							6-11-0	
	31		3-13-0							3-13-0	
	June 7	[Strange News]	7-02-0	69v	6-00-0	3-00-0				7-02-0	
	14		5-08-0		3-05-0	2-00-0				5-08-0	
	21	[Cupid & Psyche]	4-12-0		2-04-0					4-12-0	
	28		4-12-0		1-10-0					4-12-0	
	July 5					11-00-0(nd)					
	12										
		Totals	111-08-0	69v	43-09-0	67-12-0		111-01-0	62v	111-08-0	(0-07-0)

* Income estimated equivalent to half-gallery repayments

MOVE TO FORTUNE THEATRE

131

IV.18   FALL-WINTER 1600-1601

Fol.	Date	Details	Income Fol.	Literary	Product.	Fol.	Total	Fol.	Repay	Balance
	Aug. 16		70v		6-12-0					
	23									
	30									
	Sept. 6				4-00-0					
	13			1-00-0	0-08-0					
	20				3-00-0					
	27									
	Oct. 4									
	11									
	18									
	25									
	Nov. 1									
	8									
	15				4-00-0					
	22									
	29									
	Dec. 6									
	13			1-10-0	1-12-0					
	20		71	2-00-0	1-00-0					
	27			2-00-0	0-19-0					
	Jan. 3			0-10-0	1-00-0					
	10	[Phaeton]		6-00-0						
	17			0-10-0						
	24			0-10-0						
	31			3-10-0						
	Feb. 7			1-00-0						
	14			1-12-0						
	21									
	28									
	Mar. 7		85v	2-00-0	7-16-6					
				21-12-0	30-07-6		85v 51-19-6		——	51-19-6
	Totals									

IV.19   SPRING-SUMMER 1601

Fol.	Date	Details	Income	Fol.	Literary	Product.	Fol.	Total	Fol.	Repay	Balance
	Mar. 14			86	2-08-0						
	21										
	28										
	Apr. 4				0-10-0						
	11				4-05-0						
	18				6-00-0						
	25			86v	1-04-0						
	May 2	[Blind Beggar B G]			0-15-0	0-16-0					
	9				0-10-0	4-10-0					
	16	[Blind Beggar Alex.]			2-00-0	3-05-0					
	23			87	5-05-0	10-00-0					
	30	[Jew of Malta]				5-10-0					
	June 6			87v	3-15-0	3-13-4					
	13				2-10-0	20-15-7					
		Totals			29-02-0	48-09-11	87v	77-11-11			

IV.20　　FALL-WINTER 1601-1602

Fol.	Date	Details	Income	Fol.	Literary	Product.	Fol.	Total	Fol.	Repay	Balance
	July 4			91	4-00-0	8-07-0					
	11	[Six Yeomen]		92		4-12-0					
	18				3-05-0	1-04-0					
	25				2-10-0						
	Aug. 1				3-15-0						
	8	[Mahomet]		92v	0-10-0	6-09-4					
	15			93	1-00-0	35-10-8					
	22	[Life of Wolsey]			3-00-0	1-10-0					
	29				1-10-0	3-06-0					
	Sept. 5			93v	3-10-0	3-03-6					
	12				0-10-0	0-13-4					
	19				2-00-0						
	26	[3 Blind Beggar]		94	2-10-0	5-02-9					
	Oct. 3			94	0-10-0	10-13-9					
	10				2-00-0	3-04-0					
	17	[West Indies]			2-00-0						
	24				2-00-0						
	31				3-00-0						
	Nov. 7			94v	2-10-0	4-17-6					
	14			95	4-15-0	2-00-0					
	21	[Guise]			2-00-0						
	28										
	Dec. 5	[Crack Me This Nut]			1-00-0	1-04-6					
	12					0-05-0					
	19	[Hercules]		95v							
	26				6-00-0	1-05-0					
	Jan. 2				9-00-0	3-01-3					
	9	[Judas]		96	1-10-0	3-12-6					
	16				6-10-0	1-10-0					
	23										
	30			104		3-19-0					
	Feb. 5										
	13					0-12-0					
	Totals				68-15-0	106-03-11		174-18-11			

IV.21   WINTER-SPRING-FALL-WINTER 1602-1603

Fol.	Date	Details	Income	Fol.	Literary	Product.	Fol.	Total	Fol.	Repay	Balance
	Feb. 20			105		1-07-6					
	27										
	Mar. 6										
	13										
	20				3-00-0						
	27										
	Apr. 3										
	10										
	17										
	Apr. 24			105	5-00-0	2-00-0					
	May 1					1-10-0					
	8	[Malcolm]		105v	12-00-0						
	15				1-00-0						
	22			106	6-00-3	10-07-0					
	29				7-00-0	4-05-0					
	June 5				1-00-0	4-16-0					
	12	[II Cardinal Wolsey]		106v		10-00-0					
	19	[Love Parts Friendship]									
	26										
	July 3				13-00-0	1-10-0					
	10	[Jephtha]		107	1-05-0	1-05-0					
	17				1-10-0	1-02-0					
	24				2-00-0	1-10-0					
	31				8-00-0						
	Aug. 7										
	14				4-00-0						
	21										
	28										
	Sept. 4			107v	0-05-0						
	11	[Mortimer]			0-10-0						
	18				5-15-0	6-18-0					
	25				0-10-0	1-12-0					
	Oct. 2	[Earl Hertford]		108	2-10-0						
	9				9-00-0						
	16										
	23				4-00-0						
	30										

135

Fol.	Date	Details	Income Fol.	Literary	Product. Fol.	Total	Fol.	Repay	Balance
	Nov. 6			4–00–0					
	13			2–00–0					
	20			6–00–0					
	27		108 v	4–00–0					
	Dec. 5			4–00–0					
	12								
	19			0–15–0	8–18–0				
	26			5–00–0					
	Jan. 2		109	0–10–0					
	9			1–00–0					
	16			5–00–0					
	Jan. 23								
	30								
	Feb. 6		109	2–00–0					
	13								
	20								
	27								
	Mar. 6		109 v	2–00–0					
	13			8–00–0					
		Totals		131–10–0	57–00–6	188–10–6			493–00–10

IV.22 WORCESTER'S (1602-03)

Fol.	Date		Details	Income Fol.	Literary	Product.	Fol.	Total	Fol.	Repay	Balance
	Aug.	21		115	2-00-0	23-09-0					
		28	[Oldcastle]	115v	-10-0	16-03-0					
	Sept.	4			11-10-0	3-13-4					
		11	[Biron]	116	2-00-0	2-16-4					
		18									
		25		116v	4-00-0	6-16-0					
	Oct.	2			5-10-0	1-13-0					
		9			1-00-0	-01-2					
		16	[Two Brothers]	117	6-10-0	-10-0					
		23		117v	5-10-0	23-09-0					
		30			-05-0	1-00-0					
	Nov.	6		118	3-00-0	7-02-8					
		13	[Marshal Osric]		-13-0	1-00-0					
		20	[Lady Jane]								
		27			11-00-0						
	Dec.	4	[Christmas Comes]	118v	1-10-0	22-08-8					
		11			2-00-0	1-19-0					
		18									
		25									
	Jan.	1				-10-0					
		8									
	Jan.	15	[1 Black Dog]	119	3-00-0	-18-4					
		22		119v	3-10-0	3-10-0					
		29	[Unfortunate General]		4-00-0	3-10-0					
	Feb.	5			3-00-0	7-15-0					
		12	[2 Black Dog]	120	4-00-0	1-00-0					
		19			3-00-0	6-02-0					
		26			2-00-0						
	Mar.	5				1-00-0					
		12			9-00-0	-10-0					
		19	[Woman Killed]	120v	8-10-0	8-10-0					
			Totals		88-08-0	145-06-6		233-14-6			

V.1 SUMMARY OF PERFORMANCE INCOME

Season	Company	Total	Wks	Average	Per.	Average
S-S 1592	Strange's	181-10-5	19	9-11-0	105	1-14-6
F-W 1592-93	Strange's	48-19-0	5	9-15-0	29	1-13-8
F-W 1593-94	Sussex's	50-09-0	7	7-04-1	30	1-13-7
S 1594	Sussex's -Queen's	15-16-0	2	7-18-0	8	1-18-6
S 1594	Admiral's	6-03-0	1	6-03-0	3	2-01-0
S 1594	Admiral's & Chamberlain's	4-11-0	2	2-05-6	10	-09-0
S-S-F-W 1594-95	Admiral's	339-07-0	39	8-14-0	218	1-11-1
S-S 1595	Admiral's	107-02-0	10	10-14-0	57	1-17-6
F-W 1596	Admiral's	224-15-0	27	8-06-5	150	1-09-11
S-S 1596	Admiral's	115-06-0	15	7-13-9	85	1-07-1

V.2 SUMMARY OF LITERARY EXPENSES, APPROVALS AND COLLABORATIONS

Season	Wks	Total	Average	F	O	I	A	S	U	Sh	Do	Ro	Bi	Ju	EA	Ca	Ce	Da	De	Dr	Hy	Hn	Hd	Jo	Mu	Po	Ra	Sm	Wl	C
F-W 1596-97	16	7-10-0	-09-4						2																						2
S-S 1597	22	4-00-0	-03-4						1																					
F-W 1597-98	22	30-10-0	1-07-9	5	2	3		7	8	5	3		1			1			1	2	1			1							3
S-S 1598	20	83-00-0	4-03-0	11	5	5		10	34	3	4		2			8	8		8	8			3		2				8	10
F-W 1598-99	30	111-19-0	3-14-8	15	9	3	2	20	30	8	9	3	1	1		4	1	1	8	8	1			2	2	2	1		3		3
S-S 1599	15	21-05-0	1-08-4	3	3	3		15	3	4	9		1			1		1	4	1	2			1		2					3
S 1599	18	32-10-0	1-16-1	3		7		15	2	2	2			6		2			2	4	1	2			1	2	2				3
F-W 1599-00	18	71-15-0	3-19-9	8	8	1		23	12	12	7		2	1		5	5		3	5	3	2	6	3		2			3		8
S-S 1600	20	43-09-0	2-03-5	7	4			16	8	7	1		2			5	3		1	5	2	5	1		2						6
ROSE TOTAL	196	405-18-0	2-01-4	52	10	39	3	98	100	46	36	7	13	7		8	34	8	32	21	6	14	2	4	9	8	1		14	41
F-W 1600-01	30	21-12-0	-14-5	1	4	1		10	7	1	7					1	2		2	2		2									3
S-S 1601	14	29-02-0	2-01-6	5	5			16	8		13		1	1		3	4		3	3	1	2				2	1				6
F-W 1601-02	33	68-15-0	2-01-8	6	7	4		30	14	11	13	2				5	4		6	6	2	1		1		3					9
1602-03	56	131-10-0	2-06-11	14	10	10	6	41	12	21	4	5	11	5		10	3		2	1	1	2			4					7
FOR. TOTS.	133	250-19-0	1-17-7	26	17	26	11	97	41	12	22	37	8	12	15	18	12	9	2	9	12	1	3	5	4			6		25

V.3   SUMMARY OF PRODUCTION EXPENSES AND APPROVALS

Season	Wks	S-Total	U-Total	C-Total	Average	S	U	EA	Sl	Dn	Ju	Sh	Do	Bl	Je	Lɛ	Dɪ	Ty
S-S 1596	15			32-03-04	2-02-10	8		8										
F-W 1596-97	16	11-05-00	17-00-00	28-05-00	1-15-01	8	4	1	6	3	1					1		1
S-S 1597	22	4-09-00	5-16-00	10-05-00	-09-04	2	1	2		1	3	2	1			2		
F-W 1597-98	22	12-12-07	3-04-08	15-17-03	-14-05	8	3	1	2	1	3	2	1			2		
S-S 1598	20	23-01-04	13-19-00	37-00-04	1-17-00	8	9						6	2				
F-W 1598-99	30	105-11-00	96-13-00	202-04-00	6-14-09	26	6				4	5	17					
S-S 1599	15	36-01-00	18-18-00	54-19-00	3-13-03	7	8				1	1	4					
S 1599	18	10-08-00	2-02-04	12-10-04	-13-09	3	1				1	2				1		
F-W 1599-1600	18	11-07-00	28-02-06	39-09-06	2-03-09	8	4					5	4			1		
S-S 1600	20	45-04-00	22-08-00	67-12-00	3-07-07	11	5					10	1					
ROSE TOTALS		259-18-11	208-03-06	500-05-09		89	41	12	6	5	7	25	36	3		5		1
F-W 1600-1601	30	1-00-00	29-07-06	30-07-06	1-00-03	5	7				4	4		1				
S-S 1601	14	16-03-04	32-06-07	48-09-11	3-09-03	1	12				1	1				5		
F-W 1601-02	33	80-04-07	25-19-04	106-03-11	3-04-04	17	43	4			4	9				13		4
S-S-F-W 1602-03	56	37-13-00	19-07-06	57-00-06	1-00-03	16	6	3			1		12					
FORTUNE TOTALS		135-00-11	107-00-11	242-01-10		39	68	7			6	14	12	1		18		4

V.4 SUMMARY OF PLAYWRIGHTS' INCOME

ADMIRAL'S MEN (1597 - 1603)

Season	Ca	Ce	Da	De	Dr	Hy	Hn	Hd	Jo	Ml	Mu	Po	Ra	Sm	Wl	We	Total
F-W 1597-98		2-05		9-00	3-00		1-10		1-00		10-15						30-10
S-S 1598	4-10	19-15		9-10	13-05	7-10	1-00				3-15	4-00					83-00
F-W 1598-99	17-10	15-09	2-00	20-05	19-05			10-00	2-00		1-05	10-00			4-05		111-19
S-S 1599	1-00	7-10		4-05								8-10					21-05
S 1599	5-10	3-10		11-00			1-10		5-10								32-10
F-W 1599-00		10-18	9-10	15-15	8-13	2-12	8-02				4-13						71-15
S-S 1600		14-00	7-00	2-15	1-10	1-10	11-05				1-19						43-09

MOVE TO FORTUNE

Season	Ca	Ce	Da	De	Dr	Hy	Hn	Hd	Jo	Ml	Mu	Po	Ra	Sm	Wl	We	Total
F-W 1600-01		8-10	1-15	3-00		6-10	5-15						4-12				21-12
S-S 1601			6-00	4-10		1-09	5-15						1-08	-10			29-02
F-W 1601-02		9-00	8-00	-10	-15	4-10	11-15		2-00		2-00			4-15			68-15
1602-03		23-05	7-00	10-05	1-15	6-00	2-10	2-00	10-00	7-15	7-00			5-00	1-00		131-10

WORCESTER'S MEN (1602-03)

Season	Ca	Ce	Da	De	Dr	Hy	Hn	Hd	Jo	Ml	Mu	Po	Ra	Sm	Wl	We	Total
F-W 1602-03	7-03		3-14	11-05		8-04		26-05		1-00				23-14			88-18

V.5   CONSOLIDATED WEEKLY ACCOUNTS SUMMARY

Season	Wks	Per	Income	Literary	Product.	Fol.	Total	Average	Repay	Balance	Cum. Balance
S-S 1592	19	105	181-10-5								
F-W 1593-93	6	29	48-19-0								
F-W 1593-94	7	30	50-09-0								
S-S 1594	2	8	15-16-0								
S-S 1594	1	3	6-03-0								
S-S 1594	2	10	4-11-0								
F-W 1594-95	39	218	339-07-0								
S-S 1595	10	57	107-02-0								
F-W 1595-96	27	150	224-15-0								
S-S 1596	15	85	115-06-0		32-03-4	71v	32-03-4	2-02-10	39-09-0	(7-05-8)	
F-W 1596-97	16	75	95-07-0	7-10-0	28-05-0	22v	35-15-0	2-04-8	20-00-0	15-15-0	15-15-0
S-S 1597	22	109	132-06-0	4-00-0	10-05-0	22v	14-05-0	0-12-7		14-05-0	30-00-0
F-W 1597-98	22		65-16-0	30-10-0	15-17-3	44v	46-07-3	2-02-1		46-07-3	76-07-3
S-S 1598	20		59-03-5	83-00-0	37-00-4	48	120-00-4	6-00-0	10-14-0	109-06-4	185-13-7
F-W 1598-99	30		236-09-0	111-19-0	202-04-0	53v	314-03-0	10-09-5	236-09-0	77-14-0	263-07-7
S-S 1599	15		103-17-0	21-05-0	54-19-0	63	76-04-0	5-01-7	103-17-0	(27-13-0)	235-14-7
S 1599	18		7-03-0	32-10-0	12-10-4	64v	45-00-4	2-10-0	7-03-0	37-17-4	273-11-11
F-W 1599-1600	18		95-14-0	71-15-0	39-09-6	67v	111-04-6	6-03-6	95-14-0	15-10-6	289-02-5
S-S 1600	20		111-08-0	43-09-0	67-12-0	69v	111-01-0	5-11-0	111-08-0	(0-07-0)	288-15-5
Rose Totals				405-18-0	500-05-9		906-03-9		617-08-4	288-15-5	
F-W 1600-1601	30			21-12-0	30-07-6	85v	51-19-6	1-14-8			
S-S 1601	14			29-02-0	48-09-11	87v	77-11-11	5-10-9			
F-W 1601-1602	33			68-15-0	106-03-11	104	174-18-11	5-06-0	[93-00-11]	211-09-0	211-09-0
S-S-F-W 1602-03	56			131-10-0	57-00-6	109v	188-10-6	3-07-4	[93-00-11]	188-10-6	400-00-6
Fortune Totals				250-19-0	242-01-10		493-00-10		[93-00-11]	399-19-11	
Rose Totals				405-18-0	500-05-9		906-03-9				
Grand Totals				656-17-0	742-07-7		1399-04-7				

SELECT BIBLIOGRAPHY

Adams, John Quincy. 1917. *The dramatic records of Sir Henry Herbert*. New Haven, Yale University Press.

    1934. The *Massacre at Paris* leaf. *Library*, fourth series, 14: 447–69.

    1946. The author plot of an early seventeenth century play. *Library*, fourth series, 26: 17–27.

Albright, E. M. 1927. *Dramatic publication in England, 1580–1640*. New York, Heath.

Arber, Edward (ed.). 1875–94. *A transcript of the registers of the Company of Stationers of London: 1554–1640 A.D.* 5 vols. London, Birmingham.

Ashe, Dora Jean. 1954. The non-Shakespearean bad quartos as provincial acting versions. *Renaissance Papers*, 57–62.

Baldwin, T. W. 1927a. *The organization and personnel of the Shakespearean company*. Princeton, Princeton University Press.

    1927b. Posting Henslowe's accounts. *Journal of English and Germanic Philology*, 26: 42–90.

Beckerman, Bernard. 1971. Philip Henslowe. In *The theatrical manager in England and America*, ed. J. W. Donohue, Jr. Princeton, Princeton University Press.

Bentley, G. E. 1971. *The profession of dramatist in Shakespeare's time, 1590–1642*. Princeton, Princeton University Press.

    1984. *The profession of player in Shakespeare's time, 1590–1642*. Princeton, Princeton University Press.

Bevington, David. 1962. *From mankind to Marlowe*. Cambridge, Mass., Harvard University Press.

Brombert, Murray. 1950. The reputation of Philip Henslowe. *Shakespeare Quarterly*, 1: 135–9.

Byrne, M. St. Clare. 1932. Bibliographical clues in collaborate plays. *Library*, fourth series, 13: 21–48.

    1966. Prompt book's progress. *Theatre Notebook*, 21: 7–12.

Cerasano, C. P. 1985. Revising Philip Henslowe's biography. *Notes & Queries* 230: 66–71.

Chambers, E. K. 1923. *The Elizabethan Stage*. 4 vols. Oxford, Clarendon Press.

Chillington, Carol. 1979. Philip Henslowe and his 'diary'. Unpublished Ph.D. dissertation. University of Michigan.

    1980. Playwrights at work: Henslowe's not Shakespeare's *Book of Sir Thomas More*. *English Literary Renaissance*, 10: 439–79.

Collier, John Payne. 1845. *Henslowe's Diary*. London.

Defoe, Daniel. 1738. *The complete English tradesman*. 2 vols. Fourth edn. London.

De Roover, Raymond. 1948. *Money, banking and credit in mediaeval Bruges*. Cambridge, Mass. Mediaeval Academy of America.

Edwards, James. 1960. Early bookkeeping and its development into accounting. *Business History Review*, 34: 446–58.

Evans, G. Blakemore. 1973. An Elizabethan theatrical stock list. *Harvard Library Bulletin*, 21: 254–70.

Fleay, F. G. 1890. *A chronicle history of the London stage 1559–1642*. 2 vols. London, Reeves and Turner.

    1891. *A biographical chronicle of the English drama 1559–1642*. New York, B. Franklin.

Foakes, R. A. (ed.). 1977. *The Henslowe papers*. London, Scolar Press.

Gossen, Stephen. 1579. *The School of Abuse*. London.

Gray, Henry D. 1917. The purport of Shakespeare's contribution to *1 Henry VI*. *Publications of the Modern Language Association*, 32: 367–92.

Greg, Walter Wilson (ed.). 1904–8. *Henslowe's diary*. 2 vols. London, A. H. Bullen.

(ed.). 1907. *Henslowe's papers*. London, A. H. Bullen.

1919. 'Bad' quartos outside Shakespeare – *Alcazar* and *Orlando*. *Library*, third series, 10: 193–222.

1922. *Two Elizabethan stage abridgements: The Battle of Alcazar and Orlando Furioso*. London, The Malone Society.

1925. Prompt copies, private transcripts, and the 'playhouse scrivener'. *Library*, fourth series, 6: 148–56.

(ed.). 1931a. *Malone Society Collections II, 3*. London, The Malone Society.

(ed.), 1931b. *Dramatic documents from Elizabethan playhouses*. 2 vols. Oxford, Clarendon Press.

1937. From manuscript to print. *Review of English Studies*, 13: 190–205.

1939. A fragment from Henslowe's diary. *Library*, 19: 180–4.

(ed.). 1950. *The tragical history of the life and death of Doctor Faustus by Christopher Marlowe: a conjectural reconstruction*. Oxford, Clarendon Press.

Greg, W. W. and E. Bothwell (eds.). 1930. *Records of the court of the stationers' company*. London, Bibliographical Society.

Guiney, L. I. 1919. Ben Jonson and Henslowe. *Notes & Queries*, 136: 271.

Haaker, Ann. 1968. The plague, the theatre and the poet. *Renaissance Drama*, new series, 1: 283–306.

Hart, Alfred. 1932a. The time allotted for representation of Elizabethan and Jacobean plays. *Review of English Studies*, 8: 395–414.

1932b. The length of Elizabethan and Jacobean plays. *Review of English Studies*, 8: 139–54.

1934. Acting versions of Elizabethan plays. *Review of English Studies*, 10: 1–28.

1941. Did Shakespeare produce his own plays? *Modern Language Review*, 36: 173–83.

1942. *Stolen and surreptitious copies*. Melbourne, Melbourne University Press.

Holdsworth, William. 1903–66. *A history of English law*. 16 vols. London, Methuen.

Hoppe, Harry R. 1946. *John of Bordeaux*: a bad quarto that never reached print. In *Studies in Honor of A. H. R. Fairchild*. University of Missouri Studies 21: 121–32.

Howard-Hill, T. H. 1983. The censor and four English promptbooks. *Studies in Bibliography*, 36: 168–77.

Hoy, Cyrus. 1976. Critical and aesthetic problems of collaboration in Renaissance drama. *Research Opportunities in Renaissance Drama*, 19: 3–6.

Hudson, Kenneth. 1982. *Pawnbroking: an aspect of British social history*. London, The Bodley Head.

Hume, Robert D. (ed.). 1980. *The London theatre world, 1660–1800*. Carbondale, Southern Illinois University Press.

Hyde, Mary C. 1949. *Playwriting for Elizabethans 1600–1605*. New York, Columbia University Press.

Ingram, William. 1971. The closing of the theatres in 1597: a dissenting view. *Modern Philology*, 69: 105–15.

1978. *A London life in the brazen age*. Cambridge, Mass., Harvard University Press.

Isaacs, J. 1933. *Production and stage management at the Blackfriars theatre*. London, Oxford University Press.

Jenkins, Harold. 1934. *The life and work of Henry Chettle*. London, Sidgwick and Jackson.

Kirschbaum, Leo. 1938. A census of bad quartos. *Review of English Studies*, 14: 20–43.

1945. An hypothesis concerning the origin of the 'bad quartos'. *PMLA*, 60: 697–715.

1955. *Shakespeare and the stationers*. Columbus, Ohio, Ohio State University Press.

1959. The copyright of Elizabethan plays. *Library*, fifth series, 14: 231–50.

Klein, David. 1967. Time allotted for an Elizabethan performance. *Shakespeare Quarterly*, 18: 434–8.

Lambarde, W. 1970 [*c.* 1596]. *Perambulation of Kent*. Bath, Adams and Dart.

Langhams, Edward A. 1975. A Restoration Actor's part. *Harvard Library Bulletin*, 23: 180–5.

Lawrence, William J. 1927. *Pre-Restoration stage studies*. Cambridge, Mass., Harvard University Press.

Lesko, Kathleen M. 1979. A rare Restoration manuscript prompt-book: John Wilson's *Belphegor* corrected by the author. *Studies in Bibliography*, 32: 215–19.

McMillin, Scott. 1972. The ownership of *The Jew of Malta*, *Friar Bacon* and *The Ranger's Comedy*. *English Language Notes*, 9: 249–52.

1973. The plots of *The Dead Man's Fortune* and *2 Seven Deadly Sins*: inferences for theatre historians. *Studies in Bibliography*, 26: 235–43.

1976. Simon Jewell and the Queen's men. *Review of English Studies*, 27: 174–7.

Marder, Louis. 1970. Chettle's forgery of *The Groatsworth of Wit* and the 'shake-scene' passage. *Shakespeare Newsletter*, 20: 42.

Milhous, Judith. 1979. *Thomas Betterton and the management of Lincoln Inn Fields, 1695–1708*. Carbondale, Southern Illinois University Press.

1980. Company management. In Robert D. Hume (ed.), *The London Theatre World 1660–1800*, pp. 1–34. Carbondale, Southern Illinois University Press.

1981–2. United Company finances, 1682–92. *Theatre Review*, 7: 37–53.

Miller, Edwin Haviland. 1959. *The professional writer in Elizabethan England*. Cambridge, Mass., Harvard University Press.

Nashe, Thomas. 1599. *Lenten Stuff*. London.

Peele, James. 1569. *The pathewaye to perfectnes in the accomptes of debitour, and creditour*. London.

Rabkin, Norman. 1976. Problems of collaboration. *Research Opportunities in Renaissance Drama*, 19: 7–14.

Ramsay, G. D. (ed.). 1962. *John Isham: mercer and merchant adventurer*. Northants Record Society, 21.

Ramsay, Peter. 1956. Some Tudor merchants' accounts. *Studies in the history of accounting*, ed. A. C. Littleton and B. S. Yamey. London.

Rhodes, Ernest L. 1976. *Henslowe's Rose: the stage and the staging*. Lexington, University Press of Kentucky.

Rhodes, R. Crompton. 1923. *Shakespeare's first folio*. Oxford, Basil Blackwell.

Ringler, William A. 1968. The number of actors in Shakespeare's early plays. in G. E. Bentley (ed.), *The seventeenth century stage*. Toronto, University of Toronto Press.

Rutter, Carol Chillington. 1985. *Documents of the Rose playhouse*. Manchester, Manchester University Press.

Sanders, Norman. 1953. Greene and his editors. *PMLA*, 48: 392–417.

Saunders, J. W. 1964. *The profession of English letters*. London, Routledge and Kegan Paul.

Schoenbaum, S. 1966. *Internal evidence and Elizabethan dramatic authorship*. Evanston, University of Chicago Press.

1975. *William Shakespeare: a compact documentary life*. Oxford: Oxford University Press.

Sheavyn, P. 1909. *The literary profession in the Elizabethan age*. Revised J. W. Saunders, 1967. Manchester, Manchester University Press.

Sisson, C. J. 1936. *The lost plays of Shakespeare's age*. Cambridge, Cambridge University Press.

1954. The Red Bull company and the importunate widow. *Shakespeare Survey*, 7: 57–68.

1960. The laws of Elizabethan copyright: the stationers' view. *Library*, fifth series, 15: 8–20.

1972. *The Boar's Head Theatre*. Edited by Stanley Wells. London, Routledge and Kegan Paul.

Van Dam, B. A. P. 1929. Alleyn's player's part of Greene's *Orlando Furioso* and the text of the Q of 1594. *English Studies*, 11: 182–203; 209–20.

1934. The Collier leaf. *English Studies*, 16: 166–73.

Wallace, Charles W. 1909. *Three London theatres of Shakespeare's time*. University Studies IX, no. 4. Lincoln, Nebraska, University of Nebraska Press.

1910–11. The Swan theatre and the Earl of Pembroke's servants. *Englishe Studien*, 43: 340–95.

1966 [1913]. *The first London theatre*. New York, Benjamin Blom.

Yamey, B. S. 1940. *The functional development of double-entry bookkeeping*. London, Publications of the Accounting Research Association No. 7.

GENERAL INDEX

INDEX OF PLAYS

gument between a young white redneck from Louisiana or Mississippi and a black from Cleveland or Chicago is names start flying. . . . And the fists start flying. I saw this happen in the field, as a matter fact. . . . When you see racial incidents developing and weapons lying around, it gets pretty tense.[95]

Behind the lines, discrimination and unequal treatment were even more widespread. Black officers often watched swimming pools empty when they approached. Black enlistees noted that administrative staffs were predominantly Caucasian, and that the most menial tasks were often reserved for the "brothers." "You would see the racialism [racism] in the base-camp area," former specialist Haywood T. Kirkland recalls. "When the brothers who was shot came out of the field, most of them got the jobs burning s— in these fifty-gallon drums. Most of the white dudes got jobs as supply clerks or in the mess hall."[96]

Powerless Positions

Support personnel who worked at monotonous, unimportant jobs often felt like spectators in the war. Many experienced guilt for not being in the heart of the conflict. Others struggled with feelings of powerlessness and with the conviction that they were wasting their time. One soldier wrote bitterly to a friend,

While in the field under combat conditions, ethnically diverse soldiers drew together into tight-knit units. Behind the lines, however, problems with racism were common.

Long Binh, USA. I'm not really in Vietnam. . . . I'm living in a moderate-size town which combines the worst features of the Midwest and the South. . . . The only Oriental food I've had is at a bad Chinese restaurant on post. I've never seen a Vietnamese village, been in a local hut or talked to someone who raises rice for a living. . . . Nothing is [real], except the office, the mess hall, my room and my books.[97]

Although military protocol was usually fairly relaxed in the boonies, rules were more strictly enforced for soldiers in the rear. Appearance was a high priority. Orders were to be implicitly followed, rank dutifully observed. Many soldiers were driven to fury by officers who wanted to "play war" and embellish their own power and prestige. Soldiers spent their days painting captain's bars on helmets, detailing a superior's jeep with special glossy paint and pinstripes, picking up cigarette butts, and other meaningless activities. "You're supposed to rake your sand," one veteran recalls. "The sand around your tent had to be raked and they would inspect twice a week. And, I swear to God, I'm not telling you a lie, it had to be raked east to west. It couldn't be raked north-south—they'd raise hell. It's crazy!"[98]

"Birds"

Some GIs battled bureaucracy behind the lines, while helicopter crews, pilots, and medics worked in the thick of the fighting, providing backup and aid to combat units. Soldiers valued such support as much as they valued the buddies who fought by their side. "A grunt's best friends were the medics who tended him, the firepower that supported him, the helicopters that rescued him,"[99] writes author and Vietnam veteran Bernard Edelman.

Helicopter crews were some of the main players in the war. They inserted and extracted fighting units into and out of landing zones, often in the thick of enemy fire. They transported the injured to hospitals. They used their machines as gunships complete with rocket launchers and machine guns to take part in the fighting themselves. "I had an M-60 machine gun in the door," explains a former gunner, "I'd do a whole acrobatic trip of shooting be-

hind and underneath the helicopter to spray the area."[100]

Helicopter crews operated out of base camps and maintained grueling schedules, responding to orders to fly at a moment's notice. Most took enormous risks in order to perform their duties. One member of a helicopter crew recalls, "When they would fire from the ground the bullets looked like baseballs or beer cans coming up at you. . . . When they'd get closer, they'd suddenly seem to speed up and whiz by."[101]

Men who served in the noisy, shaking "birds" eventually became hardened to the danger they faced and developed a cool-headed, daredevil approach to both flying and the war. Most were highly skilled at what they did, as one new member of a medevac (medical evacuation) team described in a letter to his mother.

> The pilot noticed that the patrol [on the ground] was receiving intense mortar and small-arms fire. So he decided to circle overhead. All of a sudden, out of nowhere, two U.S. jet fighters came swooping down and bombed and rocketed the VC [Viet Cong] positions. . . . Before I knew it, we were down in the zone with the VC firing all over the place. No sooner, the wounded were hustled aboard. . . . When they were aboard, we swooped up and cut off the trees in the way. Then the bird started swaying back and forth like crazy. That's to keep the enemy from hitting us.[102]

Helicopters served vital functions, including inserting fighting units (left) and transporting wounded (above).

"Air and Arty"

Helicopters provided a variety of invaluable services, but bombers and fighter jets gave the greatest support to ground forces when they were in battle. Bombing raids were vital to America's military strategy in Vietnam, and those men who flew planes and made up the crews (navigators, gunners, and bombardiers) played a vital role in most large battles. Ground troops pinned down by enemy fire had only to radio their coordinates to headquarters, and air support would be on its way. The arrival of bombers and jet fighters regularly turned the tide in battle and inspired struggling GIs to take the initiative and fight harder.

Flight crews were viewed as some of the elite troops of the war. They served long hours, often sleeping in flight gear while snatching a few hours rest between assignments, and operated under high stress and in dangerous conditions. Most took great pride in performing well, and saw themselves as professionals. "Whatever I set out

to do I try to do the best job I can," recalls one veteran. "I studied alot. I really knew my airplane, I knew the missions, I knew the tactics. . . . I just immersed myself in my work and gave myself very little free time. And when I was free, I just drank."[103]

One of the best-known fighter squads was the Flying Black Ponies, formally known as U.S. Navy Light Attack Squadron Four. These crews flew in planes larger and less maneuverable than small fighter jets, but often daringly skimmed the treetops in order to drop their explosives on target. "We interfaced with the air-cavalry pack," remembers pilot Kit Lavell. "They flew helicopters. . . . We'd integrate and work targets with them. We'd stay above, and when they ran into trouble we'd come in with the heavy stuff."[104]

American soldiers regularly relied on "air and arty" (air power and artillery) to rescue them from tight spots. Providing air support was risky business, however. American patrols often fought in close proximity to the enemy, and if an incorrect coordinate was called in or if air crews were inaccurate in their drops, bombs could land on friend rather than foe. Friendly fire from aircraft was a very real hazard to GIs on the ground.

To further challenge air crews, the enemy often attacked under cover of darkness or during bad weather, conditions that made air strikes even more dangerous and difficult. Their schemes did not always work, however, since American pilots were as daring as they were skilled. "Sixty percent of my combat missions were at night, mostly in bad weather," says Lavell. "We did not have sophisticated navigational equipment in our airplanes. We literally flew seat-of-the-pants and had to fly underneath the clouds. . . . On more than 80 percent of the missions we took fire."[105]

Medics

Just as flight crews were valued for the aid they supplied from above, medics, known as corpsmen in the

Foot soldiers depended on air support (above, a fighter bomber attacks a Viet Cong base camp) and artillery (right, an American firebase).

navy and marines, were some of the most vital and beloved support forces on the ground.

Trained to give medical care to wounded GIs in the field, combat medics regularly endured all the hardships and stresses of "humping the boonies" with their unit. Their jobs were to care for casualties, so they were usually in the thick of the fighting, relying on cover fire from other members of the unit while they aided wounded soldiers.

A medic's purpose was to help, not kill, and constantly seeing the ugliness of war was particularly difficult. Many experienced post-traumatic stress disorder on returning home. Despite the hardships and trauma, however, medics found their jobs rewarding and even ego-building. Some entered the war with only a high school education but were regularly called "Doc" by their men. All were respected for the miracles they pulled off in the field. "You can stop bleeding with a belt, you can stop bleeding with a piece of string out of a poncho," observes one former medic. "You can stop a sucking chest wound with the cellophane off a cigarette pack. You can use [a man's] chin strap to secure things. I learned that first aid is a matter of primitive wits."[106]

Many medics were part of medevac teams, who evacuated casualties out of the midst of battle by helicopter. Again, these jobs were extremely risky since they were often performed while under heavy enemy fire. Many medics were wounded and killed in the course of saving others. They worked with the conviction that they performed a vital task and were appreciated by the men they served. Former marine corpsman Douglas Anderson says:

The people had begun to trust me. They knew if they got hit that I would come after them. . . . People would give me the goodies out of their C-ration packets. If there was an air mattress to be had, the doc got it. . . . And I know that if I had been hit and there was no way to get out of there, they would have grabbed me up in a poncho and carried me a hundred miles if they had to.[107]

Nurses and Doctors

Doctors, nurses, and hospital medics faced their own unique challenges as they tended the sick and wounded in military hospitals throughout South Vietnam. Those who were assigned to large bases had access to modern equipment and adequate facilities that eased the burden of saving lives. For instance, the hospital at Da Nang was the largest combat casualty unit in the world, complete with orthopedic wards, surgeries, recovery wards, intensive care wards, POW wards, and hundreds of staff. Patients were housed in portable barracks, and benefited from monitors, respirators, and everything else that was needed to provide excellent care.

Even the best facilities were not perfect, however. Wards often flooded during monsoons. "There'd be rats in the water; sometimes there'd be snakes there. That bothered me more than anything,"[108] one veteran navy nurse who served in Da Nang remembers. Incoming mortars knocked out electricity at times, and then nurses and medics had to scramble to care for critical cases until emergency power could be restored. Occasionally mortars hit the wards, wounding nurses, doctors, and patients alike.

Most military hospitals were smaller and conditions more challenging than at Da Nang and other major bases. Staff regularly worked long hours; shifts were commonly twelve hours long. Many nurses and medics had time to snatch only a four- to six-hour break before they returned for another shift. Many medical personnel worked six days a week, changing dressings, helping with surgeries, and performing dozens of other medical duties. "We didn't have any running water. We had big napalm tanks with holes cut out of them, and that's what we kept the water in. We didn't have enough bandages, we were short of IV fluids, and I remember using outdated penicillin because that's all we had,"[109] one nurse who served in Pleiku describes.

When hospitals came under attack, nurses had to be sure that their patients were safe before they could seek shelter. At times, nurses were attacked by patients themselves, usually Vietnamese POWs who had been wounded and were being treated. One nurse attested to the fact that female prisoners were particularly vicious. "I remember one night I brought a dinner tray to one of them, and she was on a bed with two casts on her legs, having had abdominal and eye surgery. . . . I gave the woman a tray and turned around to get a sheet, and she had picked up a fork and was going right into my back."[110]

"Strength to Die"

Nurses in Vietnam were regularly struck by the horror and tragedy of war as they struggled to care for young men who were injured in combat. In Keith Walker's *A Piece of My Heart,* Christian McGinley Schneider relates one unforgettable experience that occurred on her first day in the emergency ward.

There is a wonderful line in a poem by Thomas Hardy that really gets me; the line is "Alive enough to have strength to die." And that is exactly how this boy was. He was a really good-looking boy—Jimmy was his name—with blond hair, and half of his face had been blown away, and the first thing the nurse said to me was "Cut off all of his clothes." They give you these huge scissors to cut off the clothes, and I was trying to comfort him—He was wide awake even though half his face was gone, and he was scared. I remember cutting off all his clothes and the horror of taking one of his boots off and his foot still being in the boot. . . . I remember that nurse saying, "Draw four tubes of blood, type-cross him, and get it over to the lab right away." I remember drawing the blood, and he begged me not to leave. . . . I said, "I just have to run across the hall to the lab. I promise I'll be right back." I was right back, and he had died in the time that I had left him alone. . . . And I never forgot that; I never again left anyone, because you realize that when they say that, it's like they know that they are going. . . . It's a horrible thing; I never forgot it.

Building Walls

Doctors saw the same horrors of war as nurses, and the stress of trying to patch up men whose bodies were horribly torn and mutilated led many to drink, use drugs, and have mental breakdowns. "Sometimes the only way I could handle the casualty scene was to ignore the big picture around me and just keep busy," one physician remembers. "Patching holes, putting intravenous drips in arms, necks, groins. Putting in chest tubes. . . . Ripping off clothes. Splinting limbs. Examining. Working. Touching."[111] Doctors were often older than military nurses and the fighting men, however. Many physicians had families at home and confidence in their own skills that added to their stability and ability to endure the war with greater equanimity.

Nurses, on the other hand, were usually young and inexperienced. Many were shy, uncertain, and self-conscious about being women in the predominantly male world of the military. In addition, nurses had to cope with many emotional demands from their patients that doctors were spared because of their sex and their profession.

One of a nurse's most important roles was to show compassion for her patients, comforting them when they were afraid, letting them know that they were cared for, and reassuring them that their sacrifice was appreciated. But as they attended to and befriended patients who were suffering and dying, many nurses grew too emotionally involved. They fretted over recovering

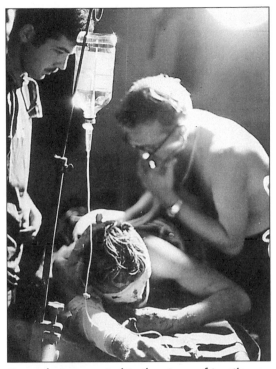

Some doctors reacted to the stress of treating a continuous stream of horribly injured soldiers by drinking, using drugs, or suffering mental breakdowns.

soldiers who returned to the field; they became distraught over the death of a favorite patient.

In order to remain functional and maintain a professional manner, many nurses smothered these emotions. They continued to care for their patients, listened to their stories, and maintained a cheerful, positive demeanor, but inside they became detached from the suffering that was all around them. Nurse Anne Simon Auger says, "I found I'd built up walls real effectively. I was patient and tender with the GIs. . . . I was very professional, but I was distant. . . . Because of the walls I'd put up I didn't listen to them, didn't hear what they might be trying to tell me even just in gestures or whatever. I wasn't open to them because I was so closed to myself."[112]

Despite the control they exerted over their emotions, nurses were unable to curb the powerful hatred they developed for the enemy. Many found it particularly difficult to care for Vietnamese POW patients. Auger observes, "This POW was personally responsible for the deaths of six . . . GIs. When he was wheeled onto my ward, something snapped. I was overwhelmed with uncontrollable feelings of hate and rage. I couldn't go near this guy because I knew, without any doubt, that if I touched him I would kill him."[113]

"Things I Wouldn't Have Done at Home"

Although they became war-hardened, nurses still valued the camaraderie they had with their coworkers, and, like combat troops in the field, testified that friendships were the best part of their war experience.

Such friendships were not enough to counteract the effects of fatigue and stress that built up as the months passed. Many nurses suffered from insomnia, despite the fact that they were always physically and mentally exhausted. Many spent their spare time going to parties in order to avoid being alone with their thoughts. Some involved themselves in casual physical relationships with doctors or other GIs in an attempt to find warmth and safety in an unsafe world. "You just wanted to have a relationship to have some happiness and security on your off hours," one nurse says. "And sometimes your feelings and your actions were like they had no consequence. I mean you might've done some things . . . I'm not saying they're terrible things, but they are things I wouldn't have done at home."[114]

Although doctors and nurses were pushed to the limits of endurance by the demands of the war, most believed that their sacrifice was worthwhile because of the comfort they brought to their patients. Nurse Jane Hodge says, "The fact that we were in Vietnam might not have been right, but the guys who were being shot up weren't the ones that had that choice to make. That's why I think I was able to work and live under the conditions that we did for a year."[115]

Deep in Enemy Territory

Although not seen technically as support forces, covert-action troops that carried out secret, undercover missions for the military in Vietnam played a vital role in aiding ordinary GIs. They concentrated on gathering information, attacking and destroying strongholds deep in enemy territory, and helping to weaken and demoralize a foe who would otherwise have been a greater threat to ordinary combat forces. Some units were part of the Phoenix Program, a top secret project set up by the army and the CIA to identify, capture, interrogate, and/or assassinate Vietnamese who offered vital support to the enemy. Members of the Phoenix Program reportedly were responsible for some twenty thousand assassinations during the war.

Covert-action units were commonly marine recon (reconnaissance) teams, Army Special Forces units (Green Berets), Army Long Range Reconnaissance Patrols (LURPs, whose mission was essentially inspection and exploration), and Navy SEALs (sea, air, land guerrillas), also known as Black Berets or "green-faced frogmen." All were accorded great respect due to their skill, their daring, and their accomplishments. All were physically fit, rigorously trained, familiar with a variety of weapons, and skilled in hand-to-hand combat and night fighting.

Guerrilla warfare was a key part of special force operations. Mike Beamon, former scout for the Navy SEALs, explains a technique used for capturing the enemy. "A lot of times we would sit in a bush as close as two or three feet from a trail and watch people walk back and forth for hours until somebody came along with a gun, and then we'd grab them, just reach right out of the bush and grab them by the ankles. . . . The

Navy SEALs (pictured) were one of the covert-action units in Vietnam that carried out secret missions.

level of concentration and commitment was just incredible."[116]

Barefoot with Painted Faces

In order to carry out guerrilla tactics, covert units laid aside their regular uniforms and did all they could to blend into their surroundings. Some dressed in black like the Viet Cong. Others wore dark loincloths and sandals. Many let their hair and beards grow, and painted their faces in camouflage patterns. "On patrol we traveled stripped," one says. "There was no insignia, no identification, no cigarettes, no American anything. If we were caught, there was no way in the world—outside of the fact that we were Americans—that you could identify us with the U.S. military."[117]

Some covert units dropped into remote regions by parachute. Some were inserted by helicopter, which touched down in several locales to confuse any enemy who might be watching. Navy SEALs, trained as frogmen, often traveled by boat upriver, then swam ashore under cover of darkness. With great stealth, all special force units slipped into and out of villages in the dead of night, knocked out weapons arsenals, kidnapped and killed Viet Cong leaders, set booby traps, and left a trail of fear, death, and demoralization behind. Mike Beamon observes:

Us, being in there barefoot, they didn't hear us, they didn't hear any helicopters, they'd come up and the guy is dead. Sometimes we'd paint green

on their face, which would mean the green-faced frogmen were in there. We'd go back and read intelligence reports and see that the people were really afraid that the green-faced frogmen were lurking. . . . Finding a loved one with a green face and stabbed . . . was incredible terror.[118]

Getting Away with Murder

Although covert forces were originally some of the best and brightest young men to be found in the military, troublemakers and lawbreakers were inevitably drawn into their midst by the prospect of excitement and glory. Says Bruce Lawlor, who served in Military Intelligence:

Barry Sadler was the worst thing that ever happened to [the Green Berets]. He came out with this song ["Ballad of the Green Berets"] and all of a sudden the Green Berets no more were an elite small unit. They got all kinds of cowboys in there, and the cowboys wanted to go out and shoot and kick down doors and beat up people. . . . The Special Forces became overpopulated with cowboys.[119]

Such reckless "cowboys" were prone to commit atrocities, and, after a time, even ordinarily law-abiding guerrilla operatives performed acts that they would not ever have contemplated in civilian life. Some became hardened by the demands of the job. Some came to believe they were above

The Mission

Covert force units were the specialists of the military, men who walked on a razor edge of danger to accomplish their missions. Despite the glamour and prestige they acquired, their deeds were often breathtakingly brutal, as Navy SEAL Mike Beamon describes in Al Santoli's account of the war, *Everything We Had*.

> When we'd go out on a mission, we'd take a whole handful of pills, and some of those were Dexedrine. When I hit Dexedrine I'd just turn into a pair of eyeballs and ears. That's probably why I don't remember too many of the details real well, because it was just like I was on a speed trip the whole time I was in the field. . . .
>
> When we would go in [to a village] I'd be barefoot, I would move up to a hootch. This is maybe during a real stormy night; they're not expecting Americans to be out there in the middle of a storm, they're not expecting them to come walking in at two o'clock in the morning in the middle of a Viet Cong stronghold. . . .
>
> Around my head I wore a triangular green bandage. I'd take it off and tie it into a knot in the center and walk over to the bed—I knew exactly what bed this guy was sleeping in. I had a Navy K-bar knife. . . . The blade is about seven or nine inches long, razor sharp. . . . I would go over to the person and I would hold their nose shut so they'd take a breath with their mouth, and I'd take this rag . . . and cram it down their throat so it would get down to their larynx, at the same time bringing that knife up under their neck, so that if they moved at all they would be cutting their own throat. . . . .
>
> I would take the gag, grab it from behind their head, the knife under the throat, and literally pick them up just by the head. . . . I would pass him to the prisoner-handler. All this time no words are spoken. We were incredibly well rehearsed. This has all taken about a minute, maybe a minute and a half. . . . We would pull back and start to move for our exit. I would usually sit by the hootch for about five minutes and listen and, while I was doing that, hook a grenade on the door, flatten the pin and run a fishing line across the door so if anybody opened it up, they would drop the grenade and of course they would be killed. . . . It was something you just didn't think about. You just did it.

the law. Others discovered that they got pleasure from causing others pain. They used their assignment as an excuse for all kinds of unnecessary cruelty—rapes, murders of innocent women and children, cutting off ears, cutting out hearts, and so forth. "There was a certain joy you had in killing, an exhilaration that is hard to explain,"[120] one stated.

Serving in such forces was an incredibly dangerous proposition, however. Due to death and injury, it was unusual for SEAL teams to be intact for as long as five months. Thus, many guerrillas lived as if there was no tomorrow, even after returning to base or to a town. They drank too much, used drugs, and defied their superiors. They stole automobiles, destroyed property, and used any excuse to brandish their weapons and intimidate those around them.

Because most outsiders were aware of the risks guerrilla fighters took and admired their daring, they were usually allowed to act as they pleased. "I'd create quite a bit of havoc," says Mike Beamon, "and they would say, 'SEALs are supposed to be crazy. Leave him alone. He's going to die tomorrow.'" [121]

Most men knew that what they were doing was wrong. One man, looking back on his experience in LURPs, says, "I started disliking myself for what America, the war, and bein' in the Army had caused me to become." [122] Still, they rationalized their actions as being part of the job, and the military appeared to support such rationalizations. "You think no crime is a crime durin' war, 'specially when you get away with it," [123] another veteran notes. Many covert units were even given medals, extra R&R, and other rewards by superiors who chose to overlook their barbarity and focus on their accomplishments.

Human Damage

Men who worked in covert operations were not the only American troops who enter-

tained doubts about the rightness of what they were doing in the war. Many young soldiers, once exuberantly patriotic, were shaken by growing feelings of disillusionment. They had come to Vietnam to be heroes, then found themselves in a bizarre, senseless world where morality was lacking, where killing was the highest purpose, and survival the only reward.

There was no way to feel good about what was happening in Vietnam. One GI wrote to a friend in 1970,

Really, the physical and human damage done over the last few years is much greater than I realized—especially the human damage. . . . Not just the dead, but the GIs who can't talk in coherent sentences any more, or the ones who have found they love to kill, or the Vietnamese, who must have been a very gentle, graceful people before the war turned them into thieves, black marketeers and prostitutes. . . . I feel like I'm at the bottom of a great sewer. [124]

Chapter 5

The Insanity of War

As the war dragged on, new recruits assigned to Vietnam entered the war with different attitudes than they had in the mid-1960s. Most still believed in their country and were willing to fight, but few were as naïve as those who had joined earlier in the decade. All knew that they were going into a long war that showed few signs of ending. All realized that they were taking part in a conflict that was highly unpopular at home, and that was causing dissension even in their own ranks.

Few soldiers made a conscious decision to oppose the war, although some protested against it when they returned home. Many, however, as they progressed through their tour of duty, found it harder and harder to justify their presence and their actions in South Vietnam. They grumbled to each other, avoided combat, and expressed their rebellion by wearing love beads, letting their hair or beards grow, or painting peace symbols on their possessions. Some compressed all their frustration into four letters, "UUUU," which they scrawled on their helmets—"the unwilling, led by the unqualified, doing the unnecessary for the ungrateful."[125]

Betrayed

The basis for widespread disillusionment among American troops was the growing conviction that the war was wrong, and that the United States should not be involved in Vietnam. They had been told they were fighting to preserve democracy, to protect the United States from Communist invasion, and to help the Vietnamese people. In fact, South Vietnam had never had a democratic government; those that had prevailed since World War II were in effect dictatorships, often repressive ones. And even if South Vietnam became Communist-controlled, the country's size and strength was nothing compared to U.S. might. One man recalls:

When pressured, I upheld our presence in Vietnam by a rather feeble belief in the Domino Theory. But often I wondered how that tumbling column of dominos . . . could possibly complete a chain reaction. . . . Try as I could, I simply could not visualize a fleet of North Vietnamese sampans and junks overcoming the U.S. Navy and landing an invasion force on the shores of California.[126]

The argument that America was in Vietnam as a favor to the Vietnamese people was feeble as well. The South Vietnamese army did not seem eager to fight the Communists any more than the South Vietnamese people seemed eager to have Americans in their country. In fact, many South Vietnamese hated and feared U.S. troops in response to the widespread, apparently pointless destruction caused by the war. One navy corpsman who provided supplies to villagers observes, "I spent a great deal of time discussing the problems of Vietnam with the Vietnamese people, what they felt and what they thought about Americans and their involvement. I learned right away the war was not the right thing to do from the people's point of view."[127]

Since it was all-too-apparent that official justifications of the war were weak and illogical, soldiers grew inclined to brush off standard patriotic speeches and slogans with skeptical responses such as "What a crock," or "Who's kidding who?" Still, they asked themselves, if they were not fighting for no-

In the later years of the war, more soldiers expressed their opposition to the American presence in Vietnam.

ble reasons, what were they fighting for? The options were disturbing—to preserve America's reputation as a world power; to enrich U.S. corporations who sold the military war material; or simply to further a national blunder from which Presidents Johnson and Nixon could not withdraw without losing pride and prestige.

Many soldiers came to the conclusion that the answer was a combination of all of the above, and their anger flared against the government that they saw as devious and corrupt. The leaders of the war came in for blame as well, since they allowed so much suffering and dying to continue. On his return to the United States, soldier and author Al Santoli's convictions were confirmed when he found himself face-to-face with Secretary of Defense Melvin Laird in a veterans hospital.

The Honor of War

Many men who served in Vietnam grew angry over the sacrifices America asked them to make in the war. In Wallace Terry's *Bloods*, combat photographer Stephen A. Howard gives his final assessment of the conflict which he entered in part to fulfill his mother's dreams that he do his part for his country.

Vietnam taught you to be a liar. To be a thief. To be dishonest. To go against everything you ever learned. It taught you everything you did not need to know, because you were livin' a lie. And the lie was you ain't have no business bein' there in the first place. You wasn't there for democracy. You wasn't protecting your homeland. And that was what wear you down. You were programmed for the fact as American fighting men that we were still fighting a civilized war. And you don't fight a civilized war. It's nothing civilized about—about war. . . .

I think we were the last generation to believe, you know, in the honor of war. There is no honor in war.

My mama still thinks that I did my part for my country, 'cause she's a very patriotic person.

I don't.

Melvin Laird came to inspect the hospital. . . . I'm wheeling this guy on a stretcher who is quite obviously missing both legs. . . . Well, I realized it's Melvin Laird and now's my chance. My first impulse was to strangle him. . . . And then I thought, "Well, [s——], if this person with me, this guy on the stretcher, isn't enough. . . ." Just that Laird has to live with knowing that he's sending all these boys over there to have this happen to them. . . .

As they walked by, single file, bald-headed Melvin Laird in his three-hundred-dollar suit, I looked right for his eyes. . . . And that son of a bitch walked head on—didn't even look to the right or left of him. . . . He didn't bat an eye and he didn't look.[128]

Antiwar Movement

Soldiers who felt betrayed by their government also felt intense hostility toward antiwar protesters at home. Opposition to American involvement in Vietnam had started almost as soon as the war began, and was first centered around pacifists and students on college campuses who saw the conflict as immoral, racist, and economically motivated. By 1969, the antiwar feeling had become widespread. The high cost of the war was leading to higher taxes and serious inflation, affecting everyone from businessmen to housewives. The revelation of the My Lai massacre (the mass murder of several hundred Vietnamese civilians by U.S.

combat troops in the village of My Lai) proved incontestably that American soldiers were hurting rather than helping the Vietnamese people. Polls showed that over half of all Americans felt that the war was a mistake. A one-day moratorium against the war in October 1969 resulted in millions of working people staying home in protest.

Many times, protesters included American soldiers on their lists of those responsible for perpetuating the war and its evils. GIs naturally resented such animosity. The knowledge that their efforts were not valued and supported at home was both depressing and demoralizing. One man wrote home, "It hurts so much sometimes to see the paper full of demonstrators, especially people burning the flag. Fight fire with fire, we ask here. Display the flag, Mom and Dad. . . . It means so much to us to know we're supported, to know not everyone feels we're making a mistake being here."[129]

Adding to GIs' resentment was their conviction that protesters and draft dodgers had no credible basis for opposing the war, and that they did so without first-hand knowledge of the stupidity and unfairness of the conflict. Many soldiers felt, consciously or subconsciously, that those at

Antiwar protesters carry signs showing bleeding American, South Vietnamese, and North Vietnamese flags.

home were not only cowardly and intent on degrading servicemen's sacrifices, but they were usurping the right of GIs to be the valid voice of protest. One tried to express this feeling:

To so many of us the peace phalanx [army] parading American streets were the spoiled, gutless middle class kids who cowered in college classrooms to escape the battlefield and who, to soothe their cowards' consciences and regain their lost self-respect . . . now campaigned with . . . envy to destroy what honor and prestige we might earn through our courage and sacrifices in battle.[130]

Feeling Bad

It was hard for soldiers to fight a "crazy" war that made no sense, and hard to know that they lacked support from the American people when they were risking their lives for their country. Alone, and surrounded by so much killing and dying, soldiers often felt intensely lonely and homesick, and relied on letters from friends and family for comfort. "Mom, I appreciate all your letters," wrote one GI. "I appreciate your concern that some of the things you write about are trivial, but they aren't trivial to me. I'm eager to read anything about what you are doing or the family is doing. You can't understand the importance these 'trivial' events take on out here. It helps keep me civilized."[131]

At times, news from home only added to their misery, however. One man wrote his wife,

My RTO [radiotelephone operator], who has 28 days to go, cracked up. He was shaking and crying, not loud, but the tears were running down his face. . . . [In] the last couple of letters he has received from home, his wife has said she didn't care whether he came back or not. . . . It is bad enough over here. But when your wife writes [s——] like that, it completely destroys a man.[132]

Despite difficulties and disillusionment, however, soldiers still had orders and assignments to carry out, and they relied on a variety of private motivations and reasons to get them through. Some chose to see the war as their job, a project that had

A dejected American infantryman holds his head in his hands after reading a letter from home.

to be completed before they could go home. "My goal was work, do anything to keep busy to pass the time as quickly as possible,"[133] states veteran Myron Yancey. Some were determined to gain the respect of others in the unit, to become the most macho, the man with the most kills to his credit. Regulars in combat units sometimes fought because they loved to cause pain, or for "payback"—to retaliate for the loss of a friend. "If anybody got hurt, we wanted revenge more than anything else," says one veteran. "Every time we got psyched up for a patrol it was to pay 'em back. . . . Payback was all we were doing."[134]

Goodness and Humanity

Many soldiers were able to maintain a positive focus and retain their goodness and humanity amidst the savagery of the war. For some, it was as simple as nurturing friendships with buddies, performing kind or unselfish acts for other men in the unit, or having a pet to love.

Although American troops slaughtered an incredible number of animals—from snakes and rats to chickens and water buffalo—in the course of their search-and-destroy missions, they had a weakness for dogs, particularly neglected or mistreated strays. "They adopted dogs, none of them very big, who grew fat and playful. They were cuddled, scratched, teased, talked to,

A soldier cradles two puppies he found on a search-and-destroy mission.

wormed, washed and overfed. . . . There were puppies everywhere,"[135] wrote one newspaper correspondent who visited the area.

Dogs were not the only pets of choice, however. In 1969, records showed that soldiers returning to the United States carried with them a total of thirty-three cats, nineteen reptiles, twenty monkeys, twenty-six birds, and one fox.

Other GIs reached out to South Vietnamese civilians, whose poverty and war losses touched and saddened them. Some gave extra support—money or gifts—to a well-liked servant or a favorite prostitute from the nearby town. Some volunteered their services to schools and hospitals. One man says, "Sometimes I would collect food

Something for the Children

Many soldiers became hardened and disillusioned in Vietnam. Others retained their humanity and focused on aiding those who were being hurt by the war. Bruce McInnes was one of the latter, and his passion for helping children is expressed in a letter to his mother, published in *Dear America: Letters Home from Vietnam,* edited by Bernard Edelman.

One day when I wasn't scheduled to fly, my platoon leader, Capt. Roy Ferguson, asked me if I wanted to go to the orphanage in town with him. We picked up some things some friends had sent him and went down to the Vinh-Son Orphanage and School, run by eight sisters of the Daughters of Charity of St. Vincent de Paul. . . .

I was at once ashamed and proud. Proud because we in America have so much, and ashamed because we take our good fortune for granted, wasting so much that these people, especially the children in this orphanage, so desperately need. Things like blankets and sheets, clothes for little boys and girls, even shoes. . . .

The shame of it all is that these children had nothing to do with bringing all this on themselves. It's hard to sympathize with someone who causes his own misfortune. These children, though, are the victims not of their generation, but of yours and mine. Many are orphans because their parents have been killed. They haven't died of old age or heart attacks . . . they've been killed by terrorism while defending their homes, their country, their freedom. Others are orphans as a result of the assistance we have given to their country. We have fathered many children, unable to take them home, their mothers unable to care for them. You and I must do something for these children, for this orphanage (so it) can expand its work and care for children who now walk the streets with no one, no one at all.

Vietnamese orphans receive a push on their swings by three American soldiers, who bought the swing set for the orphans.

that we didn't eat to take to an orphanage or give it to refugees. . . . I taught English to the orphans. If a house was destroyed someplace, me and my driver and some Vietnamese would rebuild the building."[136]

Some soldiers fell in love with girls they met, married them, and brought them back to the United States after the war. This was easier said than done. The military discouraged such marriages and required a great deal of paperwork before the woman could leave the country. Often a soldier's term of duty ended, and he was required to return home without his chosen bride. Some couples never saw each other again. Despite such complications, in 1969 alone, over 450 American soldiers received permission to marry South Vietnamese women and remove them from the war zone.

Some good-hearted GIs encountered animosity and opposition from those who lacked such generous impulses. Interpreter Emmanuel J. Holloman, who helped provide reparations to South Vietnamese civilians who had lost property or family members, says, "I expected the Vietnamese to give me hell sometimes. That came with the job. But some of my own people hated me. Guys would call me gook lover. Sometimes worse. They would call me turncoat or traitor. That was the worst part."[137]

Mistrust and Intolerance

While some soldiers possessed qualities that enabled them to retain their humanity, other men lacked such balance and perspective. They had assumed that they would become friends with the Vietnamese civilians. Instead they were often ridiculed and scorned, or seen as easy marks for beggars and thieves. "I thought we were supposed to be over there to help these people and right off the bat I feel like a total idiot, like a tourist in some country where everyone hates the rich Americans,"[138] comments one man.

The fact that any civilian, no matter how innocent and friendly they seemed, might throw a hand grenade the moment a soldier's back was turned, heightened GIs' mistrust of the Vietnamese. Many soldiers found it safest and most practical simply to assume that all Vietnamese were hostile and treat them accordingly. South Vietnamese civilians were regularly mistreated and abused on the slightest pretense, and soldiers expressed shock and outrage when their misbehavior was censured by superiors.

Racism also played a role in GIs' attitudes toward the Vietnamese. Men who held racist views found it easy to believe that the Vietnamese did not suffer as intensely as Caucasians and that their deaths were unimportant except as a measure of victory or loss. Even GIs who were more fair-minded were sometimes inclined to lump all natives in a group, scorning them as nothing but "dinks" and "gooks." Ironically, this latter group of GIs included blacks. "Yeah, we called the Vietnamese gooks too. Almost everybody took on some racist feelings, no question. When you're in combat you don't really think about the right and wrong of it,"[139] one black veteran says.

Like men in covert forces, once ordinary American soldiers began believing that accepted rules of humanity did not apply to the Vietnamese, almost any behavior became legitimate. In addition to burning villages, killing farm animals, and poisoning wells, soldiers sometimes killed villagers simply because they were in the wrong place at the wrong time.

Hootches full of children and old people were sprayed with bullets on the off chance that the enemy might be hiding inside. Old persons, running to warn families that the Americans were coming, were liable to be shot as well. "It wasn't s'posed to be nobody out at nights but the Marines," one veteran observes. "Any Vietnamese out at night was the enemy."[140]

Rapes of village women occurred, with murder often following. Villagers suspected of having knowledge of Viet Cong or North Vietnamese army activities were threatened and killed, sometimes by being taken up in a helicopter and tossed out. Black vet Haywood T. Kirkland says, "This brother and the squad leader, a white dude, for some reason thought they could interrogate this man. This man wasn't speaking any English. They did not speak any Vietnamese. . . . I turned around and

Ear Collectors

GIs who carried out covert operations and became experts at guerrilla warfare were both fascinating and frightening to ordinary soldiers. Drawn from the army, navy, and marines, these tough soldiers were the stuff that legends were made of, as an anonymous veteran relates in Mark Baker's book, *Nam*.

We hung out at a bar halfway between [Da Nang] and Quang Tri. That's where I met this guy called Eighty-nine. Eighty-nine got the name because he killed eighty-nine men in one day. . . .

When his unit came in the bar, everybody else in the joint would shift out of the way. . . . A lot of them had one long braid down one side of their face. Some part of their heads was shaved. . . . .Eighty-nine and his men was Marine Recon [Marine Reconnaissance]. I had a lot of respect for them. They were all crazy, but I respected them. They were ear collectors.

They lay these ears on the bar. The guy who had the most ears that didn't match up in pairs had to buy rounds for all the rest the whole night. . . . I was fascinated with this group of men. . . . I don't remember how I actually got to talking to this guy Eighty-nine, but I found out that he really believed in what he was doing. That was the difference. We were there because we didn't want to go to jail or whatever our reason was, but he was there because he believed it.

I kind of felt sorry for them in a way. They got there and found out that their talent was killing and they were damn good at it. They had a taste of killing and they all liked it. Now when the war ended, what were they going to do? Once you reach the peak it's all downhill.

the man was gone. I didn't actually see him pushed, but he was gone. It took a long time for me to believe it."[141]

At times, soldiers mutilated those they killed as payback for atrocities committed by the enemy. The most macho GIs cut off victim's ears and wore them on thongs around their necks. "When we first started going into the fields, I would not wear a finger, ear, or mutilate another person's body. Until I had the misfortune to come upon those American soldiers who were castrated. Then it got to be a game,"[142] says one.

Massacre at My Lai

Wanton violence against the Vietnamese was highlighted by the My Lai massacre in March 1968. During that incident, a U.S. infantry company entered the hamlet of My Lai in the Quang Ngai province, apparently on a routine search-and-destroy mission. The area was known to harbor many Viet Cong, and the GIs had suffered casualties earlier in the week from booby traps and snipers. Thus, some approached the hamlet with murder on their minds. Their subsequent actions sparked hours of mayhem that had lifelong repercussions for all concerned.

No resistance was offered by villagers, but some GIs began shooting as they entered the village. The violence quickly escalated. Hootches were burned, animals slaughtered, women raped, a Buddhist monk shot at point blank range. Many of the soldiers shouted and laughed as they carried out their work. "The boys enjoyed it," one ex-GI points out. "When someone laughs and jokes about what they're doing, they have to be enjoying it."[143]

Lieutenant William Calley was in charge of one of the platoons, and as the morning progressed, he directed the roundup of some seventy villagers. At his orders, they were pushed into a ditch and sprayed repeatedly with automatic-weapon fire. Author Seymour M. Hersh, who first brought the story to America's attention in 1969, writes,

> One further incident stood out in many GIs' minds. Seconds after the shooting stopped, a bloodied but unhurt two-year-old boy miraculously crawled out of the ditch, crying. He began running toward the hamlet. Someone hollered, "There's a kid." There was a long pause. Then Calley ran back, grabbed the child, threw him back in the ditch and shot him.[144]

Before the day was over, almost five hundred women, children, and old persons lay dead. The killing went on so long that men took rest breaks, smoking cigarettes, or eating C-rations.

Not everyone took part in the killing. American helicopter pilot Hugh Thompson risked his life when he set his machine down in the midst of a group of angry GIs and rescued several injured villagers. Thompson and several other men complained of atrocities committed that day,

Helicopter pilot Hugh Thompson (left) helped initiate the investigation into the My Lai massacre and its leaders, including Lieutenant William Calley (above).

and their complaints helped lead to an investigation of the incident. Criminal charges were eventually brought against eighteen officers. For all but Calley, however, charges were dismissed or the men were acquitted.

Calley was later convicted of over one hundred counts of murder. Many of the rest of the company—grunts who obeyed orders—bore their own personal punishment for what they had done. They brooded on the incident, felt deep remorse, and even years later would cry in shame for what they had done. "It was the worst thing that ever happened to me,"[145] one man acknowledges.

Escaping the War

Many GIs were deeply ashamed when they began to enjoy the act of killing, when their initial reluctance to take a human life was replaced by a feeling of power or a thirst for revenge. Even those who did not kill out of anger or pleasure were troubled that they had become so calloused to the violence and the ugliness of the war. One man, after viewing the bodies of three enemy sappers (commandos) he and his men had killed that morning, immediately went on to the mess tent and ate an excellent breakfast. He later stated, "I felt bad that my price was so low—that I could see what I did and just go on in and have breakfast.

It made me question what is really important to me. Is life? What do I take your life for, a dollar and a half? I tried to tell myself, ah, they're just gooks. But they weren't dead animals, they were dead people."[146]

Both men and women were disturbed by their growing hatred of the Vietnamese and the tendency to regard their deaths as meaningless because they were "the enemy." One helicopter gunner observes,

> You begin . . . to understand how genocide takes place. I consider myself a decent man, but I did mow those people down from my helicopter. . . . I tried to compensate in my head that most of the people we were wasting were the enemy. But I could appreciate in a black way that you can take anybody given the right circumstances and turn him into a wholesale killer. That's what I was. I did it. Bizarre. That's what it was. It was very bizarre.[147]

In reaction to those feelings, and to the shocking acts they witnessed and carried out, many began experiencing mental and emotional breakdowns, insomnia, crying jags, and other unexpected behaviors. A few went on shooting sprees. Others deserted from the army. Alcohol use increased as some tried to ease the memory of too many horrors and the frustration they felt at having been placed in an unbearable situation. "I did a lot of drinking over there," says one female communications specialist. "I started to drink to cover feelings. I was one of those people who dealt with it by not dealing with it, and so a lot of my spare time was spent hitting the booze bottle and playing my guitar, anything that would make it go away for awhile."[148]

Many GIs used marijuana as a form of relaxation and release, because the drug could be easily purchased from many Vietnamese. "It was very powerful stuff and everybody got real happy. . . . Most of the time I hated everything about Vietnam. But when I was stoned I could really ap-

Two soldiers try to recover their equilibrium after a firefight. Some were overwhelmed by the horrors of combat and experienced emotional breakdowns.

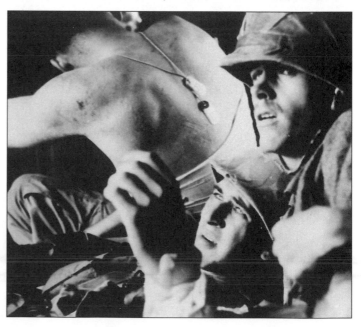

preciate the beauty of the country," [149] one veteran testifies.

Heroin and amphetamines were also popular. Heroin became widely available after 1970, and small vials were purchased for as little as two dollars in powder form. GIs used it, like marijuana, to ease anxiety, and because it seemed to make time pass more rapidly. Many mistakenly believed that they could not become addicted if they did not inject the drug, and by 1971, at least 10 percent of GIs in Vietnam were "hooked" and had to cope with their addiction when they returned home. Amphetamines were often administered by medics to help ease men's fatigue. Many men believed "uppers" made them better fighters, and amphetamines were at least partially responsible for some of the unnecessary violence that was committed during the war.

Ghosting and Sandbagging

Drugs and alcohol helped many soldiers cope with the boredom, the loneliness, and the horrors of war, but for others, mental escape was not enough. Men who were no longer willing to face the perils of patrol pretended to be sick, invented a death in the family which entailed a leave back to the United States, or went AWOL (absent without leave) for a short time. Such avoidance mechanisms were termed "ghosting." The penalty for getting caught was a sentence in the stockade or jail, but even that was a means of avoiding combat.

Some men took even more drastic measures to get out of fighting. They stopped taking their malaria pills so that they would really become ill. The most reckless inflicted a minor wound upon themselves, or convinced a friend to do it, in order to get into the hospital for at least a few days. One man recalls,

> I told this friend of mine . . . that I was going to throw a grenade around the corner of this hootch and stick my leg out. I wanted to go home. I wasn't going to do this anymore. I didn't know how to reconcile what I was doing. I was standing there, shaking and crying, and he's telling me, "You're stupid man. You're stupid. You're going to blow your leg off. . . ." He talked me out of doing it. [150]

In time, whole units dared to rebel against missions that seemed particularly hopeless or pointless. Some mutinied and refused outright to go into a fight where they believed they might all be killed. Sympathetic officers often cooperated by not reporting them to superiors. Other units "sandbagged"—that is, when they were sent on night patrols or other perilous assignments, they took refuge in a safe locale and radioed in fabricated reports as if they were carrying out their mission.

Fragging

When superior officers were unsympathetic and refused to cooperate with sandbagging schemes, or when an officer constantly endangered men's lives due to ambition or stupidity, a few GIs resorted to "fragging"—murder or attempted murder. The term came from the use of fragmentation grenades, which were popular because they could be tossed into an officer's sleeping quarters, where they exploded without leaving fingerprint evidence. Grenades were not the only weapons used for fragging, however, and some battle-hardened GIs did not hesitate to punish a superior for almost any offense, as one soldier explains:

> A friend of mine put sixteen rounds in a staff sergeant's back in Vietnam. The staff sergeant . . . was just an incredibly short-tempered, evil man. They would go out humping for eighteen days, come home, and he'd hold a full field inspection. . . . You had to unload, clean your weapon, stand a full field inspection, and you only got three hours' sleep that night. . . . Sleep is the most valuable thing in the world over there. If anybody [f——] with your sleep, you want to take their ass off.[151]

Fraggings were usually collaborative attempts, not personal vendettas, and oc-

curred more often later in the war, when increasing numbers of soldiers questioned their willingness to suffer and die for those who were unappreciative of their sacrifice.

War's End

By 1970, fewer and fewer soldiers wanted to be involved in the war. The rock song, "We Gotta Get out of This Place," by the Animals, expressed the fondest wish of most men and women who served in Vietnam. Cathleen Cordova, once a member of Army Special Services, writes, "The majority of the guys aren't concerned with issues, moral judgments or politics. Most of them are young guys who didn't want to come here, and they just want to get out in one piece."[152]

To everyone's relief, a cease-fire was signed on January 27, 1973. American forces came home shortly thereafter. The suffering was not at an end, however, as veterans who returned home quickly learned. Author Mark Baker writes, "Simple things [had changed] in a year—clothing, hairstyles and television shows—but nothing had changed as much as they had. They had seen too much, done too much. And now they found out that they had hoped for too much."[153]

Chapter 6

Somber Homecoming

GIs reacted to the news that they were going home—whether at the end of a one-year tour or at the end of the war—with great happiness. Most men and women were overjoyed that they had survived the conflict and could return to "the World."

Some felt nervous, however, at the thought of giving up a life that had become very familiar. They were sad at the thought of losing friends, afraid that reality would not measure up to their dreams of the future. One young woman says, "When it was my turn to go home, I got sick the week before. To this day, I don't know whether it was psychological or not. I had dysentery and I lost about fifteen pounds in a week. But I also was getting more and more anxious. I couldn't eat. I couldn't even swallow. I had a hard time breathing."[154] GIs who left after the cease-fire was signed in 1973 often felt angry that America was withdrawing without winning the war, that all the years of sacrifice had been for nothing.

For many soldiers, departure from Nam was abrupt. GIs found themselves in the air or on an aircraft carrier steaming across the Pacific within hours of coming out of the field. Some did not have a chance to shower and change into clean clothes before they were on their way. Many were thinner and more silent than when they had arrived. Some were on crutches or strapped to stretchers.

Despite the drawbacks, however, most were jubilant when reality finally sank in. "Me and my buddy Al rotated out at the same time. . . . I looked at Al and I started laughing. I said, 'Al, I think we made it.' He started laughing. We laughed so hard that we were crying. We couldn't stand up. My sides ached. We made it."[155]

Welcome Home

A soldier not only left Vietnam abruptly, but due to the wonders of air travel he often arrived back home within hours of leaving the war zone. The experience could

The Kid Is Coming Home!

Nothing could top the elation felt by young GIs who looked forward to returning home; a letter to loved ones often heralded the happy occasion. Editor Bernard Edelman notes that different versions of the following letter circulated in Vietnam, but this one was sent by private David Bowman, and published in *Dear America: Letters Home from Vietnam.*

Dear Civilians, Friends, Draft Dodgers, etc.,

In the very near future, the undersigned will once more be in your midst, dehydrated and demoralized, to take his place again as a human being. . . . In making your joyous preparations to welcome him back into organized society you might take certain steps to make allowances for the past twelve months. . . .

A veteran returning from Vietnam raises his arms in jubilation.

Show no alarm if he insists on carrying a weapon to the dinner table, looks around for his steel pot when offered a chair, or wakes you up in the middle of the night for guard duty. . . . Pretend not to notice if he acts dazed, eats with his fingers instead of silverware and prefers C-rations to steak. Take it with a smile when he insists on digging up the garden to fill sandbags for the bunker he is building. Be tolerant when he takes his blanket and sheet off the bed and puts them on the floor to sleep on. . . .

When in his daily conversation he utters such things as 'Xin loi' and 'Choi oi' just be patient, and simply leave quickly and calmly if by some chance he utters "didi" with an irritated look on his face because it means no less than "Get the h—— out of here." Pretend not to notice if at a restaurant he calls the waitress "Numbuh 1 girl" and uses his hat as an ashtray. . . .

Last but not least, send no more mail to the APO, fill the ice box with beer, get the civvies out of mothballs, fill the car with gas, and get the women and children off the streets—BECAUSE THE KID IS COMING HOME!!!!!

Love, Dave

be disorienting and overwhelming. There were so many people in U.S. airports, so many bright lights, so many restaurants, so much civilization.

Family reunions made up for the discomfort for some. "They met me with roses," one army nurse remembers, "and my brothers had these torches across the front lawn and a huge sign, 'Welcome Home Lt. Crissy.'"[156] For others, homecoming was an emotional letdown. "I got out of Vietnam the sixth of June, got home the eighth," recalls one man. "All of a sudden I found myself at one or two in the morning standing outside Oakland Air Force Base in my dress greens. I was out of the Army. . . . How anticlimactic it was. Nobody met me at the airport. Nobody knew I was coming home."[157]

Everyone—GIs, family, and friends—soon discovered that twelve months of war had changed returning veterans. Colors appeared too bright after the greens and browns of Vietnam. Air conditioned supermarkets were unbearably cold. Beds were too soft. Welcome-home parties seemed inane and pointless. Old friends, old routines, and old pleasures were no longer fulfilling. One man observes, "I dropped back into the old neighborhood and nothing had changed. They were the same people in the same situation with the same head. . . . It was like I never left. But I *did* leave. I wasn't the same anymore."[158]

Veterans were no longer the naive youths they had been before the war. They no longer saw things from the standard, middle-class "American" perspective that their parents did. Some men were physically scarred and disabled—blind, amputees, paraplegics, and quadriplegics permanently confined to wheelchairs and beds. Most had witnessed life at its worst, and were confused, disillusioned, battleworn, and angry.

Yet now, they were expected to be "normal" again, and that was difficult.

Soldiers dodge enemy fire as they rush to board a helicopter. After such harrowing experiences, many vets found it difficult to readjust to civilian life.

(VVA), was established in 1978. Its aims were to change the public's perception of Vietnam veterans as well as promote issues that were vital to veterans' recovery and well-being. Over the next twenty years, the VVA grew to include over fifty thousand members and worked to help veterans rebuild a sense of self-worth, gain access to benefits, pass laws which supported increased job training and placement for unemployed vets, and create the Vietnam Veterans Assistance Fund, which provides financial assistance to vets in need.

Such actions improved the economic status of those who were disabled or unemployed, gave vets the opportunity to get together, to share experiences and problems, and to let the public know of their war-related problems. "I feel better when I talk about Vietnam and get it out of me every once in a while," says one vet. "You can't keep it inside you. If it's in you it stays in you."[177]

Changing Misconceptions

As light was shed on those problems, public feelings grew more sympathetic. By the mid-1980s, Vietnam vets were honored in Veterans Day parades across the United States and hailed as heroes who had been unjustly treated in the wake of the war. Politicians and the press spoke of lessons learned—that no matter how unpopular a future war might be, America's greatest responsibility was to her fighting forces, who deserved unswerving support for their willingness to serve.

The attention did much to heal old wounds, although some veterans remain skeptical. "I think there's a national guilt complex emerging over the way they all

Delayed Stress

Like many Vietnam veterans, nurse Anne Simon Auger was not aware that she was experiencing delayed post-traumatic stress disorder nine years after the war. In Keith Walker's *A Piece of My Heart,* Auger describes the moment of discovery that eventually motivated her to join a support group and work out her emotional problems.

About nine years after I got out of Vietnam, I read an article in the paper about this guy in Oregon who'd gone berserk and shot somebody. At his trial they named his condition delayed stress syndrome. I had never heard of it before. But the article described some of the symptoms. And I kept saying, "That's me, that's me! This is exactly it. I can't believe this!" So that evening I brought the article to [my husband] Rick and said, "Don't laugh, but. . . ." Rick and I are very open about everything, talk about absolutely everything, but I never talked to him about my nightmares or my depressions. I didn't want to burden him, I guess, or I didn't want to talk about it. I'm not sure which. I asked, "Did you ever notice things like that about me and just not say anything?" And he said, "Yeah, exactly. . . ." So I spent six months reading up on delayed stress. And it was a relief just to find out what it was that was making me do this stuff. But I still had the nightmares. I still had the depression. I'd go through periods of relative calm and serenity, and then I'd turn around and start screaming at the kids, or at Rick, or the dog. I'd ventilate that way for a while, and then we'd go back to serenity again.

From living on the brink of death and coping with responsibilities beyond their years, veterans had become ordinary citizens who were slightly out of synch with society. "One day you have a license to kill," says one. "The next day, a cop pulls you over for speeding. One day you're with people you'd trust with your life. The next day you have to sit alone in the far corner of the bar so nobody will see you and identify you as a Vietnam veteran."[159]

"Anything, but Vietnam"

The disgrace of being a Vietnam veteran hit some GIs the moment they returned to the United States. Strangers approached uniformed soldiers in airports, asking them how many innocent civilians they had killed. Some spit on them, pushed them, called them "baby killers" and "Nazis."

Even civilians who were not hostile viewed returning vets warily, unsure of what to say, uneasy in the presence of those who represented much that was controversial and unpopular in America. A great many people avoided talking about Vietnam with returning veterans. "The minister of our church never mentioned Vietnam to me when I returned," remembers one veteran. "He knew where I'd been. He knew my family. But he never asked me how I felt about my time over there. He never said a word."[160]

Others chose to treat the topic casually—out of embarrassment or a dislike of getting too personal—and confined their comments to such innocuous remarks as

"Oh, were you in the war?" and "I'll bet you're glad to be home." One soldier who lost his leg in combat observes, "When I got back to the real world, it seemed nobody cared that you'd been to Vietnam. As a matter of fact, everybody would be wondering where have you been for so long. They would say, how did you lose your leg? In a fight? A car wreck? Anything, but Vietnam."[161]

Fitting into the Old Routine

Despite such discourtesy and indifference, the majority of veterans quietly resumed normal routines on their return and set about finding jobs, going to college, getting married, and getting on with their lives. Some had a year of military service left and put in their time on bases around the United States. Some went back to jobs they had held before being drafted or sought out new opportunities in law enforcement, education, and business. The majority went on to enjoy lives and careers comparable to other ordinary Americans, while a number rose to positions of honor and prestige due to their accomplishments after the war.

For some veterans, however, the transition was not as easy. Many decided that the discomforts of Vietnam were better than the dullness, aggravation, and superficiality of civilian life and reenlisted. "I missed the place," one nurse says. "I missed the intensity, the people, all of it, so much. I said, 'Please let me go back,' but they wouldn't let me, and it's a good thing."[162]

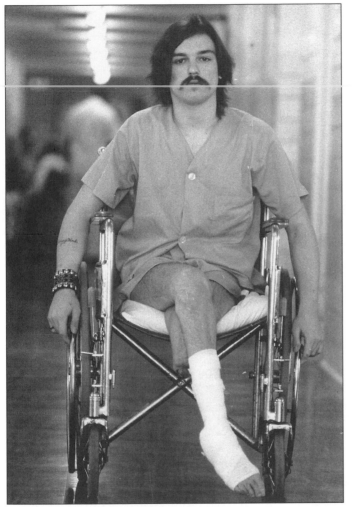

People were often uncomfortable talking to wounded vets about Vietnam and the injuries they had received there.

For many, jobs were hard to find. They had gone to war shortly after high school and had little or no work experience. Now they were at the bottom of the work ladder and had to be satisfied with menial posi-tions, despite the fact that they had been given important as-signments in Vietnam. Many got angry over such injustice and drifted in and out of work for years. The most disillusioned turned to crime—drug running, bank robbing, and the like. "Do-ing stick-ups was like being in Nam going on patrol," explains one vet. "I had a reason for do-ing what I was doing, some sense of priorities. It gave me direction and a sense of being."[163]

Psychological Turmoil

Lawbreaking was only one of many ways that vets expressed their emotional and psychologi-cal turmoil on returning home. Many made an enormous effort to lead normal lives but found that their memories, their anger, and their disillusionment were crippling. Atrocities they had wit-nessed—perhaps even commit-ted—left many feeling debased and depressed. Some felt great rage at the government and the military who had turned them into trained killers. They be-came antiwar activists; Vietnam Veterans Against the War was organized in 1967. Some felt guilty for surviving when friends had died. "To this day it's still hard for me to find my place," says one. "Now I'm a civilian. I'm not in the military anymore. That elation of going out and killing and

Memories of Nam

The aftereffects of serving in Vietnam were unexpected and terrifying, especially for veterans who did not get proper attention or care. In his book *Bloods,* author Wallace Terry includes specialist Charles Strong's account of flashbacks he began having after leaving the army in 1972. Strong served in Vietnam from 1969 to 1970.

I started having flashbacks. When I would lay down and dream at night, my mind would play tricks on me. I still had my jungle boots and fatigues. And when it would rain real hard, I would put them on and go wherever I wanted to go. I would be ducking around in the bushes, crawling around just like you do in actual combat. And I would do silly stuff like breaking out the street lamps, and they put me in jail a couple of times for being disorderly.

But I did a really strange thing. I had this little .22 [revolver]. Something prompted me to turn it into the police department. It was a good thing, too. Because I got real mad at my wife one day. I put on my fatigues, and put this ice pick at my side. When I couldn't find her, I just totally demolished the house. People called the police, but they couldn't find me. I just lightly eased out of the house and went across the street, where there were some high bushes. It was dark and stuff, and I moved just like I learned in Vietnam. I thought I could keep running forever. But after thirty minutes, I cooled off and got out of the bushes and went back over to the house. The neighbors said they didn't know what was wrong with me. The police didn't take me to jail but to the hospital, where they put me in the psychiatric ward for four days. And the psychiatrist told me I loved my wife too much. Nothing about Vietnam.

having somebody try to kill you, the comradery [camaraderie] I had with men was something I've never found since then. You look for that."[164]

These unresolved feelings of disillusionment, bitterness, and depression surfaced in unexpected ways. Some vets developed physical symptoms such as trembling hands, insomnia, hallucinations, or flashbacks during which they lost touch with reality. Many were irritable, seemed to lack affection for loved ones, and experienced irrational attacks of anger. Panic attacks were common, too. "That first Fourth of July was the hardest thing for me to get through. I was in a big store and somebody threw firecrackers. I crouched down. People laughed at me. I felt like somebody dropped a safe out a window on me,"[165] recounts one veteran.

Some men had repeated nightmares where they woke up screaming. "At first I would wake up with my arms and hands all scarred from hitting the walls," recalls another. "I was having dreams in which I would run out of ammunition and we were getting overrun. And this VC is coming at me with a machine gun. I jump him, and I'm killing him."[166]

To numb their pain, many veterans turned again to alcohol and drugs. Their marriages broke up after unpredictable, distant, and violent behavior drove away bewildered spouses. Some men went to prison as a result of brawling, abuse, robbery to support drug habits, and the like. Some became intensely fearful, even paranoid, and carried a gun at all times. "A lot of vets back here in the World just picked up rifles and started shooting people," one man comments. "I can understand that. They could not adjust. They [the military] just threw us back into a place that we were untrained to live in. They should have had to train us to come back into the World."[167]

Some vets became so desperate and so deeply unhappy that they attempted suicide. The Veterans Administration (now the Department of Veterans Affairs) estimated that at least twenty thousand Vietnam veterans took their own lives in the years after the war. One survivor says, "I took thirty Seconal tablets and a bottle of aspirin. . . . Then I called everybody I knew

Some vets could not successfully adjust to civilian life. Here, a Vietnam veteran convicted of bank robbery sews shirts in prison.

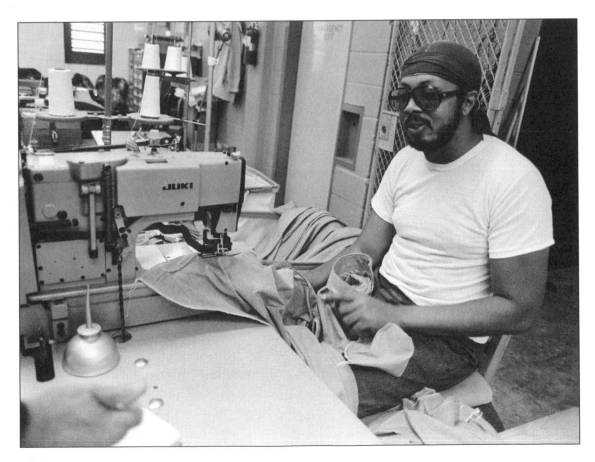

and told them goodbye. It was my last plea for somebody to help me, to say that I was worth it. A couple of vets came over and got my ass. If it wasn't for them, I wouldn't be here today."[168]

Too Little Help

In time, experts came to understand that tormented veterans were experiencing symptoms of post-traumatic stress disorder, a condition that can develop after an individual experiences traumatic or life-threatening events. The Veterans Administration (VA), a government agency established in 1930 to administer benefits for veterans, eventually acknowledged that at least half a million Vietnam veterans suffered and still suffer from the disorder. Other specialists place the number much higher because many vets experienced milder symptoms and did not seek help for them.

In the 1970s, such expressions of pain were poorly understood, however. "I think the Army made a drastic mistake in that they didn't do any deprogramming [to counteract the effects of the war]. . . . We got home from Vietnam and we were out of the Army. Never once did anyone talk to us about what was going to happen, but I don't think they knew what was going to happen to us either,"[169] observes one Army nurse.

Veterans usually suffered alone, not even aware that there were others who shared their anguish. The military did little or nothing to help ease their reentry to society. One man says bitterly, "I went to Wal-

English Muffins

As one nurse describes in Mark Baker's book, *Nam,* veterans who returned from Vietnam sometimes experienced violent, irrational bursts of anger over mere trivialities. Family and friends often tried to ignore or overlook such outbursts, unaware that the eruptions were symptoms of serious, stress-related disorders.

My dad had this toaster that was very touchy. You had to drop the English muffins in just right for them to go down automatically. I couldn't get the English muffins to drop in. I'd stand there and drop them in easy, and then drop them in hard, then I'd slam them in. My father would say, "Look, just like this." He'd pick up an English muffin, drop it in the toaster and they'd go down right away. . . .

I got downstairs one morning before my folks got up and those G[—— d——] English muffins would not go down. I threw the toaster against the wall. I picked it up and threw it against the wall again. I kept throwing it against the wall until I couldn't throw it anymore. I'd been home about a week when that happened. There were a billion trillion crumbs everywhere.

My dad never said a word. He just looked at me. I said in a small voice, "The English muffins wouldn't go down. You know?"

ter Reed [Army Medical Center] first. They put me in a situation with about thirty-four people in a room. How in the hell are you gonna talk to me about my problems with thirty-four other problems in your face? I went to the VA hospital in Baltimore, and they gave me two aspirins and told me to go to bed and call in the morning."[170]

Those veterans who received help often did so from local support groups. Veteran Charles Strong, who suffered from flashbacks and violent rages, says, "When I came back from Vietnam, I was not given any psychological assistance from various organizations like the VA. I had to use my relationship in the church to help me adjust to civilian life."[171]

Not only did they receive little assistance from the government, Vietnam vets received no official recognition of their service and their sacrifice, a fact that they deeply resented. Nurse Pat Johnson says, "I remember feeling very angry when the POWs [prisoners of war] were released from Iran [in 1981]—about the big deal

that they [Americans] made about them. I was happy for them that they had recognition but was also feeling very angry that the country couldn't rally around the Vietnam people."[172]

"A Room by Myself"

Public indifference to the veterans' plight, combined with their own psychological upheaval, led many ex-GIs to believe that America as a whole hated and despised them for the role they played in the war. In fact, such was not really the case. A 1979

Veterans resented the government's lack of assistance and recognition of the troops' sacrifices.

survey showed that antiwar hostility was actually directed more toward military and government leaders than at fighting men themselves.

Soldiers did not understand this, however. Confused by their feelings, convinced that no one cared about them, certain that their war experiences were too horrible and shameful to share, most withdrew into silence. Those who did talk generally related personal experiences or incidents that were funny or easy to tell. Many tried to conceal the pain and confusion of war, and dealt with their memories, their fears, and their physical symptoms alone and as best they could. "I would sometimes sit in a room by myself," one man remembers. "I didn't want to bother with nobody. Just be in a room by myself. Don't want to be in this so-called World. I'd be sitting there thinking about Nam. Tell myself, many's the time, 'Why didn't I die in the Nam, like they told me? I don't belong here in this World.'" [173]

It would take over a decade before veterans and the nation as a whole began to come to terms with the devastation left by Vietnam.

Chapter 7

Legacy of Vietnam

On March 29, 1973, the last U.S. ground forces left South Vietnam, marking the formal end of American involvement in the war. Peace was short-lived, however. Hostilities resumed between the Communists and the South Vietnamese government later that year, and fighting continued until April 1975, when Saigon, capital of South Vietnam, fell to the North Vietnamese army. Hundreds of thousands of South Vietnamese fled for their lives in the coming months. In America, millions of Vietnam veterans who had struggled so hard to hold back the Communist incursion faced the final, terrible truth—all their efforts had ended in failure. "The day we pulled out is the day they [the Communists] moved back, so the whole fight was for nothing," veteran J. C. Wilson says. "The guys that died died for nothing. We were fools, is what we were."[174]

The unsatisfactory conclusion to the war only added to the painful memories that plagued the young men and women who had participated in the conflict. Admittedly, some felt that their experience in Vietnam had been positive despite the hardships. One man observes, "Nam has been beneficial in coping with life. I look around at my problems and I say, 'Damn, this is nothing compared to the hell and s— I had to go through in Vietnam.'" Another says, "One of the ways that Vietnam changed my life the most is precisely the territory of compassion, kindness and caring—deeply human concern. I saw in Vietnam among men . . . more capacity for understanding and sensitivity and love than I had ever before encountered in my life."[175]

Most vets however, experienced a deep sense of pain and dislocation that did not quickly fade. Even some who believed that they had escaped unscathed found that, years later, they were relying heavily on alcohol, going from job to job, and having nervous breakdowns.

A feeling of isolation pervaded their lives. Only 10 percent of their generation

North Vietnamese troops wave a flag in front of the presidential palace in Saigon after the city was captured in April 1975.

had gone to Vietnam, so they could not assume that they were surrounded by others who had served, as was the case with men who had participated in World Wars I and II. The public's attitude made veterans cautious about revealing their pasts as well. One ex-GI, asked to share his war experiences for a book, informed the author, "When I was on the phone with you today confirming our interview, the guy sitting

two years at the desk across from me said, 'You in Nam?' He's a vet, too, and I didn't even know it."[176]

Self-Help

Tired of feeling isolated and powerless, some veterans decided to help themselves and each other. They began organizing and exerting pressure on the Veterans Administration to establish storefront counseling centers—staffed by veterans—in major cities around the United States. Through the efforts of a small group of veteran-activists, the Council of Vietnam Veterans, now known as the Vietnam Veterans of America

No Grudges

While many veterans struggle with anger and hatred, others remain at peace with themselves and their world. In Mark Baker's book, *Nam,* one unnamed veteran gives his perspective on the Vietnamese people both in his neighborhood and in the war.

> The town I live in has settled quite a few of the boat people and the refugees. We have a local newspaper and they do a lot of articles that run, "This is the latest boat people family that we've rescued from the jaws of death."
>
> . . . There are several Vietnamese children that live a few houses away. They know I'm a Vietnam veteran. At first they were sort of afraid of me. I don't know why. Maybe it's because I'm in a wheelchair. . . .
>
> I don't hold any grudges against the Vietnamese. The kids love me now. They know I'm a real sucker. The little girl came over selling Girl Scout cookies and I bought about ten dollars worth. They've got me pegged. . . .
>
> I saw the Vietnamese people [in Vietnam]. I worked with them and shared a common experience with Vietnamese soldiers as well as Americans. I found them to be just like us, only a different color and a different culture. . . . They weren't the insensitive, inscrutable people that Orientals are made out to be. They were just as saddened by someone being killed as anyone of us. The only thing I feel bad about is that we didn't allow all of them the opportunity to get out of Vietnam if they really wanted to before we let it fall.

Vietnamese refugees crowd on a boat in the Gulf of Thailand. Many veterans held no grudges against the Vietnamese.

treated us when we got back," remarks veteran Greg Skeels. "Well, no thanks. What's done is done. I just want to be left alone."[178]

A number of vets are still left with a lingering feeling of cynicism and distrust for their government, which they express by teaching their children to run to Canada before fighting in another war or by refusing to register to vote. "I never have registered to vote, and I'm not going to. I don't think that much of the country *to* vote,"[179] veteran Roy Rosson states with deep bitterness.

More veterans retain a positive outlook but continue to direct the nation's attention to issues that the government has been slow to address—among them veteran homelessness and unemployment, post-traumatic stress disorder, the toxic aftereffects of Agent Orange, and the problem of Americans who remain unaccounted for in Southeast Asia.

Post-Traumatic Stress Disorder

Hundreds of thousands of Vietnam veterans remain homeless, in prison, or repeatedly in trouble with the law due to delayed or chronic post-traumatic stress disorder (PTSD) and/or an addiction to drugs and alcohol. Despite limited resources, the National Incarcerated Veterans Program, established by veterans for veterans in the 1980s, works to educate and aid those who have served sentences and have difficulty returning to society. In 1989, the Vietnam Veterans of America called for improved treatment programs in penal institutions to aid incarcerated veterans who currently receive little or no help at all.

Outside of prisons, more help became available to veterans with PTSD after 1980. PTSD centers have been established by the Department of Veterans Affairs (formerly the Veterans Administration) where veterans can work through their guilt, anxiety, rage, and confusion in sympathetic settings. The National Center for PTSD, also sponsored by the Department of Veterans Affairs, carries out a wide range of activities in research, training, and public information. Many veterans are unaware that such aid exists, however, or are too disillusioned with the government to seek its help.

Agent Orange

Veterans are also highly concerned by chronic and worsening health problems that have been linked to Agent Orange, a herbicide used in Vietnam to defoliate the jungle and reveal enemy hiding places. Almost 20 million gallons of Agent Orange and other toxic chemicals were dispersed by plane, helicopter, truck, and handheld sprayers during the war. So widespread was its use that all soldiers who served in Vietnam now presume that they were exposed to some extent.

Shortly after the war's end, thousands of veterans began to suffer from a variety of health problems that included cancer, fevers, rashes, miscarriages, numbness and pain in the arms and legs, and other unexplained maladies. One man says,

Nobody could tell me what was wrong with me. I lost thirty pounds in a year and a half. I was skin and bones. . . . I had a terrible pain right in my liver and I just couldn't take it anymore. So I went

Getting Involved

Veterans have learned that they can improve their circumstances by lobbying their government. In Keith Walker's *A Piece of My Heart,* Lily Jean Lee Adams, who served as a nurse in Vietnam, recounts her first efforts to push for legislation that authorized research into Agent Orange. Adams went on to become involved in other veterans' issues and served on the National Board of Directors of the Vietnam Veterans of America.

I read in the newspaper how a bill in Texas had been passed to create research in Agent Orange and to provide genetic counseling. I thought, "This is what we need [in Hawaii]" so I sent the article to the representative of our state. . . . I was able to convince a lot of people to support the bill. . . . After hearing my testimony—I talked about the health problems, about my knee joint pains and how I've yet to find a doctor that can help that out. . . . And about how [my son] Daniel got adhesions and one third of his small bowel was removed and he almost died on us—the bill passed. . . .

The governor signed the bill, and I had a chat with him—changed his views about Vietnam vets, and he told me that. I got involved with other vets and coordinated a ceremony at the National Cemetery at Punchbowl on Memorial Day for all those killed or missing in Vietnam. Found myself getting very involved with the issues and feeling very good about it.

to the VA. They admitted me and kept me for about five months. They took out my spleen, my gall bladder and my appendix. They were inflamed, they said. . . . I blame it on being sprayed eight or nine times with Agent Orange in Nam. Nobody has ever seen this kind of disease before with every organ in my body eaten up.[180]

In some cases, problems showed up in veterans' children, suggesting that the herbicide had produced genetic damage. An abnormally high number of cases of spina bifida, a birth defect in which there is incomplete closure of the vertebral column during prenatal development, occurred in children born to veterans.

Other less dramatic but incapacitating conditions manifested themselves as well. One nurse/veteran whose daughter underwent three major surgeries in one year, says, "She's got all these skin rashes, problems with her knees, pains, a lot of pains. I've got a lot of things, too, Agent Orange signs and symptoms, but she has more. . . . Of course, I feel like she got a double dose, because both her father and I were over there."[181]

Vietnam veterans grew angry when the Veterans Administration denied responsibility for their health problems and initially refused to listen to their assertions that they were suffering the toxic effects of Agent Orange. Before 1989, only five of the first thirty thousand vets who filed claims were granted government benefits based on their contact with the chemical.

Convinced that many more were due compensation, veterans' organizations lobbied to promote studies that revealed the link between the herbicide and many of the diseases they exhibited. In May, 1989, a U.S. district court in San Francisco finally deemed that too severe a standard was used to determine whether veterans were suffering from exposure to Agent Orange. The government soon adopted new guidelines. Many illnesses that vets attribute to Agent Orange still remain unaccepted by the Department of Veterans Affairs, however, and veterans continue to work for greater understanding of the problem and increased aid and support for their chronic physical disability.

Planes spray Agent Orange, a chemical defoliant that may have caused severe health problems in veterans and their families.

Americans Missing in Action

Another issue of concern to Vietnam veterans is that of unreturned prisoners of war (POWs) and those soldiers who are still missing in action (MIAs). Nearly three decades after the war's end, over two thousand Americans are still unaccounted for in Southeast Asia. Many are dead, and loved ones await only the return of documents and photos that corroborate their demise. Some who were known to have been alive in captivity at the end of the war, however, may still be alive and held as POWs.

During the war years, the U.S. government's policy on POWs and MIAs consisted of playing down the issue, keeping it out of the news, and discouraging involved families from communicating with each other.

That policy did not find favor with POW families, who came together to form the National League of POW/MIA Families in 1970. The League's purpose was to obtain the release of all prisoners, to obtain the most complete account possible of all Americans missing in action in Southeast Asia, and to recover the remains of all who died while serving in the war. Families felt that they achieved significant success when almost six hundred prisoners were released at war's end in 1973.

Over time, the League has been joined by other veterans' groups, including the Vietnam Veterans of America and the Veterans of the Vietnam War, Inc., who con-tinue to work on the POW/MIA issue. They have been frustrated by bureaucracy and a lack of concern shown by both the U.S. and Vietnamese governments, but they continue to push for progress. They are also aided by the U.S. Army's Central Identification Laboratory in Hawaii, the Armed Forces DNA Identification Laboratory (AFDIL) in Washington, D.C., the Joint Task Force–Full Accounting (JTF–FA) headquartered in Hawaii, and the Defense Prisoner of War/Missing Personnel Office,

The remains of U.S. soldiers and airmen missing in action in Vietnam are repatriated in a solemn ceremony.

part of the Department of Defense. The Veterans of the Vietnam War organization states, "As long as there is one family member dissatisfied with the government's answers as to the fate of their loved one . . . we will still be in business."[182]

Monument to Sacrifice

The legacy of Vietnam has been one of pain, confusion, and broken lives. Not even greater acknowledgment of the sacrifices made by the men and women who fought and died has made up for bad memories and disfigured lives.

National commemoration was a significant step in the right direction, however. A memorial wall, erected in Washington, D.C., in 1982, gave ultimate recognition and honor to the men and women who were killed in Vietnam and stands as a monument to their sacrifice. "The Wall was more than I ever could have imagined," writes the daughter of one soldier whose name is listed there. "It touched my soul. . . . [I]t broke my heart. . . . [I]t overwhelmed my mind. . . . The Wall is a good thing . . . it Honors. . . it Remembers. . . . The Wall Heals."[183]

The Wall

Dozens of memorials have been erected across the United States commemorating the men and women who served and died in the Vietnam War. Of particular note is one in New York City, a glass wall sixteen feet high and sixty-six feet long, which exhibits excerpts of letters from American soldiers who were in the war, and serves as a site of reflection for all who visit. On the day it was dedicated—May 7, 1985—more than twenty-five thousand veterans marched across the Brooklyn Bridge and through lower Manhattan's "Canyon of Heroes" (Broadway Street), heralded by thousands of cheering New Yorkers who showered them with ticker tape and confetti. New York mayor Edward I. Koch observed on that occasion, "This welcome home was long overdue."[184]

A National Memorial

State and local monuments were moving and inspirational, but they did not speak for all of America, and could not give the national recognition for which thousands of veterans longed. That recognition came in 1982 with the creation of the national Vietnam Veterans Memorial in Washington, D.C.

Located on the Mall between the Lincoln Memorial and the Washington Monument, "the Wall" is two expanses of polished black granite, each over 246 feet long, etched with the names of the fifty-eight thousand Americans who died or are missing in the war. Names are listed according to casualty dates. The memorial makes no political statement about the war. Rather, its massiveness and stark simplicity testify to the enormity of the American sacrifice made in Vietnam. Its serene stretches inspire reflection and reconciliation. The offerings of poems, flowers, faded photos, and other tokens that visitors leave at its base personalize it and aid those who seek peace and healing in its presence. One nurse who visited the Wall by night remembers, "It was dark, and nobody could

Healing at the Wall

For many veterans who had difficulty getting over the war, a visit to the Vietnam Veterans Memorial was often beneficial. In Wallace Terry's *Bloods*, former marine Reginald Edwards relates his experience at the Wall and the inner peace it brought him.

> I met a Vietnamese soldier. North Vietnamese. In 1990. One of them leftist [left-wing or liberal] groups brought him over from Hanoi [North Vietnam]. He had been around the country trying to meet veterans, talking to veterans. Some friends of mine, some far-lefties knew him. They invited me to meet him. We spent a whole day together, talking about what it was like from his side, and see [seeing] what we experienced on our side.

> He was a grunt. He was about forty-one or forty-two. He didn't really start fighting until the late sixties. He started later than I did. He and I wouldn't have crossed paths. Now he's teacher. I liked the guy. He was a nice person. He was intelligent. He was easy to talk to. We had a translator, but he could speak English. He said basically the war was over, you know. He was looking to live in peace. It was like two veterans sitting around talking about our experiences. . . .

> When I met the North Vietnamese guy at the Memorial, he was very moved. He was very respectful of The Wall. He could see the Asian influence in the design, but he didn't know an Asian woman had done it. I told him. He was very impressed. He said it was very beautiful and sad at the same time. At first we were uptight about people knowing who he was. But when people realized who he was, they were very nice to him. He was talking to people all along The Wall. They didn't get angry with him. They didn't get upset. They were very kind to him. The vets shook his hand. I felt like the war was over.

A vet visits the Vietnam Veterans Memorial in Washington, D.C.

see me. It was the first time I really got the mourning, the grief, out. I bought a big candle and brought it back for my friend that died over there."[185]

Debate and Compromise

Just as the Vietnam War was controversial, the Wall sparked debate during its creation as well. Its design, the brainchild of Maya Ying Lin, an architectural student at Yale University, was one of over fourteen hundred entries submitted for consideration and was authorized by Congress as a fitting and thought-provoking testament to American military service in the war. Many veterans did not agree with Lin's vision.

They saw it as too abstract and impersonal, and called it "a black gash of shame" or a "giant tombstone."[186]

Because the feelings and opinions of veterans were paramount to sponsors of the project, it was decided that a more realistic representation of the Vietnam experience would be added to the memorial. A bronze sculpture, entitled "The Statue of the Three Servicemen," was erected in 1984, two years after the Wall's completion. Designer Frederick Hart describes its figures in the following words: "The contrast between the innocence of their youth and the weapons of war underscores the poignancy of their

The bronze "The Statue of the Three Servicemen" was added to the memorial in 1984.

sacrifice. . . . Their strength and their vulnerability are both evident."[187] Most Americans see Hart's sculpture as a fitting complement to the larger memorial structure.

Recognition of all who served in Vietnam was not yet complete, however. "The Statue of the Three Servicemen," did not represent the women who participated in the war, and many female veterans believed that that omission should be corrected. Led by former army nurse Diane Carlson Evans, who founded the Vietnam Women's Memorial Project in 1984, numerous female Vietnam veterans worked to create a Women's Memorial that could be placed near the Wall for all to see. Sculptor Glenna Goodacre of Santa Fe, New Mexico, was

commissioned to design a bronze statue that represents two women, one of whom cares for a wounded soldier. The Women's Memorial was dedicated in 1993. Eight trees are planted around the sculpture in memory of the eight female veterans who died in the war. Their names are also inscribed on the Wall.

Shared Responsibility

Time has passed, and America has gained some perspective on the war. The Vietnam Veterans Memorial is one of the most frequently visited sites in Washington, D.C.; war correspondent and author Wallace Terry notes, "The Vietnam veteran no longer stands in the shadows of the national memory."[188] In addition to the memorials, courses are being taught on the war in colleges and universities across the United States. Numerous movies, books, and articles have also examined the period and laid bare the injustices and misunderstandings that caused so much grief.

More remains to be done before the work is complete, however. The tragedy of Vietnam is the shared responsibility of those who fought, those who supported or tolerated a conflict marked by racism and brutality, and those who protested it but failed to recognize their obligation to support

The Women's Memorial honors the women who served in Vietnam.

those who served. The task of shouldering such responsibility and acknowledging societal wrongs may be difficult for some Americans. Author Peter Marin observes:

More than Parades

Speeches and parades helped ease the anger and frustration of Vietnam veterans who were overlooked after the war, but such tributes are not enough. According to author Christian G. Appy in *Working-Class War,* all Americans must take responsibility for their share of the social and moral cruelty of the conflict before recovery can be complete.

Eating at the souls of many veterans is the knowledge that in Vietnam they committed acts and took risks they never imagined themselves capable of—from the most heroic to the most savage—in pursuit of a cause they could neither win nor identify nor embrace. Soldiers in all wars fight for survival, but they do not find meaning in their action unless they can attach it to a just and positive purpose. In Viet-

nam, Americans had only the negative goals of destruction and survival. . . . As [author and chaplain] William Mahedy and others have argued, veterans come to terms with the war most successfully not by denying the worst of the war and their participation in it but by identifying all that was wrong about the war and sharing responsibility for it with the larger society. Only then can they fully locate what is still right and whole in themselves. . . . The recent acceptance of veterans will do nothing to help this struggle if it simply covers their experience in the warm glow of tributes and parades. It will be helpful only if America as a whole confronts the social and moral cruelty of the Vietnam War and accepts the collective responsibility to become accountable for that history and the future it continues to shape.

The "horror" of war is really very easy to confront; it demands nothing of us save the capacity not to flinch. But guilt and responsibility, if one takes them seriously, are something else altogether. For they imply a debt, something to be done, changed lives—and that is much harder on both individuals and a nation, for it implies a moral labor as strenuous and demanding as the war that preceded it.[189]

For veterans who have carried the burden alone for many years, increased public understanding and commitment will be another encouragement to leave the bitterness of the war behind.

Part of Life

The war will forever remain a fundamental part of who Vietnam veterans are, and how they see their country and their world. The war was a rite of passage, a life-altering experience, a trial-by-fire for thousands of young Americans. They were participants in its ugliness and its horrors, and only death will wipe away the memories. "When you be in combat, this lasts a lifetime," says a veteran, looking back on the conflict. "You never, ever get over this. It is a memory, a part of life that stays with you all the time. . . . You carry the scars of war around for a lifetime. This is something that you have to take to the grave."[190]

★ Notes ★

Introduction: Impossible Mission

1. Quoted in Stanley Karnow, *Vietnam: A History*. New York: Viking Press, 1983, p. 472.
2. Quoted in Christian G. Appy, *Working-Class War: American Combat Soldiers and Vietnam*. Chapel Hill: University of North Carolina Press, 1993, p. 218.
3. Quoted in *Reporting Vietnam*, vol. 1. New York: Library of America 1998, pp. 128–29.
4. Quoted in Appy, *Working-Class War*, p. 227.
5. Quoted in Karnow, *Vietnam*, p. 21.
6. Quoted in Mark Baker, *Nam*. New York: William Morrow, 1981, p. 270.
7. Al Santoli, *Everything We Had: An Oral History of the Vietnam War by Thirty-Three American Soldiers Who Fought It*. New York: Ballantine Books, 1981, pp. xv–xvi.

Chapter 1: Call to Fight

8. Quoted in Appy, *Working-Class War*, p. 11.
9. Quoted in Keith Walker, *A Piece of My Heart: The Stories of Twenty-Six American Women Who Served in Vietnam*. New York: Ballantine Books, 1985, p. 351.
10. Quoted in Karnow, *Vietnam*, p. 135.
11. Quoted in Peter Goldman, "What Vietnam Did to Us," *Newsweek*, December 14, 1981, p. 50.
12. Quoted in Bernard Edelman, ed., *Dear America: Letters Home from Vietnam*. New York: Simon and Schuster, 1985, p. 213.
13. Quoted in Baker, *Nam*, p. 33.
14. Quoted in Appy, *Working-Class War*, p. 57.
15. Quoted in Appy, *Working-Class War*, p. 72.
16. Quoted in Appy, *Working-Class War* p. 46.
17. Quoted in Baker, *Nam*, p. 40.
18. Quoted in Appy, *Working-Class War*, p. 50.
19. Quoted in Appy, *Working-Class War*, p. 35.
20. Quoted in Appy, *Working-Class War*, p. 52.
21. Quoted in Appy, *Working-Class War* p. 42.
22. Quoted in *Reporting Vietnam*, vol. 2, p. 118.
23. Quoted in Appy, *Working-Class War*, p. 86.
24. Quoted in Appy, *Working-Class War*, pp. 101–102.
25. Quoted in Appy, *Working-Class War*, p. 93.

26. Quoted in Appy, *Working-Class War,* p. 107.
27. Quoted in Appy, *Working-Class War,* p. 105.
28. Quoted in Appy, *Working-Class War,* p. 107.
29. Quoted in Baker, *Nam,* pp. 40–41.
30. Quoted in Appy, *Working-Class War,* p. 119.

Chapter 2: "Welcome to the War, Boys"

31. Quoted in Appy, *Working-Class War,* p. 118.
32. Quoted in Baker, *Nam,* p. 61.
33. Quoted in Appy, *Working-Class War,* p. 126.
34. Quoted in Appy, *Working-Class War,* p. 127.
35. Quoted in Baker, *Nam,* p. 54.
36. Quoted in Appy, *Working-Class War,* p. 124.
37. Quoted in Baker, *Nam,* pp. 67–68.
38. Quoted in Baker, *Nam,* pp. 62–63.
39. Quoted in Baker, *Nam,* p. 54.
40. Quoted in Appy, *Working-Class War,* p. 243.
41. Peter Goldman and Tony Fuller, *Charlie Company.* New York: William Morrow, 1983, p. 109.
42. Quoted in Baker, *Nam,* p. 58.
43. Quoted in Baker, *Nam,* p. 78.
44. Quoted in Appy, *Working-Class War,* p. 141.
45. Quoted in Santoli, *Everything We Had,* p. 107.
46. Quoted in Appy, *Working-Class War,* p. 183.

Chapter 3: "Humping the Boonies"

47. Quoted in Santoli, *Everything We Had,* p. 90.
48. Quoted in Appy, *Working-Class War,* p. 177.
49. Quoted in Baker, *Nam,* p. 100.
50. Quoted in Appy, *Working-Class War,* p. 179.
51. Quoted in Baker, *Nam,* p. 100.
52. Quoted in Appy, *Working-Class War,* p. 184.
53. Quoted in Baker, *Nam,* p. 166.
54. Quoted in Baker, *Nam,* p. 97.
55. Quoted in Appy, *Working-Class War,* p. 181.
56. Quoted in Karnow, *Vietnam,* p. 470.
57. Quoted in Edelman, *Dear America,* p. 89.
58. Quoted in Baker, *Nam,* p. 125.
59. Quoted in Edelman, *Dear America,* p. 23.
60. Quoted in Edelman, *Dear America,* p. 48.
61. Quoted in Baker, *Nam,* p. 115.
62. Quoted in Edelman, *Dear America,* p. 35.
63. Quoted in Santoli, *Everything We Had,* p. 92.
64. Quoted in Baker, *Nam,* p. 128.
65. Quoted in Edelman, *Dear America,* p. 85.
66. Quoted in Santoli, *Everything We Had,* p. 92.
67. Quoted in Edelman, *Dear America,* p. 68.
68. Quoted in Santoli, *Everything We Had,* p. 94.
69. Quoted in Santoli, *Everything We Had,* p. 27.
70. Quoted in Baker, *Nam,* p. 210.

71. Quoted in Edelman, *Dear America*, p. 11.
72. Quoted in Karnow, *Vietnam*, p. 472.
73. Quoted in Karnow, *Vietnam*, p. 467.
74. Quoted in Baker, *Nam*, p. 158.
75. Quoted in Santoli, *Everything We Had*, p. 157.
76. Quoted in Karnow, *Vietnam*, p. 467.
77. Quoted in Karnow, *Vietnam*, pp. 467–468.
78. Quoted in Karnow, *Vietnam*, p. 469.
79. Quoted in Santoli, *Everything We Had*, p. 107.
80. Quoted in Edelman, *Dear America*, p. 63.
81. Quoted in Baker, *Nam*, p. 121.
82. Quoted in Wallace Terry, *Bloods: An Oral History of the Vietnam War by Black Veterans.* New York: Ballantine Books, 1984, p. 311.
83. Quoted in Baker, *Nam*, p. 137.
84. Quoted in Baker, *Nam*, p. 137.
85. Quoted in Edelman, *Dear America*, p. 139.

Chapter 4: Office Pogues and Green-Faced Frogmen

86. Quoted in Edelman, *Dear America*, p. 139.
87. Quoted in Edelman, *Dear America*, p. 156.
88. Quoted in Appy, *Working-Class War*, p. 256.
89. Quoted in Edelman, *Dear America*, p. 161.
90. Quoted in Appy, *Working-Class War*, p. 190.
91. Quoted in Terry, *Bloods*, p. 285.
92. Quoted in Terry, *Bloods*, p. 272.
93. Quoted in Edelman, *Dear America*, pp. 145–46.
94. Quoted in Santoli, *Everything We Had*, pp. 92–93.
95. Quoted in Santoli, *Everything We Had*, p. 72.
96. Quoted in Terry, *Bloods*, pp. 120–21.
97. Quoted in Edelman, *Dear America*, pp. 157–58.
98. Quoted in Appy, *Working-Class War*, p. 240.
99. Edelman, *Dear America*, p. 32.
100. Quoted in Baker, *Nam*, p. 152.
101. Quoted in Baker, *Nam*, p. 153.
102. Quoted in Edelman, *Dear America*, p. 25.
103. Quoted in Santoli, *Everything We Had*, pp. 138–39.
104. Quoted in Santoli, *Everything We Had*, p. 135.
105. Quoted in Santoli, *Everything We Had*, p. 135.
106. Quoted in Santoli, *Everything We Had*, p. 67.
107. Quoted in Santoli, *Everything We Had*, p. 75.
108. Quoted in Walker, *A Piece of My Heart*, p. 254.
109. Quoted in Walker, *A Piece of My Heart*, p. 55.
110. Quoted in Walker, *A Piece of My Heart*, p. 255.
111. John A. Parrish, *12, 20 and 5, A Doctor's Year in Vietnam.* Baltimore, MD: Penguin Books, 1972, p. 296.
112. Quoted in Walker, *A Piece of My Heart*, pp. 98–99.

113. Quoted in Walker, *A Piece of My Heart,* p. 100.
114. Quotcd in Walker, *A Piece of My Heart,* p. 195.
115. Quoted in Walker, *A Piece of My Heart,* p. 275.
116. Quoted in Santoli, *Everything We Had,* p. 211.
117. Quoted in Baker, *Nam,* p. 175.
118. Quoted in Santoli, *Everything We Had,* pp. 219–20.
119. Quoted in Santoli, *Everything We Had,* p. 201.
120. Quoted in Baker, *Nam,* p. 203.
121. Quoted in Santoli, *Everything We Had,* p. 212.
122. Quoted in Baker, *Nam,* p. 301.
123. Quoted in Terry, *Bloods,* p. 306.
124. Quoted in Edelman, *Dear America,* p. 90.

Chapter 5: The Insanity of War

125. Appy, *Working-Class War,* p. 43.
126. Quoted in Appy, *Working-Class War,* p. 219.
127. Quoted in Terry, *Bloods,* p. 81.
128. Quoted in Santoli, *Everything We Had,* p. 152.
129. Quoted in Edelman, *Dear America,* p. 233.
130. Quoted in Appy, *Working-Class War,* p. 221.
131. Quoted in Edelman, *Dear America,* p. 221.
132. Quoted in Edelman, *Dear America,* p. 171.
133. Myron Yancey interview by author,

in Dallas, Oregon, January 22, 2000.
134. Quoted in Appy, *Working-Class War,* p. 229.
135. Quoted in Appy, *Working-Class War,* p. 261.
136. Quoted in Terry, *Bloods,* p. 98.
137. Quoted in Terry, *Bloods,* p. 96.
138. Quoted in Appy, *Working-Class War,* p. 133.
139. Quoted in Appy, *Working-Class War,* p. 225.
140. Quoted in Terry, *Bloods,* p. 10.
141. Quoted in Terry, *Bloods,* pp. 114–15.
142. Quoted in Terry, *Bloods,* p. 293.
143. Quoted in Seymour M. Hersh, *My Lai 4.* New York: Random House, 1970, p. 56.
144. Hersh, *My Lai 4,* p. 64.
145. Quoted in Hersh, *My Lai 4,* p. 184.
146. Quoted in Appy, *Working-Class War,* p. 259.
147. Quoted in Baker, *Nam,* pp. 154–55.
148. Quoted in Walker, *A Piece of My Heart,* p. 25.
149. Quoted in Appy, *Working-Class War,* p. 284.
150. Quoted in Santoli, *Everything We Had,* pp. 73–74.
151. Quoted in Santoli, *Everything We Had,* p. 95.
152. Quoted in Edelman, *Dear America,* p. 211.
153. Baker, *Nam,* p. 262.

Chapter 6: Somber Homecoming

154. Quoted in Baker, *Nam,* p. 280.
155. Quoted in Baker, *Nam,* p. 263.

156. Quoted in Walker, *A Piece of My Heart,* p. 49.
157. Quoted in Santoli, *Everything We Had,* p. 78.
158. Quoted in Baker, *Nam,* p. 264.
159. Quoted in Goldman, "What Vietnam Did to Us," p. 72.
160. Yancey, interview.
161. Quoted in Terry, *Bloods,* p. 218.
162. Quoted in Walker, *A Piece of My Heart,* p. 49.
163. Quoted in Baker, *Nam,* p. 302.
164. Quoted in Baker, *Nam,* p. 312.
165. Quoted in Baker, *Nam,* p. 289.
166. Quoted in Terry, *Bloods,* p. 257.
167. Quoted in Baker, *Nam,* p. 290.
168. Quoted in Baker, *Nam,* p. 310.
169. Quoted in Walker, *A Piece of My Heart,* p. 65.
170. Quoted in Terry, *Bloods,* p. 155.
171. Quoted in Terry, *Bloods,* p. 365.
172. Quoted in Walker, *A Piece of My Heart,* p. 65.
173. Quoted in Baker, *Nam,* p. 306.

Chapter 7: Legacy of Vietnam

174. Quoted in Goldman, "What Vietnam Did to Us," p. 94.
175. Quoted in Baker, *Nam,* pp. 317–18.
176. Quoted in Baker, *Nam,* p. 292.
177. Quoted in Baker, *Nam,* p. 314.
178. Quoted in Goldman, "What Vietnam Did to Us," p. 72.
179. Quoted in Goldman, "What Vietnam Did to Us," p. 74.
180. Quoted in Baker, *Nam,* pp. 313–14.
181. Quoted in Walker, *A Piece of My Heart,* p. 244.
182. Veterans of the Vietnam War, Inc., POW/ MIA page. www.vvnw.org/powmis.htm.
183. Joan Cox, "I'll Meet You at the Wall," Vietnam Veterans Memorial Wall page. www.thewall-usa.com/literary/joancox. html.

Epilogue: The Wall

184. Quoted in Edelman, *Dear America,* p. xxii.
185. Quoted in Walker, *A Piece of My Heart,* p. 406.
186. "Vietnam Veterans Statue," Vietnam Veterans Memorial, National Parks Service. www.nps.gov/vive/statuev. htm.
187. "Memorial Design," Vietnam Veterans Memorial, National Parks Service. www.nps.gov/vive/Memorial Design.htm.
188. Terry, *Bloods,* p. 353.
189. Peter Marin, "Coming to Terms with Vietnam," *Harpers,* December, 1980, p. 50.
190. Terry, *Bloods,* p. 365.

✦ Glossary ✦

Agent Orange: A highly toxic defoliant sprayed on vegetation in Vietnam.

arty: Slang for artillery; large caliber weapons such as cannons and rocket launchers.

AWOL: Absent without leave; to leave a post or position without permission.

bangalore: A piece of metal pipe filled with explosives, used to clear a path through barbed wire or to detonate land mines.

base camp: A supply base for field units and the location for headquarters, airfields, artillery supplies, etc.; also known as the rear.

battalion: A military unit composed of two or more companies, batteries, or similar units.

bird: Slang for helicopter.

boonies: Short for boondocks; the jungles and mountains of Vietnam.

boo boo: A slang term derived from the French *beaucoup,* meaning "much" or "many."

brigade: A military unit composed of one or more battalions with other supporting units.

bush: An infantry term for the field or the boonies.

C-ration: Canned rations; meals provided by the military for GIs to eat in the field.

Charlie: A derogatory term for Viet Cong.

claymore mine: An antipersonnel mine carried by the infantry.

cold war: A state of political tension and military rivalry between nations that stops short of full-scale war.

company: A military unit consisting of two or more platoons.

counterinsurgency: Political and military strategy intended to oppose and suppress rebellion.

covert: Hidden or secret.

clutch belt: A cartridge belt worn by members of the Marine Corps.

deferment: An official postponement of compulsory military service.

didi: A slang term derived from the Vietnamese word *di,* meaning "to leave" or "to go."

Demilitarized Zone (DMZ): The dividing line between North and South Vietnam.

domino theory: The theory that if one nation comes under communist control, then neighboring nations will also come under communist control.

dust-off: Medical evacuation by helicopter, also known as medevac.

enlisted person: A member of the military who ranks below a commissioned officer.

fire base: A temporary artillery camp used for fire support of forward ground operations.

114

fire fight: An exchange of small-arms fire with the enemy.

flak jacket: A heavy, fiberglass-filled vest worn for protection from shrapnel.

flashback: A recurring, intensely vivid mental image of a past traumatic experience.

flechette: A missile dropped from an aircraft.

fragging: Assassination of a military leader by his own troops, usually by grenade.

friendly fire: Accidental attacks on one's own forces in a war.

frogman: A swimmer equipped to execute underwater military maneuvers.

ghosting: A means of avoiding combat by going AWOL, pretending to be sick, or inventing family problems that entail a return to the United States.

GI: An enlisted person or veteran of the military.

gook: A derogatory term for an Asian person.

grunt: An infantryman in ground combat units of the U.S. military.

guerrilla: A member of an irregular military force operating in small bands in occupied territory to harass and undermine the enemy.

gunship: An armed helicopter.

hootch: A simply constructed hut or tent, either military or civilian.

Huey: A nickname for the UH-1-series helicopter.

hump: Infantryman's term for carrying packs and armaments up and down hills while on combat patrol.

immersion foot: A condition resulting from the feet being submerged in water for a prolonged period.

French Indochina: The former French colonial empire in Southeast Asia which included Vietnam, Cambodia, and Laos.

K-bar: A combat knife.

klick: Slang for kilometer.

LURPs: Long-Range Reconnaissance Patrol members.

MACV: Military Assistance Command/Vietnam; the main American military command unit that had responsibility for and authority over all U.S. military activities in Vietnam.

medevac: Medical evacuation of the wounded from the battlefield by helicopter; also known as dust-off.

MIA: A person missing in action.

mortar: A muzzle-loading cannon that throws projectiles at high angles.

napalm: Incendiary jelly used in bombs and flamethrowers.

office pogue: A slang term for a soldier who fills an office or administrative position in the rear.

Phoenix Program: A U.S. program aimed at Communist subversion.

platoon: A subdivision of a company, usually about forty-five men.

point man: A man walking in the forward position on a combat mission.

post-traumatic stress disorder: A condition that develops after an individual experiences psychologically traumatic events. Symptoms include memory impairment, guilt feelings, sleep difficulties, flashbacks, and hallucinations.

punji stakes: Sharpened bamboo sticks,

coated with excrement and planted at an angle in tall grass or at the bottom of pits, designed to pierce the enemy.

PX: Post exchange; a military store.

R&R: Rest and recuperation; a three- to seven-day vacation from the war.

rear: Part of a military placement farthest from the fighting front; a position some distance from the fighting.

reconnaissance: Inspection or exploration of an area.

regiment: A military unit of ground troops consisting of at least two battalions.

RTO: Radiotelephone operator; one who carries his unit's radio on his back in the field.

sandbagging: A unit's means of avoiding combat by pretending to fight while taking refuge in a safe locale.

sapper: A Viet Cong or North Vietnamese army commando, particularly carrying high explosives.

search and destroy: An operation designed to find and destroy enemy forces.

short-timer: A GI nearing the end of his tour in Vietnam.

shrapnel: Pieces of metal sent flying by an explosion.

SP pack: A cellophane packet containing toiletries and cigarettes, sometimes given to GIs along with their C-rations.

stand-down: A period of rest for a combat unit, during which time they return to base.

titi: Slang for "a little."

USO: United Service Organizations; groups that supply entertainment, social services, and spiritual guidance for the U.S. armed services during a war.

verdant: Green with vegetation.

veteran: Also vet; a person who has served in the military.

World, the: The United States; home.

Willy Pete: White phosphorus; used in grenades and shells for incendiary purposes.

Xin loi: Vietnamese idiom meaning "sorry about that."

☆ For Further Reading ☆

David Bender and Bruno Leone, eds., *The Vietnam War: Opposing Viewpoints*. San Diego: Greenhaven Press, 1984. Presents contrasting views on various aspects of the war, including reasons for American involvement, failure of the U.S. policy in Vietnam, and effects of the war on veterans.

Barry Denenberg, *Voices from Vietnam*. New York: Scholastic, 1995. A history of the Vietnam War told largely by American men and women who fought in it.

Albert Marrin, *America and Vietnam*. New York: Viking, 1992. Examines the political history of Vietnam, along with military events, social impact, and long-term effects of the war.

Neil Super, *Vietnam War Soldiers*. New York: Twenty-First Century Books, 1993. Focuses on the experiences of African American soldiers in the Vietnam War.

Richard L. Wormser, *Three Faces of Vietnam*. New York: Franklin Watts, 1993. A look at the Vietnam War from three perspectives: American soldiers who fought, American students who protested, and Vietnamese who suffered the consequences.

✯ Works Consulted ✯

Books

Christian G. Appy, *Working-Class War: American Combat Soldiers and Vietnam.* Chapel Hill: University of North Carolina Press, 1993. An account of the Vietnam War with an emphasis on the working-class men who made up the majority of the fighting force. Appy includes information on soldiers' attitudes before the war, experiences in boot camp, adjustments to the war, battle-weariness, disillusionment, and difficulties encountered after coming home.

Mark Baker, *Nam.* New York: William Morrow, 1981. Powerful and, at times, disturbing accounts of the Vietnam War, told by several men and women who served there.

Bernard Edelman, ed., *Dear America: Letters Home from Vietnam.* New York: Simon and Schuster, 1985. A compilation of letters written by soldiers while they were serving in the Vietnam War. Honest and authentic correspondence ranges from first impressions of newly arrived troops to last letters, written by those who died in combat.

Peter Goldman and Tony Fuller, *Charlie Company.* New York: William Morrow, 1983. An account of the men of one combat infantry unit who fought in Vietnam in the late 1960s, including their entry into the war and their adjustment to "the World" after their return.

Seymour M. Hersh, *My Lai 4.* New York: Random House, 1970. A report of the My Lai massacre and its aftermath, reconstructed from eyewitness accounts, written by the man who first told the story to the world in 1969.

Stanley Karnow, *Vietnam: A History.* New York: Viking Press, 1983. A comprehensive and well-balanced history of the Vietnam War by a renowned journalist.

John A. Parrish, *12, 20 and 5, A Doctor's Year in Vietnam.* Baltimore, MD: Penguin Books, 1972. A first-person account of a young doctor's service in the Vietnam War.

Reporting Vietnam. 2 vols. New York: Library of America, 1998. An anthology of book excerpts and newspaper and magazine reports written during the Vietnam War. The two volumes trace the war from the first American deaths in 1959 through the fall of Saigon in 1975.

Al Santoli, *Everything We Had: An Oral History of the Vietnam War by Thirty-Three American Soldiers Who Fought It.* New York:

Ballantine Books, 1981. A personal look at the Vietnam War through the eyes of thirty-three American soldiers.

Wallace Terry, *Bloods: An Oral History of the Vietnam War by Black Veterans.* New York: Ballantine Books, 1984. Honest, moving, and sometimes disturbing accounts of the lives of twenty black soldiers who fought in the Vietnam War.

Keith Walker, *A Piece of My Heart: The Stories of Twenty-Six American Women Who Served in Vietnam.* New York: Ballantine Books, 1985. American women who served as nurses, Red Cross volunteers, entertainers, and flight attendants in the Vietnam War tell their stories, including their experiences with post-traumatic stress disorder and Agent Orange illnesses.

Periodicals

Peter Goldman, "What Vietnam Did to Us," *Newsweek,* December 14, 1981, pp. 46–96. Survivors of Charlie Company, part of the Twenty-Eighth Infantry Regiment of the U.S. Army, relate some of their experiences in the war and during the decade following their return.

Peter Marin, "Coming to Terms with Vietnam," *Harpers,* December, 1980, pp. 41–56. A look at America's moral quandaries over the Vietnam War, and the plight of veterans who struggled with guilt and disillusionment eight years after coming home.

Interview

Myron Yancey. Interview by author, Dallas, Oregon, January 22, 2000. Yancey served as a Specialist 4 in the army from 1967 to 1968. He was stationed at Phu Bai near Hue during the Vietnam War.

Internet Sources

Joan Cox, "I'll Meet You at The Wall," Vietnam Veterans Memorial Wall page. (www.thewall-usa.com/literary/joancox. html). An essay written by the daughter of one U.S. soldier killed in action in the Vietnam War.

"Memorial Design," Vietnam Veterans Memorial, National Parks Service. (www.nps.gov/vive/MemorialDesign. htm.) Gives specific information on the design of "the Wall" and "The Statue of the Three Servicemen."

Veterans of the Vietnam War, Inc., POW/ MIA page. (www.vvnw.org/powmis. htm). The page focuses on those who are involved in the POW/MIA issue, including governments, military personnel, POWs, their families, and all others who work to locate and provide information about the missing.

"Vietnam Veterans Statue," Vietnam Veterans Memorial, National Parks Service. (www.nps.gov/vive/statuev.htm). The page provides background leading up to the erection of "The Statue of the Three Servicemen," part of the Vietnam Veterans Memorial, created by designer Frederick Hart. Photo included.

Websites

Vietnam Veterans Memorial Wall, (www. thewall-usa.com/). The site provides access to a message center, photo gallery, literary works, screensavers, and names that appear on the Wall.

National League of POW/MIA Families, (www.pow-miafamilies.org/). The website gives background information on the League plus statistics of those still unaccounted for, a book list, and ways to become involved in POW/ MIA issues.

Veterans of the Vietnam War, Inc. (www. vnw.org/). The site offers information on various topics including Agent Orange, Post-Traumatic Stress Disorder, POW/MIA issues, and others.

Vietnam Veterans Memorial, National Parks Service, (www.nps.gov/vive/). The National Parks Service promotes and regulates the use of national parks and mcmorials such as the Vietnam Veterans Memorial. It also works to educate visitors and the general public about their history and common heritage.

Vietnam Veterans of America, Washington, DC, (www.vva.org/). The website provides information about the organization's membership and services, publications, upcoming events, legislative issues and more.

✭ Index ✭

☆ About the Author ☆

Diane Yancey works as a freelance writer in the Pacific Northwest, where she has lived for over twenty years. She writes nonfiction for middle-grade and high-school readers, and enjoys traveling and collecting old books. Some of her other titles include *Civil War Generals of the Union*, *Leaders of the Civil War*, and *Strategic Battles of the Civil War*.